FLOURISHING LOVE

FLOURISHING LOVE
A Secular Guide to Lasting Intimate Relationships

Enrico Gnaulati

KARNAC
firing the mind

First published in 2024 by
Karnac Books Limited
62 Bucknell Road
Bicester
Oxfordshire OX26 2DS

British Library Cataloguing in Publication Data

A C.I.P. for this book is available from the British Library

ISBN-13: 978-1-80013-208-5

Typeset by Medlar Publishing Solutions Pvt Ltd, India

www.firingthemind.com

To Janet,
my best friend,
and flourishing love co-aspirer

Contents

Acknowledgments ix

About the author xi

Introduction xiii

CHAPTER 1
Aspiring to flourishing love 1

CHAPTER 2
Surviving domesticity 23

CHAPTER 3
Doing conflict well 53

CHAPTER 4
Humor me 77

CHAPTER 5
Lust is a must 97

CHAPTER 6
Wrangling with roving desires   123

CHAPTER 7
Getting the right sort of help   151

Notes   185
Index   215

Acknowledgments

The title and central themes of this book have undergone several iterations. From the outset, I wanted to write a book that was an affirmation of marriage, or long-term intimate partnership. I envisaged my readership to comprise spouses on the brink of ending their relationships who needed a reality check concerning realistic notions of the natural and expectable ups and downs, phase of life challenges, and romantic disillusionment all couples face, to avoid misconstruing unavoidable erosions in closeness as a sign of dire incompatibility. The book retained this focus but took on a higher purpose: a counter voice to the religious-moral cynics among us who steadfastly believe that ordinary human love is a feeble motivational source to inspire and re-inspire long-term romantic loyalty and commitment. In essence, while knee deep in writing the book over the past three years, I realized there is a great need for a pro-marriage, long-term intimate partnership void of religious-moral baggage that hitches itself to secular humanistic values.

I wish I could say I dialogued with flesh-and-blood psychologists and philosophers to cobble together my secular humanistic positions on love and marriage. However, being the introverted, bookish person

I am, my shifting ideas were chiefly the product of deep engagement with texts. Among the key authors I credit with influencing my thinking are: Aaron Ben-Ze'ev; Ivan Boszormenyi-Nagy; Alain de Botton; William J. Doherty; Martin Hagglund; Herant Katchadourian; Robert Karen; Aaron Lazare; Harriet Lerner; Esther Perel; Mari Ruti; and Deborah Tannen.

That said, credit is also due some dear married friends who kindly listened to and rebutted many of the ideas in this book over dinner: Sam Alibrando and Janette Davis; Daniel Goldin and Penny Pengra; Art and Debbie Hansen; and Tom and Melinda Peters. A thank you is also merited to my in-laws, Donna and Steve Wickersham, who have always been stalwart supporters of my books.

My dear wife Janet warrants the lion's share of the credit. For the better part of two years, she put up with me placing our marriage under the microscope, pestering her for permission to include personal information that could leave her feeling exposed, petitioning her to read my written work with fresh eyes, and tolerating an obsessive writing process that took me out of commission for days and weeks on end. This book is a testament to all she has taught me about enduring love. A shout-out is also due my son, Marcello, who was generous in providing permission to include snippets of his life in the book. Knowing he will likely read this book one day kept me honest as to how his parents' marriage was being portrayed by me. Lastly, I owe a debt of gratitude to the team at Karnac Books—Kate Pearce, Fernando Marques, Sophie-Jo Gavin, Anita Mason, and Aimee Dexter—who were everything an author would want in bringing a book to publication with efficiency and creative flare.

About the author

Enrico Gnaulati, PhD, is a clinical psychologist based in Pasadena, California, and Affiliate Professor of Psychology at Seattle University. He has published numerous journal and magazine articles and his work has been featured on Spectrum News, Al Jazeera America, China Global Television Network, KPCC Los Angeles, KPFK Los Angeles, KPBS San Diego, WBUR Boston, KPFA Berkeley, Wisconsin Public Radio, Public Radio Tulsa, and online at *The Atlantic*, *Salon*, and *Psychology Today*, as well as reviewed in *Maclean's*, *Pacific Standard*, the *Huffington Post*, *The Australian*, *Prevention*, and the *New Yorker*. He is a blogger for *Mad in America*, an internationally recognized reformer of mental health practice and policy, and the author of *Back to Normal: Why Ordinary Childhood Behavior is Mistaken for ADHD, Bipolar Disorder, and Autism Spectrum Disorder* (Beacon Press, 2013); *Saving Talk Therapy: How Health Insurers, Big Pharma, and Slanted Science are Ruining Good Mental Health Care* (Beacon Press, 2018); and *Emotion-Regulating Play Therapy with ADHD Children: Staying with Playing* (Jason Aronson, 2008). His latest book is *Peacemaking with Preschoolers: Conflict Resolution to Promote Emotional Mastery and Harmonious Classrooms* (Good Media Press, 2023).

Introduction

If you picked up this book because you're one of the growing mass of people who are cynical about what marriage, or a marriage-like commitment, can deliver in the way of life fulfillment, being of the opinion it demands too much self-denial, dignifies domestic drudgery, and can sandbag an erotic life—but you're open to being persuaded otherwise—read on.

Maybe you're among the roughly half of those in the United Kingdom or one-third of Americans who now self-identify as "religiously unaffiliated."[1] Because of the historic link between marriage and religion, as someone who has stepped back from churchgoing, you believe a host of conjugal ideals are old-fashioned, out of step with the realities of modern love. For instance, you may be of the mindset that just because you're going steady with someone doesn't lockstep you into a future marriage proposal. You certainly don't see marriage as an avenue to kick off and legitimize an active sex life. It's likely the overturning of *Roe vs. Wade* in the US troubled you greatly because you wouldn't want the fear of an unwanted pregnancy—due to limits on your access to emergency contraception or abortion—to hamper your right to explore your sexuality as freely and openly as possible. Nor would you want any restrictions on your reproductive choices to lead you to keep an accidental pregnancy and feel obligated to marry someone you only feel so-so about.

In your eyes, marriage is not a ticket that needs to be punched to consider yourself a mature adult. Perhaps you have taken, or want to take, the scenic route to adulthood. Steering clear of any premature marriage commitment has allowed you greater freedom to run with and through friendships, travel, fall in and out of love, gain sexual experience, get to properly acquaint yourself with your personal likes and dislikes. Being ready for a serious long-term commitment means seeing your educational goals in the rear-view mirror and your early career plans already materializing.

For all you know, you're in a good-enough relationship where all the signals say it could get even better if you really settle in—pledge to be the most emotionally vulnerable, fair-minded, reliable, sincere, affectionate version of yourself. But somehow you keep conflating *settling in* with *settling*, holding back from fully investing in the love you have, and holding out for some yet-to-be-discovered love that will satisfy you in every way.

When eventually entertaining a marriage commitment, you wonder whether the whole idea of taking a solemn oath "before God, till death do us part" just sets couples up to stop trying—when you're morally bound to be forever loyal, where's the motivation to keep rendering yourself interesting, kind, sexy, and lovable in your own eyes and in those of your mate? When we vow to love someone forever, aren't we making the shaky assumption that love is within our conscious control and a marital commitment made at one point in time is sufficient to override all that life throws at partners as life progresses?

One thing you know for sure you don't subscribe to is any biblical, or divinely inspired, justification for female submission and male dominance in a heterosexual marriage, and women being valorized as child bearers and rearers, confined to the domestic sphere. Being in an egalitarian relationship with equal power sharing is probably what's sacrosanct to you. So too is the credo that in a good marriage or intimate partnership, a person's better self can get bigger, and that there's always a dynamic interplay between maximizing your own personal happiness

measured against making your significant other happy. In all likelihood, the Judeo-Christian virtue of surrendering personal happiness to
cement a marital bond doesn't sit well with you.

And, if you are a member of the LGBTQ community, the moral-
religious baggage surrounding traditional marriage, doubtless, has left
you looking for ways to customize your wedlock plans. Although in
the US gay marriage is legal in all fifty states and almost 60 percent of
same-sex adult couples are married,[2] data shows that lesbians, gays, and
bisexuals who want to affiliate with a church often find themselves in a
bait and switch situation: they are welcomed, so long as they stay on the
downlow about their sex lives or aspire to celibacy and see themselves
as sinners in need of repentance.[3] Popular Catholic theologian, Scott
Hahn, has some grim words for gays and lesbians looking for the social
approval marriage can confer: "any society in which the idea of same-
sex 'marriage' can gain a foothold has already lost its marriage culture."[4]
This is no oddity. The conservative-leaning Supreme Court is poised
to undo laws that guarantee legal rights to same-sex consensual sexual
practices and same-sex marriage.[5]

Even though most of the Western world is becoming increasingly secular, in matters related to marriage and family we are still
marinating in Judeo-Christian norms as to rightminded ways to conduct ourselves, which is a turn-off for large swathes of people contemplating tying the knot. Currently, it's estimated that a mere 37 percent
of Americans believe society benefits when people prioritize marriage
and childrearing.[6] If a resurgence of hope and optimism around the
advantages of marriage and family life is to occur, we need a cultural
infusion of secular humanistic values for people to access, informing
them on how to hold themselves and each other accountable for the
betterment of their romantic union. An awareness that their conscience
is not a hot box of divine surveillance, but an inner voice reminding us
of the ways we need to do right by ourselves and others. A healthy habit
of dialing into the innate human capacity for benevolence, compassion,
and fairness, without any divine intermediary. A reliance on worldly,
not otherworldly, ethical wisdom. Acceptance of the axiom that the love
you get is always influenced to some degree by the love you offer. That
ultimately, loyalty and commitment are anchored to and sustained by
the balancing out of benefits received and burdens suffered over time in

an intimate partnership, not some expression of moral-religious duty to abide by a sacred vow sworn on one's wedding day.

These are heady topics, but they can be unpacked in graspable and humorous ways, where the reader walks away supplied with usable knowledge to apply in his or her relationship—which this book strives to do. I will draw from the latest science, ancient and recent philosophical wisdom, stories, and psychological insights from my psychotherapy practice with couples, what real life partners in long-term happy marriages and intimate unions have to say, musings from my own thirty-year marriage, and even what can be learned from comedians and cartoonists—secular sources of knowledge—to map out what flourishing intimate relationships look like and how best to maintain them.

Starting out, I address what it means to embark on a path to flourishing love based on a joint personal desire and commitment to co-invest in treating each other lovingly—*a mutual happiness project*. I bring to life some of the non-negotiables, like deeply felt acceptance of the emotional upkeep involved—the wholesomeness of something as seemingly basic as showing genuine interest in what a partner thinks, feels, says, and does—and an ongoing openness to manifest love with physical affection. I challenge notions of Christian agape love that espouse joint self-sacrifice, claiming such a roadmap may lead to satisfactory romantic unions, less so flourishing ones. Self-interest cannot be whitewashed out without compromising the quality of love given and gotten. Nor can self-interest lead to us ignoring our human obligation to meet our beloved's happiness needs. Flourishing love is neither selfless not selfish. The reader will discover that knowing your own and your significant other's likes and dislikes, creating emotional space together for them to be nonjudgmentally talked about, is the very definition of mutual respect.

Other ideas I descriptively tackle include how to employ a fairness habit of mind around household chores, childrearing responsibilities, finances, and even what transpires to ensure that a couple gets a good night's sleep. I argue that the religious romanticization of parenthood and family life obscures the fact that during the long arc of a marriage, the phase consisting of running a household and raising children is incredibly demanding. Realistically speaking, even the sturdiest couples do best surviving, not thriving, during these tumultuous years. That said, being a good parenting team can afford a couple a joint sense of mission that bonds them to offset the inevitable estrangement that creeps in. Later in life, the parenting payoff, witnessing your grown children act with good character and function like citizens of the world, is deeply rewarding.

As we shall see, it's a myth that a happy marriage is a conflict-free one. Science reveals that the disputes couples get into early in a relationship have an indefinite shelf life. A more realistic goal for couples is not to eliminate conflict but to improve relational management of it. Repair and reconciliation though humbling oneself and offering a guilty apology, creating inroads for forgiveness, is the relational know-how of happy couples. My secular approach to respectful communication and conflict resolution taps what I call "conversational ethics," or the how-to of conversing well and doing conflict better. I introduce the reader to the difference between "talking at" and "talking with"; how to honestly, yet tactfully, speak up; and the crucial step of communicating acknowledgment of someone's point of view during heated exchanges to de-escalate things. These are just some of the skills that need to be mastered if couples are to become adept at moving from prideful monologuing to humble dialoguing. I also shine a light on how couples can avoid unnecessary conflict by better appreciating characteristic masculine and feminine ways of speaking and listening.

My favorite chapter to write, and the one I'm tempted to have the reader jump ahead to, is "Humor me" (Chapter 4). Humor, irony, and an appreciation for the absurd are largely overlooked by marriage scholars as mindsets conducive to success at love—perhaps seen as too trivial a topic worthy of scientific investigation—yet such mindsets may constitute one of the most potent ways romantic partners can best adapt to and accept all the contradictions and obstacles baked into contemporary romantic unions. It augers well when couples use humor to channel friendly intent, deflect insults, confess personal shortcomings in good-natured ways, and preserve positivity during disagreements. By using pet names, terms of endearment, and private jokes, couples lubricate their close attachment. As happy couples age and they reconcile themselves to the fact that their years together are numbered, snickering replaces bickering. I assert that deft use of wit to minimize emotional harm and maximize enjoyment in a relationship is a human virtue.

I pull no punches elevating the importance of a vital sex life for flourishing love to form and last. The over-moralizing of sex by organized religion hinders full cultural acceptance of sex-positive attitudes that promise to breathe new life into erotically compromised intimate relationships. Within most religious contexts, the sexual preferences of gay and lesbian couples are negated. Yet information about the sexual turn-ons of those in the LGBTQ community can be good to include in the sexual playbook of heterosexuals. We are at an inflection point in our culture where the debate needs to shift from sex negativity to sex positivity to support marriages and long-term intimate partnerships that are at risk of dissolving. I walk the reader through how measuring women's libido in quasi-internal-combustion-engine ways, as an energy level, fueled by sexual fantasy, is problematic. Many couples' sex lives flounder due to under-appreciating the expectable effects of divergent gendered turn-ons and -offs. The "missionary position" is really the "missing it position" as far as women's orgasmic pleasure is concerned. The transition to parenthood, as well as the drudgery of domestic life, can flatline a couple's sex life.

I assert that as the years go by, if a vital sex life is to be preserved, each member of the couple must steadily accept that erotic feelings don't always spring up on their own. Carving out time and setting the mood for sex to happen may feel like a poor substitute for the spontaneous sexcapades of yesteryear, yet it can be surprisingly erotically satisfying. Mediocre sex is often the outgrowth of men being too sexually self-absorbed and women being insufficiently sexually self-absorbed. The prickliness of people, where they get too jumpy if their comfort preferences are not met, poses special challenges for couples' sex lives.

Another myth I dismantle involves the notion that once a person "ties the knot" and enters a marital commitment, amorous feelings for anyone other than their beloved fade away. Even in robust marriages, crushes on others are remarkably common, best friends of a spouse lusted after, and "back burner" lovers actively fantasized about as possible fallbacks in case an established relationship gets dismantled. These roving desires do not necessarily suggest a person is attachment phobic or is falling out of love. There's also keener cultural interest surrounding the idea that monogamy subverts people's needs for sexual variety and novelty and that for partners who desire something kinkier than their mate allows, alternatives outside the relationship need not be forbidden outright. Sometimes the answer is to courageously push the boundaries of the drab sex life they have fallen into and add some kink to their otherwise vanilla sex lives—*kinky vanilla sex*.

If committed love is to endure, it's imperative we find a way to neither automatically condone nor condemn wayward expressions of intimacy needs and sexual enticements. Mutual consent to open up a marriage/long-term partnership, with transparency and honest communication about sexual preferences and jealous feelings, is considered the high-water mark of ethicality. But ethics come into play also when nonconsensual affairs are conducted. As morally bankrupt, or slippery a slope, as it sounds, not all forms of betrayal are equal and perhaps it's possible to talk of "loving deception," or conducting an affair with secrecy and discretion, so as to emotionally safeguard a primary partner and minimize threats to a good marriage. Affairs are not always the death knell of a marriage/long-term partnership. The case of Peter is presented to illuminate pivotal steps that can be taken in therapy to best handle the emotional fallout from affairs in ways that make constructive use of anger and guilt, as well as tap opportunities for contrition and forgiveness.

The final chapter of the book should be an informative resource for both struggling couples and mental health professionals. It sketches out what might occur behind closed doors in the therapy office to give distressed couples their best shot at recovering and thriving. The stubborn myth exists that couples therapy is where troubled marriages go to die. That may be due, in part, to the standard "neutral" approach adopted by the average therapist which is *autonomy affirming*—helping clients clarify the issues and prioritize each other's personal happiness. Arguably, therapists have a competing ethical duty to be *marriage affirming*—to advise beleaguered couples to postpone any decision around separating until therapy is given a real chance. If troubled marriages or intimate partnerships are to survive and thrive—or end with optimal damage control—they are best treated by a skilled therapist, not just a competent one.

Finally, clients often draw motivational inspiration to be more attentive and loving in their primary relationships from existential themes— what ultimately matters in life is committing to being the best loving version of yourself to fortify important relationships and realizing therapy is an avenue to breaking intergenerational patterns of dysfunctional relationships, thereby gifting children with better prospects in their future romantic journeys. Evocative snippets from actual couples therapy sessions I have conducted are described to pull the reader in. Of course, I changed names and altered factual information for confidentiality reasons. But essential issues, meanings, and outcomes have been preserved. At no time do I source purely fictional accounts.

Dotted throughout the book are references to the secular idea that mortality awareness and death acceptance are motivators to push romantic partners to enact their most loving versions of themselves with each other. Befriending death as the end point of our life, and that of our beloved—not as a portal to eternity—can create that all-important sense of urgency to be a more involved, considerate, appreciative, forgiving partner. The background sense that time is slipping away and death can come out of nowhere is not a morbid preoccupation, but an ethical wake-up call. It goads us to not just live and love well now, but live and love better now. None of us want deathbed regrets—a nagging sense that we stupidly held grudges, let petty grievances fester, had our relationship priorities all whacky. Death acceptance makes us chase the deep consolation associated with knowing that when that dreaded, but inescapable, day arrives we can draw solace from the fact that we strove to love at our best, with our beloved feeling he or she was truly loved. Dying with an awareness that one has loved well and been loved well in return takes the sting out of death. I'm hoping that for this generation which has lived under the dark shadow of the Covid-19 pandemic, the death anxiety that has surfaced can be seized upon as a motivator to pursue more fulfilling love relationships.

At its core, this book is a pro-marriage, pro-long-term intimate partnership guidebook for those who trend secular in their value system. Who are not apt to rely on divine inspiration, sacred texts, religious leaders, church communities, or prayer to govern their love lives. Who put their faith in the human potential to call upon a combination of psychological resources, scientific information, common sense, raw intelligence, and innate ethical sensibilities to live life and to love as fully as possible. (A quick note: although it's cumbersome, I try to use terms like marriage, intimate partnership, and romantic union, as well as spouse, partner, and significant other, interchangeably, to be inclusive of all the committed relationship types that different-sex and same-sex couples enter into.) Pro-marriage books are almost always the exclusive purview of organized religion, as if secularists have nothing authoritative to say on matters related to vital marriages and family values. This book aims to correct that.

More people than ever are asking themselves questions such as: Why marry, or enter into a marriage-like commitment? Why stay married? Why remarry? What makes love last? Can it last? If so, are there unique rewards it offers that make life worth living? These are secular questions for secular times. Occasionally, the media rolls out the health benefits of marriage—fewer strokes and heart attacks, higher cancer survivor rates, better post-surgical recovery outcomes, lower likelihood of depression, living longer.[7] Truth be told, it's those that are fortunate enough to be in *vital marriages* that get the health and longevity bumps.

In the first study of its kind using a large representative sample of US adults to investigate health and longevity outcomes related to marital status and quality, those that said they were "very happily" married were twice as likely to report better health than those indicating they were "not too happily" married. The latter were almost 40 percent more likely to have shorter lives.[8] Other findings show that those who consider their spouse or partner to be their best friend obtain about twice as much additional emotional satisfaction from marriage or long-term partnering than those who don't classify their significant other that way.[9]

The takeaway is that it's not a lasting marriage or partnership per se that can potentially keep us alive longer and up the chances of enhancing couples' emotional and physical well-being, it's the *quality* and *depth* of their relationship that matters. It's their know-how in showing and receiving flourishing love. This book aims to make such a life-affirming endeavor tangible and realizable. If in its pages you find that to be true for you, setting you on a quest, the countless hours I have spent poring over relevant research, ferreting out the wise offerings of dubious bedfellows like philosophers and comedians, reflecting on my therapy work with couples, and taking solo writing trips on retreat in the desert at Joshua Tree and mountains in Idyllwild, California, will have been well worth it.

CHAPTER 1

Aspiring to flourishing love

O ne of the unsung heroes of the twentieth century who paved the way for marriage being considered a form of intimate friendship was a hard-driving California judge by the name of Ben B. Lindsey. In 1927, he co-authored a book titled *Companionate Marriage*,[1] in which he laid out arguments that for most people today seem yawningly reasonable, yet in those days raised more than eyebrows. He proposed that young men and women ought to be able to enter into a trial marriage for a year-long period to see if they were truly compatible. During this probationary love-test, couples were encouraged to use birth control to prevent pregnancy and parenthood before their marital bond was viable. That way, they could get to know each other with clothes on, and clothes off, not just while they were on their best behavior to ensure the clothes came off.

Once the year was up, if the couple had wind in their sails and believed they were well-matched, they could convert their provisional marriage into a more permanent arrangement. If, on the other hand, they believed they were ill-suited, they could fast-track a divorce and go their separate ways.

The good Judge Lindsey would wholeheartedly agree with the nugget penned by his clever contemporary, Mark Twain: "Love heightens all the senses except the common."[2] He accepted the notion that the forces bringing lovers together can be very different than what keeps them together. The motivation to be together during the romantic phase of a relationship goes without saying: wanting to bask in the erotic excitement and mutual adoration lovers offer each other. Getting lost in each other's eyes, the giddy laughter, the enchanting smiles, the engrossing conversations, the electrifying sensuality—all fueling a dream-like state of lovers feeling they were made for each other, a perfect fit. The romantic intensity is destined to wear off, even though lovers in love are convinced it will be everlasting. They are blind to such buzz-kill axioms served up by philosophers on matters relating to how the intensity of romantic love fades over time: "First there is the thrill, then there is the coping"[3] and "Love is skill rather than enthusiasm."[4]

For the fortunate, if the initial romance is to blossom into a deeper, more settled form of lasting intimate companionship, the high-octane *motivation to be together* has to involve some *commitment to stay together* based on a couple's realistic view of who each of them are as persons and how lovingly they are capable of treating each other. Although he did not use the term explicitly, Judge Lindsey was a forerunner of the belief that healthy marriages were best established based on *personal commitment.*[5] This term, put forth by veteran sociologist Michael Johnson, is at the heart of what makes companionate marriages/partnerships—and ultimately flourishing love—survive and thrive. Partners' attraction to each other and the quality-of-life benefits of the relationship—when mutually kept up—sustain a personal commitment to stay together. Couples who are personally committed treasure the emotional bond they have and stay involved largely because they *want to.*

On the other hand, a *moral commitment* to a marriage is rooted in the notion that spouses stay together out of a sense of *duty rather than desire.* Romance may make courting partners desire to be together, but once marriage is entered into, spouses have a moral obligation to remain together, typically based on the conjugal vows they declared in the eyes of God and religious authorities. Their commitment is to the marriage vows they took, and marriage as a divinely inspired covenant, as distinct from a commitment to make each other happy and the marriage a happy one. The popular Christian evangelical writer, Gary Thomas, captures this idea when he poses the question: "What if God designed marriage to make us holy more than to make us happy?"[6]

Holiness is about sticking with a marriage contract no matter what—"in sickness and in health, till death do us part"—whether or not you desire to make your spouse feel loved, or he or she desire to make you feel loved in return. This is reflected in the slogan: "I walked up the aisle and said 'I do,' and I've been doing it ever since." This can have absurd ramifications. A client recently disclosed that although he hadn't spoken to his wife in three years—her alcoholism and infidelity leading to their undoing—he was not pursuing a divorce, because "after all, a marriage vow is a marriage vow." It's no less absurd to know that:

> Your spouse is committed to you, but you don't know if he or she actually likes you and enjoys spending time together.

> The ideal of marriage as a "sacred union" or "holy covenant" has become more important than the direct experience of how spouses treat one another.

> Promising to love someone forever assumes love is within our conscious control and a marital commitment made at one point in time sufficient to override all that life throws at spouses as time passes.

Holiness is also about sacrifice. In the Christian tradition, Jesus made the ultimate sacrifice, giving his life for the sins of the world. In this spirit, a holy marriage is one where both spouses strive to sacrifice their own self-interest, placing the happiness of the other before their own, or preferring to suffer rather than let a spouse suffer. To achieve a good marriage, Gary Thomas exhorts his flock: "You must crucify your selfishness."[7] Selfless giving, or acting kind, generous, appreciative, patiently, or forgivingly, without any need for it to be reciprocated—agape love—is the divine barometer for married couples to follow. If spouses return the favor and act kind, generous, appreciative, patient, or forgiving—that's a secondary benefit. The primary benefit is meeting your Christian duty and bolstering your chances of being rewarded with eternal life after death.

As we shall see in the coming pages, agape love is blind to matters of fairness in intimate relationships. Humans are earthly creatures who want their intimate relationships to be fair and equitable. They know in their heart of hearts the love they give is always influenced by the love they receive. If there's overall balance in giving and getting based on mutual love and respect across the things that matter to them—sex, overt displays of affection and appreciation, support with housework, income generation, childrearing, being paid attention to, planning and going on vacations—the relationship pleasingly chugs along.

A husband who tries to be intentional in supporting his wife in the ways he knows register for her—being on time picking up the kids from school; noticing without being told the milk carton is empty and swinging by the store on the way home from work to have milk on hand the next morning for breakfast; really paying attention while she talks; offering a foot massage after a busy day—may not expect considerateness in return, but has learned it just happens of its own accord in a flourishing relationship where mutual love and respect are givens.

It's likely he's treating her lovingly not just because he loves her—gifting her his love—but, consciously or not, because *she deserves it* due to the fact that she: spontaneously came up behind him and kissed him affectionately on the back of the neck that morning; paid the mortgage on time; folded his laundry without fanfare; took extra time reading bedtime stories to their son, even though she was exhausted; and agreed to stay up late to watch a movie he liked more than she did.

As will be discussed below and in places throughout the book, one of the key problems with a moral-religious marital commitment is that spouses are motivated to make themselves lovable in the eyes of God, more than in the eyes of their beloved. That often means adhering to a moral code that can interfere with the flourishing of intimate relationships—no sex before marriage, sex mainly or only for procreation, sacrificing one's personal preferences, expectations of benevolence and forgiveness under threat of divine punishment, wifely subservience. Couples are derailed from listening to any innate human voices in their heads calling them to be fair, appreciative, reasonable, kind, affectionate, and sexually responsive strictly for their own well-being, that of their beloved, and the flourishing of their relationship.

Almost a century ago, Judge Lindsey was cognizant of how a moral-religious code can gum up the works as far as humans treating each other well simply for the sake of wanting to treat each other well. He pulled no punches:

> When people begin to take the responsibility for their own moral decisions on their own shoulders they will begin to be moral. Theology, masquerading as divinely revealed religion, has forbidden them that right long enough; and it has thereby produced, quite without anybody intending it, a monstrous amount of ethical impotence, stupid conduct, cruelty, fear, and asinine blundering on the part of human beings who would have done well enough if they had been taught to follow that inner craving for what is just, right, and beautiful which is the common heritage of all of us.[8]

Judge Linsey hints at the need for a secular approach to love that keeps spouses answerable to each other for the quality of their relationship, drawing upon their innate potential to behave compassionately. God may work in mysterious ways. In matters of human love, there's hardly any mystery. As I embark on outlining the contours of a contemporary secular ethics of love, offering the reader ideas on how to love better—getting you to view your partnership as a sort of mutual happiness project—you may be struck by the ordinariness of what I am proposing. The lack of mystery. The human virtues baked into small everyday gestures that spur intimate partners to be the best versions of themselves with each other.

Secular love ethics

Young couples wobbly in their approach to love crave romantic wisdom from old couples smooth in their methods. When such old couples speak up, young couples listen. That's the case with the OGS (original grandparents) of Boyle Heights in Southern California. The grandchildren of Barbara "Cutie" Cooper and Harry Cooper realized their quirkily lovable and lovably quirky grandparents had much to say about long-term love—having been married for seventy-three years—and judiciously documented it.[9]

Harry was a self-described Zen master, calm, cerebral, and deferential in his demeanor. Barbara was an unapologetic social butterfly and problem solver. I reached out to Chinta Cooper, one of the grandchildren, and she sent me a charming clip of an interview between them on the occasion of their seventy-second wedding anniversary. Chinta probed: "Seven decades of love. What's the secret? How do you keep it all together?" Harry wryly interjected: "It's a give and take situation. I give and she takes. No really, it's an equal situation."

Let's set aside the role of humor as an endearingly human, all-too-human, form of love. I deal with that later in the book. On the face of it, Harry seems to be asserting that the durability of his and Cutie's loving commitment rests on the faith they put in their natural desire to be fair and equitable with one another, not faithful reliance on some moral-religious imperative to love and not expect love in return. In the book *Fall in Love for Life*, narrating Cutie's well-worn advice for couples, it's human intuition that she advises couples to fall back on, not divinely channeled moral prescriptions: "So many people today don't know their own hearts speaking to them. They don't give their intuition the respect it deserves."[10]

If I was to extrapolate from what Harry and Cutie serve up as central to keeping love vital decade after decade, I'd say they're proposing that the best shot at being loved in the way you want to be loved comes from generously showing love in the way your partner prefers to be loved—from a place of emotional desire, not moral duty. In one sense, flourishing love entails adopting a *fairness habit of mind*. We don't need to match each other's considerate gestures—I took out the trash this week, it's on you to do it next week; I coached our daughter's soccer team last season, you need to volunteer to referee this season; I initiated sex the last few times, I'm holding off until you show me you want to get under the covers with me. Nonetheless, in the grand scheme of things, there has to be a felt sense of respectful reciprocity. An abiding sentiment of overall balance of benefits and burdens across what each partner feels is essentially important to them.

In my marriage, I function best when I have abundant solitude, time alone to read, reflect, introspect, and doodle on the weekends.

This is amplified by the fact that most days of the week I meet with emotionally troubled people compelling me to be engaged, present, and attuned. Of course, my wife wants me to be engaged, present, and attuned when I am at home, but she understands I have my limits, and expects only so much of me on any given day or week depending upon my client load. I feel immensely respected by this. It builds goodwill. It makes me benevolent when she wants to cut back on her own hours as a therapist to live a slower life, add yoga classes, garden more. I don't take it personally that she's not equaling my workload so as to add to the family income. I'm appreciative that she's respectful of me in the ways that matter to me and I'm respectful of her in the ways that matter to her.

In the Contextual Therapy lexicon, our "invisible ledger,"[11] or experienced balance of give and take in terms of benefits received and burdens suffered, is mostly a fair one. There's no need to keep score. We know the score. After thirty years of marriage, we have learned to make the mutual adjustments necessary to benefit our joint quality of life—because we care about each other's comfort and satisfaction. When there's fluency in this arrangement, there's no deliberate score keeping. It's simply a well-practiced, embodied way of being—mutually and silently delivered up: I tiptoe to the bathroom during the night so as not to awaken Janet, she refrains from emptying the dishwasher too early in the morning before I'm fully awake; she warms my teacup unasked, I show up to carry the groceries in from the car unasked, and so forth. Considerate gestures beget considerate gestures. British philosopher Mike Martin sums up this mutually caring disposition: "Marriage involves the coordinated pursuit of the overall happiness of two people who share a life."[12]

It wouldn't be a stretch to claim that my wife and I have adopted the Golden Rule, hook, line, and sinker: *Treat others as you would like them to treat you*. This common-sense ethical directive dates back to the time of Confucius, over 2,500 years ago. Although some version of it can be found in all the major world religions, as Greg Epstein, Humanist Chaplain at Harvard University, asserts: "not a single one of these versions of the golden rule requires a God."[13] It relies on normal human empathy, or people's capacity to vicariously experience the emotional states of others. Emotions are contagious. Others' feelings resonate with our own, providing us with emotional information on how our actions bring a smile or a frown to their faces. Empathy is what alerts us to consider our impact on others. It results in humans caring to care. It's what makes people ponder the issue: "If I put myself in your place then... I could see why you felt rejected... why you were frustrated... why you were overjoyed."

Of course, to put yourself in someone's place requires some affinity for knowing yourself. What turns you on and off. What the negotiables and non-negotiables are in terms of how you prefer to live your life. Being self-respecting in this way is foundational for other-respecting. The same rules apply to you as apply to me. If I like my preferences honored, then I need to find a way to honor yours. Loving application of the Golden Rule involves holding the dynamic tension between asserting self-interest while being open to self-giving. In a nutshell, it involves compromise: what's good for the goose is good for the gander, and goose and gander need to have in their interpersonal repertoire a capacity to find a happy medium.

Cutie Cooper has this to say about the importance of compromise in a marriage:

> The time for having singularly strong opinions is when you are a single person. Once you choose to be one-half of a pair, you must compromise, so that no one person gets what he or she wants at the expense of the other. It may take some getting used to, but reaching decisions that you both can live with can be quite romantic, since each one is a symbol of your connection.[14]

Knowing our own and our significant other's likes and dislikes and putting in the emotional labor to make space for them to be jointly asserted is the very definition of mutual respect. A case in point would be how my wife and I go about garden projects. Janet is every bit a horticultural aesthete. As am I. However, what pleases her eye is not what pleases mine. She likes leggy plants, an assortment of succulents of varying shapes and sizes, a medley of colorful planters, vegetation left alone to grow unevenly. I'm a minimalist who likes as few plants as possible, symmetrically arranged and trimmed, not busy on the eye. Our garden is a trade-off. Not her ideal. Not mine. I'm happy enough with it. She is too.

Christian love ethics often privilege self-sacrifice, not mutually respectful compromise arrived at by couples showing a good measure of self-interest. The tenets of agape love are prioritized: willful suffering of disadvantages and discomforts for the benefit of another, without need for reciprocation. As already mentioned, this is accorded divine significance since, as the Bible says, God sent Jesus to die for the sins of humanity, the ultimate sacrifice. In the Christian tradition, couples are encouraged to mirror this sort of unconditional love. It involves acting lovingly even when your spouse is a perennial grouch. Turning the other cheek when slighted, instead of just turning on him or her. The problem here is that turning the other cheek excessively makes people cheeky—or resentful. Over-giving and under-benefiting leads any self-respecting person to feel exploited; consciously or not, resentment is a natural outcome.

There's a funny line by humorist Gregg Eisenberg that attests to this inevitability: "I want to see myself as a loving person, but you get in my way."[15] This is notwithstanding how repeatedly suffering the slights of a perennial grouch without self-advocacy pushback lets that grouch off the hook for being a grouch, enabling the grouch to keep on being a grouch. Religious ethics that underemphasize self-respect and relational accountability are a brittle foundation on which to build a close-knit intimate bond.

Oddly, an agape mindset renders a person moral in the supernatural sense, winning God's favor and maximizing one's chances of eternal life in heaven after death, yet can position people to behave unethically in the secular sense, or engage in actions that cause emotional suffering in the lives of real flesh-and-blood people. All too often, an agape mindset pivots women into over-giving, believing that to give is to give in, and giving in ends up leading to so much surrender of self and interpersonal power that feelings of helplessness and hopelessness arise. Indeed, agape love often fits hand-in-glove with patriarchy and gender traditionalism, locking women into a homemaker role, and a subservient relationship with their husband, as a self-sacrificing expectation.

The website Biblicalgenderroles.com boils this point down: "In Christian marriage the man conforms his will to God's will and the wife conforms her will to her husband's will."[16] From a secular perspective, this is unethical, since it is an unequal arrangement that limits women's voices and choices. And, as I will argue below, it sidelines women from access to an egalitarian marital arrangement that abundant research shows is a precondition for a vital, lasting marriage.

All said, it's still good to have a dollop of agape love in your relationship toolkit—not to establish yourself as righteous in the eyes of God, but simply to better suffer the insufferable habits of an endearing significant other. Heather Havrilesky, the connoisseur of marital tedium, writes very transparently about the blessings and the curses of conjugal life: "Marriage requires amnesia, a mute button, a filter on the lens, a damper, some blinders, some bumpers, some ear plugs, a nap. You need to erase these stories, misplace this tape, zoom out, slowly dissolve to black." Nonetheless, self-regard can never be denied: "Surviving a marriage requires self-care, time alone, meditation, escape, selfishness."[17]

Another building block of secular love ethics pertains to how accepting our mortality can create greater urgency and willingness to hone our ability to love. The late British-American intellectual, Christopher Hitchens, always irreverent when he inhabited planet earth, once remarked: "We speculate that it is at least possible that, once people accept the fact of their short and struggling lives, they might behave better toward each other and not worse."[18] Living with fuller awareness of the capriciousness of existence—the randomness of our own death, and that of our beloved—sharpens the desire to be more intentional with what we do with our time. Embracing death as inevitable—not an abstraction, not a portal to eternity—facilitates zeroing in on the things that matter in life.

Nothing matters more than cultivating the most loving bond possible with our mate. It's deeply unpleasant to contemplate "death regrets," like our beloved dying in the midst of our holding a grudge or nursing a petty grievance. But such unpleasant thoughts can help us get ahead of these death regrets and see the tragedy and ridiculousness in holding grudges and nursing petty grievances, spurring us to mend our ways. Yale University scholar, Martin Hagglund, weighs in here: "The key to breaking habit is to recall that we can lose what we love."[19] Befriending death goads us to love our beloved as if it's not going to last. It makes us chase the profound consolation associated with knowing when that dreaded, but inescapable, day arrives we can derive solace from the fact that we strove to love at our best, with our beloved dying knowing with confidence he or she was truly loved.

In midlife, the shrinking window of earthly time becomes more pronounced. Carlo Strenger, in the psychology department at Tel Aviv University, sees this as a pivotal period in which people are driven to resort their priorities: "Life needs to be pared down to the essentials."[20] The temptation is to manage the dawning death anxiety with hedonistic pursuits, going for broke and amusing ourselves to death with sex, drugs, or fancy material purchases.

Ernest Becker, the prominent American cultural anthropologist, in his Pulitzer Prize-winning book, *The Denial of Death*, would say this life trajectory reflects mid-lifers managing their death anxiety by "tranquilizing themselves with the trivial."[21] Ultimately, a more fulfilling way of dealing with death anxiety is to engage in what he calls "immortality projects," meaningful pursuits that leave a lasting legacy to the special people in your life, and society as a whole. One such legacy is to exit the world leaving loved ones knowing they were loved, not in the abstract, but in the down-to-earth ways we treated them, day in and day out.

This definition of a love life well lived requires what the Roman Stoics would consider overcoming our insatiability in midlife, not indulging it. Our greedy needs to have it all somehow have to be supplanted by what the contemporary Stoic philosopher, William Irvine, argues is "creating in ourselves a desire for the things we already have."[22] In my marriage, this means keenly attending to how *fortunate* I am to have a wife who is as bubbly and outgoing, intellectually curious, sensual, politically plugged in, stylishly dressed, outdoorsy, enamored by a good novel, and gladdened by droll humor in her sixty-three-year-old body as she was when I first met her in her twenty-two-year-old body. I say fortunate, not blessed, because it would be disrespectful to imply that these charming qualities of hers were not due to her human efforts to be a good human being, rather divine providence.

Yet another virtuous immortality project—a healthy way to manage death anxiety—is to leave a wholesome legacy in the life of loved ones by actively undoing the dysfunctional patterns of caregiving visited upon them in their family of origin. Loving them in the ways they were entitled to be loved as children, by the mere fact that they were vulnerable beings worthy of a head start in life. Most people emerge out of childhood afflicted with what Thomas Bradley and Benjamin Karney, psychologists at UCLA, call "enduring vulnerabilities."[23] Past fateful experiences of rejection, abandonment, or plain emotional invalidation prime expectations to be treated similarly in the present by significant others. People, so afflicted, become sensitized to feeling rejected, abandoned, or disregarded, in their everyday interactions with partners which can have disruptive effects.

Another amusing line by humorist Greg Eisenberg declares: "I fully expected to be disappointed, and you didn't let me down one bit."[24] Insofar as insight can be gained into these dynamics, a person can avoid falling into the trap of reinjuring his or her partner in old ways, even turning the tide and responding favorably. An example will elucidate.

As a toddler, my thirty-six-year-old client Hugo was left to live in Honduras with relatives while his teenage mother made the trek to the United States in search of a better life for the two of them. They were not reunited until Hugo was thirteen.

The effects of this abandonment trauma emotionally permeated his marriage to Lorretta in ways that Hugo was barely aware of. Hugo was apt to become overly irritated when Lorretta did not return his texts in a timely manner, arrived home later than expected, made plans with friends without consulting with him first, or prioritized professional responsibilities over family affairs. Lorretta was convinced Hugo was "a control freak" and arguments would ensue.

In couples therapy, I tried to shift the focus onto Hugo's history of abandonment and suggested that Hugo probably experienced these letdowns as microscopic abandonments. He didn't have any control as a child to get predictable access to his mother, and now as an adult was exercising the control he didn't have, granted in desperate ways. This helped Lorretta develop empathy and understanding for Hugo. She realized that seemingly mundane steps like returning texts and arriving home on time, consulting with him first before making plans with friends, and generally being more available and reliable around the house didn't mean she was at the mercy of Hugo's supposed controlling tendencies, but actually were ways to remedy his trauma history.

It should come as no surprise to the reader when I conclude that a grounding in secular love ethics contributes to lasting flourishing intimate relationships. Science backs that up. Let's start with the data on couples who adopt a fairness habit of mind with each other. A host of studies reveal that couples—dating, cohabitating, or married—in fair and equitable relationships report high degrees of passionate and companionate love, sexual satisfaction, marital happiness and stability, fewer affairs, and confidence in the durability of their commitment.[25] Marriages where gender traditionalism exists and partners slot into hierarchical roles based on self-sacrifice and moral duty don't fare so well.

In the largest and most detailed study available of marital strengths and problems, involving over 50,000 couples, researchers uncovered that the greatest threat to a happy marriage was unequal sharing of power. Eighty-one percent of couples who believed their relationship was egalitarian were happily married, while 82 percent of couples in traditional/hierarchical marriages were unhappily married.[26] On a similar note, a research team headed up by Nathan Leonhardt at the University of Toronto, looking at mutual respect and shared power in long-term marriages, concluded: "The ideal relationship seems built upon a feeling of mutual influence, rather than one or the other feeling that someone in the relationship has a higher level of power."[27]

This is not to say that marriages where spouses have a shared religious outlook encouraging individual self-sacrifice and a belief in unequal gender roles can't last, or be satisfying, for that matter. We know from the work of Samuel Perry in the Department of Sociology at the University of Oklahoma that religiously committed couples tend to stay together and report high levels of relationship satisfaction.[28] However, there's a difference between being in a *satisfactory* relationship and being in a *flourishing* one. Being satisfied implies that you're comfortable with the ways things are. You've reached an end point, or your limit; better to keep the bar where it is, not raise it. It's a relationship B–. Not a bad grade, but not a great grade either. There's a thin line between being satisfied and being complacent.

Flourishing—a word that has its roots in the ancient Greek, Aristotelian term *eudaimonia*—and complacency aren't good bedfellows. Flourishing emphasizes the mutual desire to enlarge each other's well-being in a relationship. It involves not just showing interest in the life pursuits that provide meaning and purpose for a mate, but actively supporting them. It's about couples being authentic with each other, being real, doing away with pretense. It's about realizing a relationship's full potential. Not in a manic-like, enough-is-never-enough way. Not in a let's-reach-for-the-stars way. But in a let's-really-settle-in-together-way, digging in and locating the courage to push each other to make a good relationship better.

The British philosopher Robert Goodin touches upon what it means to genuinely settle in for couples who fully commit to each other in a we-are-together-until-one-or-both-of-hits-the-grave-so-let's-make-the-best-of-it way: "we do so with the intention and expectation of sticking with it more firmly and sometimes for different reasons than we would if we had chosen it for satisficing-style reasons alone."[29]

Back to Cutie and Harry Copper and their settling in experience as Harry reached the ripe old age of ninety-eight with his health in decline and death approaching. He had to be moved to a skilled nursing unit adjacent to the assisted living facility where he and Cutie resided. In my communications with Chinta, their granddaughter who had overseen their care, she mentioned: "Used to sleeping next to each other every night for over seventy years and spending all their days together, my grandmother naturally moved to skilled nursing to be with my grandfather."

After several weeks of hanging out most of the day in his room, sharing a twin bed and witnessing Harry become more inert and sedate, Chinta noticed that Cutie "started to inexplicably slow down herself, almost seemingly needing skilled nursing support despite a lack of physical causes for this need." Chinta, her sister, and the nursing staff were in a quandary. Should they just allow Cutie to while away the hours with Harry at the expense of her own health because it seemed to bring him so much joy? Or coax her to move back to her room at the assisted living facility and pay daily visits to Harry? The latter option was collectively decided upon.

"My grandparents were skeptical at first. After all, what was the point of life, if not to be together? But they were willing to try," Chinta recalled, adding: "Her mental health and mobility bounced back immediately. For the first time in her life, she learned how to live by herself. She went to meals in the dining room with her friends from the assisted living facility, she spent most of the day with my grandfather in skilled nursing, and then came home to her room to sleep alone."

Harry was grateful for Cutie's visits and soaked up the precious time remaining. Chinta described for me Harry's end-of-life experience and how Cutie handled it: "They cuddled and napped together, enjoying what ended up being his final days before he passed. I'm convinced that my grandmother took his death so well because she had a chance to learn how to live without him. She lived another five years. I can't imagine losing a partner of over seventy years but I'm so grateful that they were willing to put her well-being first."

I would concur with Chinta, with a twist. Harry probably knew Cutie was outliving him. What was best for her—going on with her own life—was best for him. He could die consoled, knowing, as life progressed, he had given her all the love he had to give. He could die peacefully, knowing he was exiting life having attained flourishing love.

Flourishing love—some non-negotiables

On January 3, 1993, at Pupilo's, an Italian restaurant in a strip mall in Azusa, California, owned by my younger brother Cosmo, my wife Janet and I tied the knot. Reading on the lines and between the lines of our marriage vows, its more accurate to say we unraveled the knot. Compressed in our vows was an awareness of the potential we somehow were cognizant of at the time for realizing a life of flourishing love together. Of meeting each other's essential needs. It's stunning to me, not having re-read our vows until a week before writing this chapter—a passage of almost thirty years—how their contents align with the secular ethics supporting flourishing love presented in this book! Here's what I proclaimed to Janet that day:

> Janet, we have come so far together, so much is possible.
> After all this time you still have the power to make me:
> Laugh with abandon
> Give up tired ideas
> Shiver with sexual excitement
> Take me beyond the personal and psychological
> Savor more than meat and potatoes
> You are you, I am I, we are we

with a predictability that is sometimes maddening,
sometimes reassuring, but rarely fraught with despair.
Janet, we have come so far together, so much is possible.
A fundamental mutual acceptance has taken shape,
a mutual acceptance that is not based on self-sacrifice
or foreclosed hopes and ideals.
A mutual acceptance that is the natural outgrowth of
who we each have become.
We truly have crossed paths.
Janet, we have come so far together, so much is possible.
With you my mind and body need not renounce necessary
pleasures.
With you there is no need to compromise my desire to be a man of
ideas.
With you companionship, rootedness, and family are all realizable.
Janet, we have come so far together, so much is possible.
Will you be my wife, companion, and lover for years to come?

Here's what Janet proclaimed to me:

You are my desert.
Wide skies you give me when I seek solitude and crystallized
thoughts.
Wise unmovable rock you become when commitment and vision
elude me.
Your body, like a high desert breeze reminds me that I am alive.
As four golden coyotes, you challenge, mystify, and incite me,
because you're different.
In your high noon heat you burn my skin, scratch my throat and
deny my thirst.
I forgive for I will bruise your sandy floors, chatter up your silence
and curse your thorn-edged beauty.
You, desert full of space, prod me to search for my space, ever so
internal.
You tempt, soothe, and shake my soul.
As I return from the desert, I now return to you.

Breaking the silence after we had both read aloud our vows was my father's confused voice: "What about till death do us part?" It was not that kind of wedding. Janet and I were in tight alignment regarding the *non-negotiables we mutually subscribed to*, our *shared value system*, and one of those pertained to there being no guaranteed longevity to our partnership simply by issuing a marriage vow. We were in agreement that marriage involved *mutual emotional upkeep* and without joint responsibility for this, a marriage could wither and die.

Desert themes pervade Janet's vows. She had just spent three days alone in the desert at Joshua Tree and was inspired to write what she wrote awakening at dawn one morning, observing the glistening fur coats of four coyotes frolicking nearby. We share a love of nature. I wouldn't pledge it's one of our non-negotiables, an essential need that if unmet for an intolerable length of time would put our marriage in a red zone. It's more the cherry on top, a bonus, an additive.

What's a joint non-negotiable is what occurs in spades when we are able to spend time in nature. Settling into nature's rhymes in the woods or the desert allows us to feel time is working for us, not against us. It allows us to tap the sublime experience the French writer Andre Maurois encapsulates: "A happy marriage is a long conversation that always seems too short." There's nobody else that matters and nowhere else we need to be. Conversations can be consummately settled into: paying attention and listening to each other with true interest and curiosity; wanting to know more; allowing space and time for the elaboration of compelling and genuine thoughts and feelings. That's not unique to us. That's a fundamental element of flourishing love.

What seems straightforward at first glance, though extraordinarily difficult to mutually enact in any sustained fashion, is showing true curiosity about what speakers really have to say. This is reflected in the quote by the French political activist and mystic, Simone Weil: "Attention is the rarest and purest form of generosity."[30] Overcoming our own susceptibility to be self-absorbed, opinionated, oblivious, or just plain preoccupied or distractible, is a prerequisite for true listening. It's befuddling to me that conversational ethics is not a scholarly topic for educators to pursue, or for educational institutions to require students be taught. What can be more important for society than to impart in future love partners—who might also model it for the children they raise—the know-how of good conversation?

The right to: complete a sentence or an unfinished thought; obtain eye contact while in the act of speaking; courteous turn-taking; anticipate a reasonable amount of curiosity; not be "talked at," but "talked with"; rely upon listeners not appearing indifferent to what we have to say or, in this day and age, to be unglued to their smartphones? In his wonderful book, *The Pursuit of Attention*, the American sociologist, Charles Derber, hints at conversational ethics when he refers to "attention-getting and attention-giving initiatives,"[31] but his ideas didn't really take off among university scholars.

The words used when *leaning in* with true curiosity while dialoguing are easily recognizable: "Are you saying…?" "What did you mean by that?" "That's interesting…" "No kidding, how did that go…?" "How was work today?" "I was thinking about what you just said and wanted to know more."

Affirmative responses show we both care to listen and listen to care: "That's sad…" "I'm glad you had a good time…" "You were so right on…" "I'm happy that worked out in your favor." They can take the form of positive reframing of an issue, even if it's a bit over-enhancing. Husband: "I can always tell I've put on a few pounds when my wedding ring doesn't fit well on my finger." Wife: "Maybe it's just your blood circulation being out of whack from sitting all day." Particularly impactful are the affirmative responses sincerely expressed when a partner fishes for recognition of something of importance they've succeeded at: "You met your goal of 10,000 steps today, that's great!" as well as moments of insecurity when a partner needs reassurance: "I know you can be overly critical, like your mother, but YOU ARE NOT YOUR MOTHER, you are capable of being so much kinder than her."

Sometimes, even in the best of circumstances, affirmative responses in the context of disputed points of view get coughed up rather than wholeheartedly emitted: "I hear you…" "I get what you're saying…" "I understand…" What results in people acting retentive in responding with such run-of-the-mill statements like these is their insufficient grasp of the difference between acknowledging and agreeing. They assume that acknowledging is agreeing, when they may disagree. They underappreciate that other-respect shown by uttering phrases like

"I hear you…" "I get what you are saying…" "I understand…" can be followed up with responses that reflect self-respect: "But I don't see it the same way…" "I have a different take on the issue…" "My memory of events is different…" The word respect originates from the Latin, "respectus," meaning "regard, a looking at." Mere acknowledgment of what loved ones have to say with affirmative phrases is an act of respect. To omit these from our discourse—*leaning out when dialoguing*—is always disrespectful in some shape or form. We are not graciously considering what they have to say.

Leaning out in conversations can take various forms. The listener can be soft-edged in their approach, ignoring what you have to say, appearing preoccupied, looking away while you're talking, or tinkering on a computer or smartphone. Hard-edged leaning out reactions in discussions are tangential or belligerent in nature. The former encompasses the listener mystifyingly not tracking: Wife: "Wow, after the rains in recent weeks the flowers are really in bloom." Husband: "Did you remember to make that appointment with the dentist for me, my tooth is really hurting." The latter are antagonistic: Husband: "I'd really like to buy one of those new electric Ford Mustangs." Wife: "On your salary… dah… that's a reach."

There's syncing up verbally and there's doing it non-verbally. Facial communication is its own special thing. Spontaneously meeting a smile with a smile, or a frown with a frown, conveys attunement. When this basic form of behavioral synchrony is significantly off kilter in a relationship, it can indicate a troublesome amount of emotional alienation. I am currently working with a couple where the wife desperately wishes her husband was better at reading faces. It's disheartening to her that he is "off" in his facial responses when she needs him to be "on." To see in his face that he understands the nuances of what she's communicating.

During a recent couples session, the husband blurted out: "Apparently, my face doesn't work right—my emotions don't show." We all laughed. There was a collective understanding of the problem. This emboldened the wife to not wallow in despair over her husband "not getting her," rooted in mismatched facial recognition, and accept the misattunements would have to be worked with, and worked around, because she was fully committed to the marriage and couldn't imagine any other life.

There's even evidence that with the passage of time, couples who read each other's facial expressions well start to look alike. A University of Michigan study had research subjects compare randomly ordered pictures of couples taken on their wedding day with separate shots taken twenty-five years later. Matching them for similarity twenty-five years out, the research subjects successfully figured out who was married to whom. Their facial features had converged over time.[32] Being facially in sync apparently leads partners to internalize each other, so much so that others can observe how much they belong to each other.

Let's return to my wedding day and what I wish my father had exclaimed after the vows were read aloud. Had he blurted out: "What about to have and to hold?" Janet and I would have replied with a resounding, "Amen!" Another of our shared non-negotiables, then and now, is showing and maintaining our love with physical affection. Not just sex, but spontaneous hugs, kisses, cuddles, and snuggles. As we age, we are not foot-massagers, but we are ardent hand-holders and cuddlers. Our joint bedrock assumption that the regular sharing of physical affection reflects the strength of our intimate bond is not unique to us.

In the first study of its kind, polling a representative sample of married Americans across levels of education and income, as well as ethnicity, ranging from age twenty to ninety-three, of the 46 percent of women and 49 percent of men who reported being "very intensely in love," displays of physical affection—frequency of sex, hugging, kissing, cuddling, hand-holding—stood out as linchpins of their marital happiness. In the older cohort, frequency of sex dropped off, but not spontaneous displays of physical affection.[33] So much for what the sweet, all-giving mother in *The Simpsons*, Marge, says in a rare moment of cynicism: "Passion is for teenagers and foreigners."[34]

Sylvia Plath alluringly inscribed in one of her published journals: "Kiss me and you'll see how important I am."[35] Happy couples show how important they are to each other with kisses. They are joined at the lips. Not just pecks on the cheek but getting all up in each other's faces with ample amor. It has been shown that almost 60 percent of people who deem themselves to be very happily married kiss passionately several times a week.[36] A recent research project out of Brigham Young University surveying over 1,600 people who had been in a committed relationship for at least two years concluded: "Kissing frequently could be considered a bell weather [sic] of sorts for determining if the relationship bonding is strong and the sexual quality high."[37]

The antidote to a partner who gets on your nerves is to get in his or her nerves—with a kiss. Lips have one of the highest concentrations of sensory neurons compared to any other body region. The brain's somatosensory cortex instantly processes a host of neural and chemical messages, leaving Chip Walter at *Scientific American* to conclude: "a kiss locks two humans together in an exchange of scents, tastes, textures, secrets, and emotions."[38]

I've zeroed in on two overarching non-negotiables, or givens, that buttress a flourishing love relationship: taking seriously the joint responsibility for the emotional upkeep involved and keeping the doors of physical intimacy open. Seizing upon the small opportunities to pay attention to each other more intently and be present during affectionate moments adds up over time. The goodwill bank account prospers. A delightful sense that you're freely giving the love your partner earns and getting the love you deserve kicks in. The wheels of give and get, and get and give, benevolently self-rotate. The negotiables get easier to handle—what color to paint the bathroom, sushi or Indian food when dining out, where to go on vacation, whether your daughter should do chores to earn her allowance, or just receive it. The chatter in the head of yesteryears after unpleasant interactions trying to persuade you could do better with some fantasied other dies down. The low-grade ambivalence fades. There's a steady dismantling of the unhelpful ideal that has long since set up residence in your head making you hold out for something else, something different, something better.

Stephen Levine, in his concise little book, *Demystifying Love*, mentions this secretive resistance to really committing to and settling into the preciousness of our loved one and the bond we have created together: "much of adult life is spent with the awareness of the gap between our private sense of ideal love and our actual experience of ourself and our partner in a relationship."[39] The person you believed had the potential to be irreplaceable when you declared your marriage vows has actually become irreplaceable. More awe inspiring is the palpable sense that the intimate relationship you've jointly molded over the years has become irreplaceable. First, you must survive the greatest challenge to your mutual happiness project together—domesticity.

CHAPTER 2

Surviving domesticity

On January 24, 2022, seven-time Superbowl Champion, Tom Brady, generally considered the greatest quarterback of all time, shocked the sports world by announcing his retirement: "I'm gonna spend some time with [my family] … It's not always about what I want. It's about what we want as a family."[1] Mr. Brady is not alone as a father torn between the demands of work and his wish to be a more involved parent. We know from the latest release by the Pew Research Center that 50 percent of fathers who are college graduates, like Mr. Brady, long to spend more time with their children. Sixty-two percent cite "work obligations" as the biggest obstacle to them alleviating their paternal guilt.[2]

Forty-eight days later, Mr. Brady press-released a change of heart. He was geared up to resume his football career: "These past two months I have realized my place is still on the field."[3] On the face of it, this sounds like a classic case of careful what you wish for. We will never know for sure. But, as a jock, who probably spent his fair share of time frequenting fraternity houses, we would expect him to appreciate some parallels between that lifestyle and raising children, like the stand-up comedian, Ray Romano, does: "Having children is like living in a frat house—nobody sleeps, everything's broken, and there's a lot of throwing up."[4]

Children are not given to fall in line and take orders expediently, like running-backs and wide-receivers. Especially teens and pre-teens, the age bracket of Mr. Brady's three children at the time. Before he jumped the gun and announced his retirement, a consultation might have been in order with Kittie Frantz in the Department of Pediatrics at the University of Southern California, who advises parents: "Remember, you are not managing an inconvenience; you are raising a human being."[5]

Which begs the question: What are the contours of contemporary family life that make raising children seem so incredibly inconvenient, especially for parents also trying to be spouses, or intimate partners? Or, for that matter, what challenges in the domestic sphere threaten to unravel a couple's romantic bond, whether children are involved or not?

Three stressful roles the current generation of parents are forced to assume that either didn't exist, or were less relevant, to previous generations of parents are: chauffeur, extracurricular activities coordinator, and social media/technology supervisor.

According to the National Center for Safe Routes to School, in 1969 about 89 percent of children in the USA either walked or biked to school in the morning. Today, the figure hovers between 10 and 26 percent.[6] In 1983, it's estimated that 72 percent of American teenagers between the ages of sixteen and nineteen years old were legally authorized to drive. Nowadays, only about 50 percent of those in that age group possess a valid driver's license.[7] That means a fresh abundance of parents are charged with negotiating and juggling work schedules to facilitate school drop-offs and pick-ups and coordinate rideshares with fellow parents. Car rides can be precious moments where children are a "captive audience." They feel they have no choice but to settle into prolonged conversations. Car rides can also be a nightmare, where parents and children alike experience it as a form of unwanted forced contact in an enclosed space, making it nerve-racking for all.

Nowadays, anxiety around rising economic inequality and uncertainty, stiffer competition for college admission, and the perceived irreplaceable value of a college education combined leave most parents energized to pull out all the stops, financially and logistically, to beef up their offspring's after-school activities resume. This is just one dimension of the new norm of so-called "intensive parenting." Other aspects involve being better playmates; listeners and communicators;

proponents of children speaking their minds and sharing their feelings; and advocates for their individualized needs with teachers and outside professionals.

A recent LendingTree report shows that nearly two-thirds of parents go into debt to pay for their children's extracurricular activities, and over half admit they are spending more than they can afford.[8] Along-side these findings are those yielded by a 2022 Stress in America report indicating that 70 percent of American parents report being under "extreme stress" related to their children's academic, social, and emotional development.[9] As we shall see in the coming pages, when finances are mishandled within the family, debt accrues, and over-parenting habits predominate, couples are in a red zone.

Monitoring screen time and social media is a veritable devil's choice. On the one hand, if parents are to steal time for themselves to decompress alone or as a couple, they often feel compelled to greenlight their child's usage of smartphones and tablets to access social media. In fact, during the pandemic, children's smartphone usage in the US jumped by 25 percent, and their videogaming by 20 percent.[10] That said, most parents—70 percent and upwards—are perennially concerned about the age-inappropriate content their children view online, such as violence, profanity, and disturbing sexualized imagery.[11]

Droves of parents also worry about how their children's overuse of screens leads to insufficient sleep and exercise. Monitoring and curbing their child's usage is an exercise in herding cats: "I just need ten more minutes," "I gave you ten more minutes an hour ago!" Videogames (unlike TV shows of old, before they could be taped and binge-watched) rarely have a discreet end point. You can always level up, copy and paste missions, and bump up against ambiguous climaxes that scream out to be retried. Taking away a smartphone from a thirteen-year-old who is in the middle of making a TikTok video, as a consequence for transgressive behavior—no matter how much forewarning and calmness are implemented—finds him or her reacting as if a lung is being extracted.

The frenzy of activities and responsibilities setting apart twenty-first-century family life with children ought to make it an all-hands-on-deck parental arrangement. However, surveys substantiate that women bear the outsized load of housework and childcare, even when partners' paid workloads are relatively even. Frequently, men deceive themselves into thinking they carry more of the domestic load than they do. A pandemic phase poll conducted by the Morning Consult for the *New York Times* showed that almost half of men believed they were overseeing the bulk of their child's home schooling. Only 3 percent of women agreed.[12] This spells trouble.

As I explore below, without a fairness-minded approach, a felt sense of equity between the sexes in the overall balance of perceived contributions and benefits in an intimate relation, a couple's bond can perish. That doesn't stop with an equitable division of household labor, or childcare responsibilities, when children are involved. It extends to a fairness-minded approach to money matters. Even something as seemingly humdrum—but is vital to stay mentally sharp and ungrumpy—as taking joint responsibility for the conditions that smooth the way to a good night's sleep.

If mothers, in particular, are to be disabused of feeling like they are permanently on the clock as far as their child's well-being goes, fathers have to seriously examine their "unselfconscious cluelessness" around parenting. As a society, we need to get away from the idea that the nuclear family is the exclusive milieu in which to socialize children. Religiously committed conservatives often rail against notions that it "takes a village" to raise children. Last year, Michael Youssef, senior pastor at the Church of the Apostles in Atlanta, Georgia, wrote to his followers: "I submit that it does *not* take a village to raise a child. God already designed the perfect nurturing environment for a child. It's called a family."[13]

If the Covid-19 pandemic has taught us anything, it's that parents rely on a whole phalanx of babysitters, teachers, coaches, tutors, counselors, therapists, and pastors, such that the sequestering at home orders left parents scrambling without the childrearing social supports they rely on. Two years into the pandemic, one survey showed that over half of mothers with children under age twelve reported it was either somewhat, or very difficult, handling childcare responsibilities. That was up from 38 percent before the Covid-19 outbreak.[14]

A secular mindset is that children are the future of society and it *definitely* takes a village to raise them. Parents can do their part as socializing agents, but if children are to be full-functioning citizens, they need to be seen as of the world and prepared for and launched into the world—daycare, sleepovers with friends, school, summer camps, mentoring programs, neighborhood clubs, sports teams, travel abroad programs. This not only increases their exposure to people from varying racial, ethnic, and socio-economic backgrounds, with different personalities and value systems to learn from—mini social laboratories preparing them to function best in the world—but frees parents up to sustain their intimate bond as spouses or intimate partners.

Gay and lesbian parents are often ahead of the curve in this domain, creating what political scientist Daniel Burns at the University of Dallas labels "forged families": friends, extended family members, even ex-partners where there's a quid pro quo helping arrangement and loyalty in times of needed parental support.[15]

Like the proverbial frog slowly boiling in a pot of water, even the best marriages and intimate partnerships can be dismantled ever-so-gradually by the burdens of family life. Committed couples without children fare better as far as relationship satisfaction goes. They experience more domestic bliss than hiss. That said, they are three times more likely to break up. "Staying together for the kids" can be a moral-religious prescription that hangs as an albatross around the necks of a couple, when all the indications are—from a mutual happiness perspective—they should part ways. Having children in common to raise together can also provide a sense of joint mission and solidarity with couples who feel emotionally estranged during the inevitable rough patches in a long-term partnership—even contemplating a separation or divorce—but retain a dormant potential to revive the intimate bond that for the time being has slipped away.

Hanging in over the long haul can be deeply rewarding. It can yield the win–win of couples rediscovering strong elements of the romantic attachment that existed before children came along, alloyed with the deep sense of mutual fulfillment derived from living long enough to witness that your parenting efforts contributed to virtuous character traits in your child.

Sweet spotting a fair division of labor

Mallory and Frank—in their late forties, married with two teenage daughters—arrived for their couples therapy session with a palpable cloud hanging over them. In Mallory's mind, the stalemate over a fair division of labor at home had become untenable. With a tone of "desperate times call for desperate measures," she disclosed that for the past week she had dressed her side of the bed, but not Frank's, as a pro-test statement. She had sat back to see when he'd notice. It took him a week. This infuriated Mallory. It was incontrovertible proof that Frank took all she did around the house for granted. Frank's anemic defense was that Mallory was such an "uber-competent" wife and mother, keep-ing household and family afloat, that he had long since stopped feeling responsible for domestic chores.

The typical pattern was for Frank to be "tasked" by Mallory—pick up the kids from school at 5pm, swing by the grocery store to buy pork chops, text family friends to confirm their attendance at their younger daughter's upcoming birthday party—and for him to take appropriate action. Mallory resented having to "task" Frank in this way and longed for a day when Frank might take initiative on his own, identifying and exe-cuting his fair share of domestic responsibilities. She especially resented having to send follow-up texts to see if Frank had completed tasks.

All the same, it was a running joke between Mallory and the other mothers in her friend group that their husbands were "utterly clueless" with regards to the domestic sphere. Because of this, she was unsure what was reasonable to expect from Frank, especially since she was a full-time homemaker, out of the paid workforce, and Frank put in long hours as an executive in an education technology start-up, command-ing a salary that afforded them a high standard of living.

Frank vacillated between becoming aggravated over Mallory's com-plaints and commending her for being "a force of nature" at home, juggling the family calendar, making sure food and household sup-plies were replenished, staying on top of their daughters' homework, and so much more. On the one hand, he slogged away at work, dealing with difficult clients, bearing the anxiety associated with the uncer-tainty of his job security given he worked at a start-up, not expecting support and recognition from Mallory. Why should she expect recog-nition from him? On the other hand, he truly believed that Mallory was a different species than he was at running a household. He held her on a pedestal for the level of task-orientedness she demonstrated. By comparison, he felt inept. On those occasions when he tried to step up—doing the weekly grocery shopping, monitoring their daughters' homework, carving out time to take their daughters out for breakfast before school—he surmised he was falling short of Mallory's standards as the best way to enact these responsibilities. This deterred him from trying. Besides, compared with other business executives he knew that were sole providers, he felt he was overcontributing at home.

Listening to Mallory, one got the sense it was difficult for her to fully admit she found housework onerous and tedious. That it syphoned off psychic investment in more intellectually rewarding pursuits. Having obtained a college degree in English Literature and worked for a spell as a magazine editor before motherhood, she appreciated a life of the mind. The domestic sphere confronted her with a type of mental atrophy it felt awkward to self-acknowledge. After all, she had "signed on" to be a full-time homemaker. If anyone needed to pay heed to the poignant quote by Simone de Beauvoir in her book *The Second Sex*, it was Mallory: "Few tasks are more like the torture of Sisyphus than housework, with its endless repetition: the clean becomes soiled, the soiled is made clean, over and over, day after day."[16]

The excellence and conscientiousness she brought to running the household was not satisfying her deeper needs to be a creative person—to have solitude, read, write, dialogue with educated peers. I knew one therapeutic focus with Mallory would involve taking a page from the advice of the late American humorist Erma Bombeck: "My theory on housework is, if the item doesn't multiply, smell, catch fire, or block the refrigerator door, let it be. No one else cares. Why should you?"[17]

Mallory would need to relax her domestic standards to free up time and energy for creative pursuits whether these were income producing or not. Simultaneously, Frank would need to commit to altering aspect of his "cluelessness," showing more initiative and follow-though with identifiable domestic responsibilities that he had some knack for performing.

All things considered, I knew working with Mallory and Frank that negotiating an *equal division of labor*, or 50/50 split of household duties factoring in the economic situation of the family, was unrealistic. They were locked in financially—a hefty mortgage, car payments, tuition expenses—and had no desire to downsize or implement a draconian budget. Mallory had been out of the workforce for over a decade. It was unlikely she could revive her career expediently enough to generate the sort of income that would offset what was needed if Frank was to cut back in his career to be more available and involved at home. The Gordian knot would be assisting Frank and Mallory to broker an *equitable division of labor*—a mutually perceived sense of balance to what each gives and receives predicated on the roles they have chosen more than they have drifted into, valanced by what each senses they have some unique ability at. The key would be maximizing the chances that neither party felt in any overriding and persistent way they were getting a raw deal; that they were over-giving and under-receiving.

My initial global therapy formulations to broker an equitable arrangement centered on amplifying for Mallory how she benefited from Frank's *paid labor*, and for Frank, how he benefited from Mallory's *unpaid labor*, including her *unpaid mental labor*. My working hypothesis was that Mallory would acquire a greater sense of fairness from realizing the standard of living advantages afforded by Frank's paid labor and the stresses and strains at work he endured to make this happen. Not just envying him for having a career that gets him out of the house and surrounds him with work colleagues who have interesting ideas to discuss. I would help Mallory take fuller advantage of the freedom afforded her by not having to work for pay, get over any guilt preventing her from chasing personally fulfilling pursuits, and see the value in hanging out with creatively minded peers—all lessening her feeling of being encumbered by domesticity.

Light bulbs would have to glow in Frank's head, alerting him to how he is under-giving and over-receiving in the domestic sphere, especially when Mallory's mental labor is factored in—not just executing, but *feeling responsible for*, tasks like: maintaining and updating the family calendar; deciding which meals to cook; making sure the kids keep up their hygiene; researching and signing the kids up for extra-curriculars; coordinating social gatherings; planning the itinerary for vacations; ensuring the kids get to bed on time; taking the dog for a walk, and so on. I would want Frank to appreciate how freed up he is from not just performing, but feeling responsible for performing, many of these tasks to engender a felt sense that Mallory *deserves* a break. This might result in Frank encouraging Mallory to identify and pursue outside creative interests, with them both zeroing in on what chores and responsibilities Frank might take on to free her up, with due consideration given to the demands of his paid workload.

Extrapolating from relevant social science research, if Frank and Mallory are to attain an equitable division of labor, he will need to seriously examine his "benign sexism," and she her "gatekeeping." I have to confess that when I started therapy with Mallory and Frank, I experienced his glorification of her domestic prowess as a refreshing gesture of appreciation. That was until reading the 2020 journal article, "Need some help, honey? Dependency-oriented helping relations between women and men in the domestic sphere," when it dawned on me I was woefully wrong.[18] The Israeli researchers who published this piece cleverly highlight how when men admire women as supremely suited for domestic life, they are subtly perpetuating traditional gender roles. The positivity communicated can seduce a woman into believing she is being honored in some way, instead of hoodwinked into colluding with a traditional gender stereotype. Conveying cluelessness and passivity, which can compel a woman to provide dependency-oriented help, simply reinforces notions that housework is a female enterprise that males can justifiably be reluctant to perform.

On the other hand, Mallory's "gatekeeping" does not help the situation. This entails a partner (usually the female) wielding excessive input as regards how household and childrearing tasks should be performed, often based on the belief that the other partner (usually the male) is too absent-minded or inept to complete such tasks properly. Many fathers want to be more engaged parents but feel shut out. In a 2016 National Parent Survey sponsored by Zero to Three and the Bezos Family Foundation, 40 percent of fathers (versus 17 percent of mothers) endorsed the statement: "I'd like to be more involved in raising my child but my parenting partner interferes with my involvement."[19]

Sometimes strife in family life is caused by gatekeeping female partners who complain they are receiving insufficient domestic help from their male mates, then are doubly frustrated by the quality of help offered up. Often, it's difficult to disentangle whether that female partner needs to relax her standards or the male needs to raise his. On the surface, it's all well and good if a father takes the lead monitoring an offspring's homework habits. If that father then refrains from checking the work for errors and voicing reminders about deadlines for submitting homework, is he being negligent, or attentive to assisting his offspring take more personal ownership? Learning from any natural consequences imposed by handing in homework late, or of inferior quality? These are the nitty-gritty dilemmas that frequently upset the apple cart at home, that need to be discussed with a modicum of reasonableness and fairness if joint parenting is the larger goal.

Parenthetically, research shows that men in same-sex relationships raising adopted children together exhibit higher gatekeeping tendencies than women in same-sex relationships, as well as men in heterosexual relationships.[20] This seems to suggest that gay men take their parenting responsibilities very seriously. The argument is made that because of their gender and sexual orientation, they feel under the societal microscope as regards their parenting competence in a way that lesbian mothers and heterosexual fathers are not. The internalized heterosexist discrimination may cause gay fathers to feel more insecure about their parenting abilities, propelling them to compensate by resorting to gatekeeping to strengthen their parenting identity.

Zooming out, the one area where the sexes disagree more than who snores the most is who does their fair share of housework. Again, all too frequently men deceive themselves. A recent Pew Research Center survey conducted indicates that 59 percent of women state they perform more household chores, while only 34 percent of men state their spouse or partner does more.[21] We are learning that men often underestimate their partner's workload because they fail to factor in the role of mental labor: the planning, calendaring, decision making, and monitoring of follow through falling on the laps of their partners. The lockdowns and work from home orders brought on by the pandemic did not close, but widened, the gender imbalance in household duties. One poll shows that roughly 80 percent of mothers were chiefly responsible for completing housework, even though the vast majority were employed working virtually from home, just like their husbands.[22]

For men in heterosexual relationships who are not swayed by an egalitarian ethic to up their game in the housework department, some research findings out of Germany might light a fire under them. Analyzing data from a sample of over 1,300 couples looking at links between male partners' housework contributions and their sexual satisfaction and frequency, the investigators concluded: "When men contribute fairly to housework, the couple enjoys more frequent and satisfying sex in the future."[23] I'm guessing romantic sparks would fly even more in those relationships when men conceive, initiate, plan, and execute tasks without prompting and reminders from their partners, and worry aloud about what needs to go on the next grocery list or the relative merits of their darling son taking Honor's English versus AP Math as a Junior in high school. They would have to renounce the smug attitude embedded in jocular statements like: "How many more times are my kids going to ask me if I know where something is, before they realize they're asking the wrong parent?"

Humor aside, it is well documented that female partners in heterosexual relationships often tend to judge the division of household labor as fair—even when it is highly unequal—if they experience their partner as generally supportive and appreciative. For instance, Sayaka Kawamura at the Center for Family and Demographic Research at Bowling Green State University collected data from nearly 500 married women, 59 percent of whom reported performing the lioness's share of household labor—housecleaning, laundry, cooking dinners, and cleaning up afterwards. To ascertain how much participating wives felt they "mattered" to their husbands, she asked them questions like: "How often does your husband make you feel he is there for you when you really need him?" "How often does your husband give you a sense of emotional security and well-being?" "How often does your husband make you feel he really cares about you?" and "How often does your husband make you feel you can tell him anything?"

The study discovered that the more wives felt they mattered to their husbands, the greater the likelihood they endorsed the division of housework as fair, regardless of the fact that they shouldered more of the burden. The takeaway here is that for most couples, fairness and equity issues around housework are nested in broader subjective judgments regarding the balance of important personal needs being met or unmet in an intimate relationship.[24]

It is also folly to ignore the more logical presupposition that household tasks are best divided up according to who shows a special aptitude at any given job, or dare I say, largely enjoys it. In our household, I keep the financials up to date, gather documents for tax purposes, and manage our retirement funds. I wouldn't say I relish this duty. Neither would I say it makes me miserable. As a psychotherapist who traffics in intangibles—the ambiguities around really knowing whether a client has a stronger sense of self-worth or is a more patient and loving parent—working with numbers does avail me with a tangible sense of order and control. Given that I originate from generations of gamblers— my father and grandfathers on both sides won and lost big waging on racehorses and greyhounds—my anxiety is lessened when I can take action to improve the predictability of money coming in and going out. Added to this is the cold fact that I have an affinity with numbers and am well-suited for the job.

My wife does all the gardening. It's hard, sweaty work. It's household maintenance. The front garden projects our public face to the world. We want that to be an inviting face. Dishevelment is unacceptable. That demands upkeep. But mostly, I see the delight in her eyes rearranging pots, clipping at plants in ways that save their wildness, making our front and backyards bird friendly, being of nature, in nature. It gives me great satisfaction to witness her derive joy from gardening, as well as to aesthetically enjoy the fruits of her hard labor. It instills in her a sense of security knowing I'm good with numbers. When I furnish her with financial updates, trust is bolstered by keeping her in the loop.

We don't think of this as a sexist arrangement, more a slicing and dicing of who is best at what, which tasks are likable and unlikable, measured against prominent family needs. Curiously, it is not an arrangement we consciously and deliberately brokered. It is one we unconsciously maneuvered into based on a felt sense of what was rea- sonable and fair. For the most part, she leaves me alone to do what I do well for the family. I mainly leave her alone to do what she does well for the family. Here and there, we overtly express our gratitude. It all works.

An objective allocation of housework duties along the lines of skill and desirability happens to be one of the wise offerings served up by older successful couples in the Marriage Advice Project. Karl Pillemer, a leading American sociologist, and his team interviewed over 700 indi- viduals who had been married for an average of forty-three years to obtain insight into what kept their union a happy one. Concerning how to avoid conflict around housework duties, there was the common strat- egy of assigning tasks based on who had the most interest or aptitude. Common sense prevailed: "Much conflict over chores occurs because the wrong person is assigned to the job." As life progressed, as regards a perceived fair division of labor axis, areas of skill and interest won out over stereotypical gender-based assignments.[25]

Same-sex couples, lacking any social script on how to divvy up household responsibilities similar to straight couples, often land on an equitable arrangement that is smoothly negotiated. One of the most elegant examples of this is contained in Hazel Barnes' biography (the University of Colorado philosopher who popularized existentialism in America through her translations of thinkers like Jean Paul Sartre) describing family life with her long-term female partner Doris:

> Without setting up rules, we fell into a division of labor, based on the principle of letting each one do what she could do best or disliked least. Thus, Doris, who excelled in cooking, making of it almost a hobby, took over preparation of meals. I clean up afterward. Being more mechanically inclined than I am more dexterous, she usually sees to repairs and "fixing up." But I manage to most of the details of keeping the house in order. She does almost all the driving. I take care of deskwork connected with shared expenses for the house, keep up with social correspondence in matters in which we are both concerned. And so on. This kind of habitual procedure saves time and bother.[26]

The fluency of Hazel and Doris' approach to domestic life is enviable. They are not ensnared negotiating and renegotiating what each needs from the other. As we shall see, this is more easily achieved in matters related to household chores and childrearing in a committed intimate partnership than how to divide up and spend money.

Money matters

Splurging on an engagement ring and wedding are thought to augur well for a marriage. The old slogan, "diamonds are forever," continues to resonate for legions of couples embarking on their conjugal journey believing that coughing up a fortune on a ring with a precious stone somehow leads to a longer-lasting bond. The average cost of an engagement ring in the US in 2022 was $5,225.[27] This Ringspo.com survey even discovered that 46 percent of respondents spent more on an engagement ring than on their first car. Current figures put the average cost of a wedding between $29,000 and $31,000, not including the honeymoon.[28]

Of the estimated 75 percent of couples who plan to accrue debt to cover wedding costs, about 61 percent do so with credit cards.[29]

It turns out that spending lavishly on a hoped-for fairy-tale marriage does not emit an auspicious afterglow, but a baleful dark shadow. In a unique research project out of the Department of Economics at Emory University, looking at links between wedding spending and marriage duration, surveying over 3,000 ever-married Americans, it was revealed that the duration of a marriage is either not associated, or inversely associated, with wedding-related expenditures.[30] This squares with what robust research uncovers pertaining to correlations between consumer debt and divorce—the more debt a couple assumes, the greater risk their intimate partnership will dissolve.[31] Maddeningly, the messages commodifying love and marriage perpetuated by the wedding industry are the reverse of what couples need to give them an auspicious start. That said, there's some sage advice that can be extrapolated from the Emory University study regarding the type of wedding that lowers the risk of divorce—spend frugally, but invite many.

Materialistic values are endemic in American capitalist culture, spilling over to other countries. They center on people being obsessed with deriving a sense of self-worth from accumulating wealth and consumer possessions in order to project popularity and status. The leading scientist investigating the effects of materialistic values on marriages is Jason Carroll at Brigham Young University's School of Family Life. Based on his extensive research, Carroll deduced that spouses who rate high on materialism are less satisfied with their marriages and invest less in their quality. He speculated that this is due to materialism squaring with a "possession-oriented" as opposed to a "relationship-oriented" approach to personal happiness.[32]

With these ideas in mind, I gave it my best shot helping a same-sex female couple mired in money disputes. Grace and Louise came out as lesbian in their later forties. The guilt they carried about ending their heterosexual marriages caused them to recoil from advocating for a fair financial divorce settlement. It left them both less well off than they should be.

Grace was an immigrant from South America who was used to an affluent lifestyle, having been raised in a family supported by intergenerational wealth derived from the cattle industry. She was perpetually frustrated that her career as a city planner did not generate a salary to fund the luxurious lifestyle deeply familiar to her.

Louise was a relatively successful architect, who had grown up in a middle-class home in Southern California living with the psychological legacy of a father who had died an impoverished alcoholic. Grace needed to live large. Cutting back was not part of her vocabulary. Louise went against her better instincts and tried to go along with Grace's need to live large, inwardly thinking that the wrong things were being prioritized to make their marriage a happier one. Grace insisted they go into debt to fund her leasing a Range Rover in addition to them taking expensive cruises around the world. She became infuriated when Louise questioned her spending needs: "Don't you love me and want me to be happy?"

My interventions with Grace and Louise found me repurposing ideas from stalwart psychologists who had influenced me in my early years in the profession. This included figures such as Erich Fromm in his perennially relevant book, *To Have or To Be*, who defined "mental greed" as having "no satiation point, since its consummation does not fill the inner emptiness, boredom, loneliness, and depression it is meant to overcome."[33] And Paul Wachtel in his equally perennially relevant book, *The Poverty of Affluence*, who declares: "what really matters is not one's material possessions but one's psychological economy, one's richness of human relations and freedom from the conflicts and constrictions that prevent us from enjoying what we have."[34]

I pushed back with Grace and Louise:

> Obviously having a degree of material comfort is important, especially if your current and future financial situation can fund it, but what if you're chasing a rainbow by prioritizing luxuries to make you happy over more human endeavors like being emotionally honest with one another, acting kind, considerate, patient, and appreciative with each other?

Comments such as these resonated with Louise, not Grace. They brought an essential disagreement in value systems around money to a head. Within months, Louise filed for divorce.

On a different note, one of the most contentious issues in an intimate relationship or marriage is whether or not to combine finances.

Based on a 2019 Insider and Morning Consult survey of approximately 2,000 Americans, we know that 37 percent of married millennials and 27 percent of married boomers keep their finances separate.[35] What does the most current science offer in the way of wisdom regarding co-mingling resources versus keeping them separate for the emotional well-being of a marriage or committed intimate partnership?

In a massive study tapping representative samples from individualistic cultures like Great Britain and the United States, as well as a collectivist culture, Japan, findings pointed to how "keeping money separate was associated with lower levels of relationship satisfaction compared to keeping money partially pooled, and to keeping money totally pooled." The authors prescribe a course of action that may not land well with many intimates, especially millennials: "the one-time logistical decision of whether or not to pool finances may have the power to influence couples' relationship satisfaction over time."[36]

Granted, there are a host of situations that might warrant keeping finances partially or completely separate—sizable debt or resources brought into a marriage by one or both spouses, divorce and remarriage where there are children from an ex-spouse and inheritance concerns, a compulsively spending partner. Generally speaking, for the long-term flourishing of an intimate relationship, co-mingling of finances can foster basic trust. Joint knowledge of what's coming in and what's going out, and what's being set aside for retirement, can have unifying effects.

"Financial togetherness" of this sort mitigates against perceptions of what's "yours" versus "mine," creating a sense of "we-ness," of real partnership. It can fortify a sense of mutual commitment, both parties being "all in," "fully committed," accepting mutual dependence. One partner may bring more money into the relationship, or make more, but when encountering genuine love from a partner with lesser means, be unconcerned with the unevenness. In fact, as "interdependence theory" scholars argue, it's very plausible that when couples pool their resources, and accept their financial interests and obligations as shared, generosity wins out over greed, and couples emphasize each other's financial security and the emotional and bonding benefits this ensures.[37]

The bottom line as regards the high-water mark of negotiating money matters in the long-term flourishment of intimate relationships is summed up in an in-depth interview study of sixty-four happy couples from across the United States. Three themes stood out. First, the most adept at finances worked the numbers and paid the bills, with transparent communication about his or her actions. Next, they strove to live within their means. Finally, they had little debt, or were determined to pay off the debt they had accumulated.[38] From a scientific perspective, rather than a moral-religious one, this has a bearing on what ought to get inscribed in marriage vows. Maybe "till death do us part" should be switched out for "till debt due do us part!"

Sleep syncing

As my wife and I edge into our sixties, the morning "sleep report" has become a sacred observance. There's a keen fascination to know what, if any, sleep aids were ingested to bring on and preserve sleep; how many times each of us got up to pee; and whether either of us kept the other up by snoring, tossing and turning, tugging at blankets, talking in our sleep, lumbering across the bedroom to the bathroom to do our business, or anywhere else in the house to curate wakefulness into sleepiness. On the infrequent occasion where one or both of us sleeps uninterrupted through the night for a glorious seven or eight hours of sleep, we react like we have hit the jackpot.

Bear in mind that about 90 percent of the time, we go to bed at the same time, swear off any use of smartphones or laptops, agree to turn on our through-the-wall air conditioner to keep the temperature below 70 degrees in the bedroom, close our thick curtains to block any incoming streetlight, have lights out at the same time, insert foam ear plugs, cuddle, then assume our respective sleep positions and hold hands. Added to this is the fact that we sleep on a California king-sized bed—the granddaddy of all beds—and are both sensitive to restraining whatever body movements and noise we can to preserve each other's sleep. Holding fast to these conditions allows us both—more often than not—to get a minimum seven hours' sleep a night, factoring in stopgap periods of wakefulness.

On the face of it, you'd think my wife and I were an anomaly—a neurotic mess—pertaining to pulling out all the stops to get a good night's rest. The available science on these matters says otherwise. Several years ago, opinion columnist Margaret Carlson wrote "sleep is the new sex."[39]

Survey numbers back this up. Six in ten Americans crave sleep over sex.[40] Everybody talks about it, desires to have more of it, and is secretly envious of friends, family members, and co-workers who cop to getting lots of it.

The scientific data supporting the benefits of couples bedding down together and coordinating their sleep habits are robust. A recent study by Henning Johannes Drews at Germany's Center for Integrative Psychiatry used state-of-the-art medical equipment to measure couples' brain waves, body movements, respiration, muscle tension, and cardiac activity, while sleeping together and separately. Compared to sleeping apart, co-sleeping led to a 10 percent increase in participants' rapid-eye movement (REM) sleep, as well as less overall fragmented REM sleep.[41] REM sleep is generally considered to be pivotal for optimizing learning, memory, and mood. It's also associated with mortality. In several long-term studies involving middle-aged men and women, it has been shown that for every 5 percent reduction in REM sleep, there is a 13 to 17 percent increase in mortality rates.[42] Another study spearheaded by Heather Gunn out of the Department of Psychiatry at the University of Pittsburgh found that couples who sleep together, and are relatively synchronized in terms of falling and staying asleep at the same time, had a reduced risk of heart disease.[43]

The positive effects of well-synchronized sleep habits extend beyond the medical realm. Generally speaking, couples who sleep in the same bed and co-adapt to each other's preferred sleep–wakefulness conditions and cycles report less emotional conflict and greater relationship satisfaction.[44] Gender seems to be a factor. Compared to men, women tend to prefer a partner going to bed at the same time, need about twenty minutes' more sleep each night to feel rested the next day, and are roughly twice as likely to suffer from insomnia.[45] Regarding the latter, the wife of a friend once announced over dinner: "How do you expect me to go to sleep when I have to keep everyone in the family alive? I go to bed every night thinking about all I have to do the next morning right when I wake up. And you wonder why I don't sleep well!"

Needless to say, in a heterosexual context, on average, it's quite possible that women need men to adapt to their sleep preferences, rather than the reverse, to maximize women's chances of obtaining sleep of sufficient quality and quantity. Paradoxically, when men accommodate, it can actually contribute to them sleeping better. Along these lines, a 2018 study in the journal *Sleep Health* concluded: "A male's sleep duration is predicted by the female partner's sleep duration, but not vice versa."[46]

Which brings us to one of the most disputed sources of disturbed sleep in women: her mate's snoring. The English novelist Terry Pratchett once opined: "A marriage is always made up of two people who are prepared to swear only the other snores."[47] Snoring statistics don't buttress any equal probability outcome between the sexes. About 44 percent of men versus 28 percent of women aged thirty to sixty snore.[48] On the issue of snoring, males are more likely to be the culprit and females disproportionately affected, leading sleep expert Wendy Troxel to write: "Pair a woman, the sex more prone to insomnia … with a man, who is more likely to snore, and the result is often that neither party is sleeping well, and at least one party (often the woman) is increasingly resentful."[49] This speaks to the dyadic nature of sleep and the joint accountability a couple is charged with to do whatever is in their power to ensure both sleep well.

The best outcomes for remedying disrupted sleep due to snoring or disordered breathing happen when couples see it as a "we" problem. Israeli sleep researcher Dana Zarhin conducted in-depth interviews with seventy snorers and their sleep partners and ascertained that any constructive resolution is predicated on couples sharing the viewpoint: "unconsciousness does not exempt snorers from moral accountability."[50] She introduces the concept of "blameless accountability," or the snorer being nonjudgmentally coaxed to take personal responsibility for how his or her physiological problem impairs the sleep and quality of life of a partner, whereby the caring thing to do is seek medical help.

Sometimes the requisite medical intervention is use of a continuous positive airway pressure (CPAP) machine to treat sleep apnea-related respiratory gasping and loud snoring. This device pumps air into the mouth and nose through a mask while the afflicted person sleeps. It's not pretty. A client who wears one told me when he straps it on, he looks and sounds like Darth Vader. He's so embarrassed, he insists his wife sleep in a different room. Yet, in one of the few studies of its kind, Rosalind Cartwright at Rush University Medical Center found that men were more likely to follow through with using a CPAP machine to treat their obstructive sleep apnea if their wives shared a bed with them.[51]

By now, it should be clear to the reader that my bias tilts in the direction of couples exercising generous amounts of mutual sensitivity and adaptability to safeguard a co-sleeping arrangement. Give a little over here—use a nasal spray to reduce snoring, agree to one less blanket, wear ear plugs—get a little over there—tiptoe to the bathroom through the night, wear an eye mask while the other one reads with a night light, wait to come to bed until a partner is fully asleep. I can even get sentimental about it—in a scientific way.

Take the results of a recent study published in *Frontiers in Physiology*, titled: "Human heart rhythms synchronize while co-sleeping."[52] Heart rhythm data were collected on four heterosexual married couples and four pairs of same-sex intimates. In both groups of co-sleepers, heartbeats were bidirectionally adjusted, as if they were unconsciously communicating with each other, engaged in a reciprocal fine-tuning melody—two hearts attempting to beat as one. It's arguable that evolution designed humans to derive a primal sense of security from bunking up together, drifting into dreamland draped over each other's bodies, melding together with bodies unconsciously communicating with each other. If danger presents itself: I've got your back—and your front, and your side.

We can't get too sentimental about synchronous bedtimes and sleep habits. It's estimated that 75 percent of couples go to bed at different times at least four times a week and that anywhere between 25 and 40 percent of couples regularly sleep apart.[53] The reasons for this are myriad. Everything from the disruptive effects of snoring, incompatible work schedules and demands, to one partner being a night owl and the other being a morning lark. All the same, sleep experts gravitate towards advising couples to maintain bedtime rituals that allow for them to snuggle and have moments of togetherness, even if they sleep apart or go to bed at different times. For instance, in a recent *Wall Street Journal* interview, Wendy Troxel offers this advice to couples who have mismatched sleep-wake preferences: "Spend quality time in bed when you are both awake. And then when the lark is ready to go to sleep, the owl gets out of bed, goes on with their evening, and returns to bed when sleepy."[54]

Of course, coordinating and obtaining good-quality sleep with the arrival of a baby—on up into the early childrearing years—is a veritable dancing target. Wendy Troxel speaks for most parents with her hard-boiled comment: "sleeping the way you did before you had children is like finding the Holy Grail."[55]

Avoiding the over-parenting/under-partnering trap

Interviewing mother-mathematicians for an article questioning the biological basis of so-called "mommy brain," Bonnie Jacob at the Rochester Institute of Technology in New York quotes an amusing utterance by the pediatrician of one of her subjects: "Once the baby is born and you deliver the placenta, your brain goes with it."[56] Jacob makes the point that the mental fuzziness visited upon mothers of newborns is not due to sudden onset brain impairment. It's about the combined effects of chronic sleep deprivation and stress associated with the awesome responsibility of caring for a vulnerable infant. A recent survey sponsored by the online sales company *Personal Creations* reveals that 43 percent of new mothers only get about 5.5 hours of sleep daily, which amounts to 900 hours of lost sleep annually. Almost 40 percent change an average of 5.5 diapers each day, which amounts to over 2,000 annually. Thirty-eight percent of new mothers spent about three hours daily feeding their babies.[57] No wonder so many new mothers feel discombobulated.

The dominant narrative in our culture, informed by Judeo-Christian thinking, is that mothers should be self-effacing and all-giving in response to their children's needs. The popular syndicated journalist, Robert Quillen, captures this ethos well: "A mother is a person who seeing there are only four pieces of pie for five people promptly announces she never did care for pie."[58]

Let's not forget the word "matrimony" originates from the Latin word "mater," or mother. Marriage and motherhood are conflated. Getting married for the main purpose of baby-making and subjugating one's selfhood to care for babies still permeates definitions of true womanhood. It is taboo for mothers to even hint at disliking being needed so much—of periodically despising having to renounce so much personal freedom and self-care to address their children's relentless neediness. There's so much cultural pressure for mothers to bury and deny any mixed feelings about motherhood and just appear enthusiastic and devoted.

Yet, when mothers are given a platform to be real and disclose their raw feelings, many of them acknowledge not just the ecstasy of motherhood, but the agony—*maternal ambivalence*. A case in point is Sandra Steingraber's candid account of breastfeeding her daughter Faith, in her book, *Having Faith: An Ecologist's Journey to Motherhood*: "Faith is the consumer, and I am the consumed … I am milk. My milk is me. When Faith cries for me, she cries for milk, for the breast stuffed into the mouth. It is all the same thing. I am eaten. I have never felt more alive. I am eaten. I have never felt more abolished."[59] Mothers often talk of "feeling completed" by motherhood. A silent majority probably also feel depleted. The theme of "loss of self" is a common aspect of maternal ambivalence.

Emma Chapman and Peter Madsen Gubi at the University of Chester in England extensively interviewed a group of women with children about motherhood's ups and downs, documenting the loss of selfhood that haunted them. Many of them spoke of "feeling trapped," of resenting having their freedom of movement restricted. Juggling all the demands of parenthood required they go on automatic pilot, emotionally speaking, leaving them feeling numb inside. Periods of boredom were hard to bear. There was a dislike of the "mundanity of motherhood." One mother found herself "yearning for adult conversation" and weary, "watching *Peppa Pig* for the seventy millionth time."[60]

It's more socially acceptable for fathers to be ambivalent about parenthood. What's not socially acceptable is to reveal some of the dark reasons why. Watching a mother nurse her infant is nothing short of a love affair in motion. It needs to be that way. Offering up a full breast for eager sucking, with sensual skin-on-skin contact and enchanting mutual gazes, is fundamental for healthy mother–infant bonding.

Some leading infant researchers alert us to the fact that: "Babies are wonderfully sensual beings: delicious, soft, cuddly, kissable, touchable, and after two months full of smiles, giggles, and gurgles. They play and tease and suck contentedly."[61] Fathers can't compete. Feeling like an excluded third-party is part of the job description. Babies are wonderfully suited for mothers to get a healthy dose of their sensual-intimacy needs met while good bonding moments happen. It's perfectly natural for fathers to feel jealous. It helps when that jealousy is counterbalanced with a sense of enthrallment over his baby receiving such a good start in life due to his partner's eager maternal affection.

The impetus for fathers to act out these natural feelings of jealousy is great. What father has the emotional maturity to say, "Darling, when I watch you get all goo-goo eyed with our son I get jealous and worry I'll never get your body back"? Avoidance and withdrawal are classic ways to cope with underlying jealousy—overworking, staying out late, coming across as detached and distant. Displacement is another—getting irritated with one's partner for minor reasons. It should come as no surprise that the transition to parenthood is a high-risk period for male partner infidelity. Thwarted feelings of jealously can also play out negatively in the father–child relationship—being unavailable to interact and play; acting impatient when caretaking; finding fault with a child's athletic or academic abilities, personality traits, or friendship choices.

A father's jealousy-based under-parenting can fuel a mother's over-parenting. Her "mama-bear" tendencies emerge. Witnessing her male partner be short-tempered, critical, and under-involved naturally makes her want to compensate and be overly indulgent and provide easy praise.

Since it's socially unacceptable for mothers to be overt with their ambivalence, negative feelings can get covertly expressed. Directing blame due to the effects of sleeplessness, physical depletion, loss of independence, shrinking friendship networks, and vexing work-life/home-life challenges at her helpless infant is unthinkable. Her partner can become an eligible target: complaining about shoddy kitchen clean-up, shunning physical touch and sex, refusing to let him have a night out with friends.

It's my belief that the mishandling of maternal ambivalence and paternal jealousy helps explain what abundant research over the past four decades has shown: rates of marital satisfaction plummet for new parents and don't return to pre-parenthood levels until after children leave the house. In fact, comparing couples with and without children, studies show that the rates of decline in relationship satisfaction are roughly double that for couples with children than for childless couples.[62] Paradoxically, as marital satisfaction decreases for new parents, so too does their risk for divorce.[63] Somewhat cynically, summing up these findings for TheConversion.com, Matthew Johnson, Psychology Professor at Binghamton University in New York, comments: "having children may make you miserable, but you'll be miserable together."[64]

There's actually a silver lining in this gloomy appraisal. Parenthood may interfere with a romantic connection, but one way to maintain a sense of overall relationship solidarity is to make space for *commiserating with each other* over the unavoidable frustrations baked into raising children. Out of earshot of children, it's perfectly acceptable to vent and complain together how their behavior drives you bananas: "Can you believe how she talked back to you? You'd think you'd robbed her of her childhood when all you asked her to do was take out the trash!" This is one way to maintain a bond. Obviously, sharing proud parenting moments is also bonding: "What a great night we all had together as a family! I'm glad we insisted that the kids turn off all electronics, leave their room, and join us for family movie night. They were huffy, but we didn't take the bait!"

Striving to work as a co-parenting team in ways that foster children's independent functioning—so they can be more self-reliant over time—incrementally frees parents up to have separate time together as a couple, thereby keeping their romantic spark alive. Studies looking at *authoritative parenting* substantiate this. This style of parenting involves mixing high behavioral expectations with loving support. Pushing children beyond their limits in reasonable ways, holding the line, offering encouragement, listening—but not capitulating—to their frustrations. They may have a voice, and you respect that voice, but executive decisions fall within the purview of parents. It's not pleasant being on the receiving end of children's edgy voices when they push back in unrefined ways in the developmental pursuit of being more refined in their personal assertiveness. Parents have mixed feelings about this. Hence the title of the self-help book: *I Want My Children to be Independent Headstrong People. Just Not While I'm Raising Them.* Some examples from my distant parenting years will help flesh out a fuller appreciation of these dynamics.

When my son, Marcello, was thirteen years old, as a family we discussed him attending a summer soccer camp to bone up on his skills before the fall season. My wife, Janet, and I got buy-in from him. To his credit, he agreed to a two-week camp at the University of California, Santa Barbara, even though none of his friends would be attending and he would not know a soul. The drop-off was nerve-racking for both him and us. The camp was staffed with young adults whose managerial skills were wanting.

Marcello was on the younger end of attendees, but as a teenager was loath to have his parents linger around while the older boys with stubble on their chins watched on. Janet and I left on a wing and a prayer.

Three days later, we got a distress call from Marcello. He was roomed with three monolingual Spanish-speaking boys from Mexico whom he could not converse with, found the coaches to be overly strict, and complained that some of the older teenagers had snuck beer into their rooms and were about to get in trouble. We didn't know how accurate his disclosures were or how much he was embellishing due to possibly feeling homesick. His frustration mounted the more we held our ground as parents wanting to know more, probing to see if he had discussed room change options with the staff. Eventually he erupted: "Mom… Dad… I've made up my mind. It's my final offer. I'm coming home in two days!" (To this day, we have a family joke: "That's it. I've made up my mind. My final offer is…"). Long story short, we put a call in to the staff, kindly asking if he could be placed in a different room, which they agreed to. The rest was on Marcello. He remained for the whole two weeks. Granted, he didn't have a stellar experience, but he did find a way to have a jovially antagonistic relationship with the coaches. His soccer skills improved. The marital payoff: Janet and I had a peaceful two weeks with the house to ourselves, catching up on movies on our to-watch list and having longer uninterrupted conversations than we were used to.

The soccer camp experience helped Marcello get his sea legs away from home. It was precedent setting. When he turned fifteen years old, Janet and I decided to build on this precedent. With his input, we researched options for him to have a community service experience overseas. He warmed to the idea of a program in the Dominican Republic, where his labor would contribute to the building of a school classroom, he got to paint murals and tutor local kids. That said, he was adamant that two weeks was his limit. I insisted on a month. That way, he could really settle into being in a new culture, absorb what it had to offer, and confront the sort of hardship that as a white child of privilege was unfamiliar to him. Happy with his first real girlfriend and fretful about missing her, Marcello pushed back hard: "Dad, you're about to ruin my summer. I hate you. When I turn eighteen, I'm out the door and not looking back." I held my ground. Janet was torn. Her head was with me. Her heart with him. I didn't sleep so well that night.

When the drop-off day at JFK airport arrived, Janet and I handed Marcello off to a very pleasant young woman holding up a placard with "Visions Service Adventures" printed on it. She was a stranger and off he went into a sea of strangers. Janet and I were bug-eyed. Speaking for myself, I had to muster the right kind of denial to deal with the primal anxiety knocking at my door. From JFK airport, Janet and I drove into Vermont. We had a lovely time visiting Middlebury College, winding our way further north, stopping at breweries to watch the US women play in the World Cup, ending up at the Hotel Vermont in Burlington. During the days ahead, we rode bikes around Lake Champlain. We decided we were having such an enjoyable time, we ate the cost and cancelled our plans to go to Montreal. Couples with children still need to create unforgettable memories to fortify their loving bond. The whole time, we were watchful not to let the murmur of anxiety between us color our experience. After all, our flesh and blood was in a distant land with total strangers, none of whom we had met, or would ever meet, trusting that projecting him into the larger world would make him more worldly and competent.

When Marcello returned from the Dominican Republic, he was a more self-possessed version of himself. Months later, he told me that he left a boy, and returned more of a man. The hate and anxiety I had to absorb had a favorable outcome for his character development. It helped that Janet and I were on the same page, co-processing and co-managing our anxiety with the greater goal of our son being resilient, socially conscious, and worldly.

An emotional intensity often swirls around authoritative parenting. Jointly holding the line as a child or teenager pushes back hard with a divide and conquer mentality—threatening to drive a wedge between an otherwise loving couple, enlisting one or the other parent to collude with their cause that they're being unfairly treated—when they're subtly trying to take the easier path forward is unfun. When parents succeed at holding their ground, largely maintaining a united front, giving enough space for everyone's frustrations to be aired and honored, it's best for the child's character development, the parent–child relationship, and the spousal or intimate partnership bond. It's a win–win all the way around. In our current cultural parenting milieu, that's easier said than done.

"Intensive parenting is now the new norm in America" was the headline Joe Pinsker, staff writer at *The Atlantic*, used in 2019 to lay out the most recent science specifying how across all walks of life, not just among the resource privileged, parents scurry to shell out money to give their kids a leg up with the best education and extracurricular opportunities.[65] The general public is more apt to label this "helicopter parenting," or caregivers hovering overhead, like helicopters, prepared to land and ensure that children are making the right moves at the right time. Being exquisitely hands-on in one's childrearing approach is the standard by which most parents now judge themselves. It's a fear-driven model. Fear that their children will fall behind in the race to the top. Leaping in to prevent perceived harm. Leaping in with an anxious desire to guarantee successful outcomes with their children, not just step back and create opportunities—as if their self-worth is knotted to that of their children's, rising and falling based on their children's successes and failures. This state of affairs is amusingly depicted in the easily accessed online cartoon of a boy lying on the living room floor watching TV, with his mother yelling from an adjoining room, the caption reading: "Please turn it down—Daddy is trying to do your homework."

It's not that overly hands-on parents are terribly misguided. All the data indicate that for the current generation, it will be a rougher road to traverse to match their parents' level of career success and standard of living, let alone own a home—criteria that most middle-class Americans assume are givens for a shot at the good life. It's that their anxiety regarding their children's future prospects tilts them to over-parent and under-partner. This can backfire for both children and an intimate partnership. A 2015 research article in the *Journal of College Counseling*, tapping the self-reports of almost 200 undergraduates on the level of overprotectiveness they were raised with and how much they persevere to attain life goals, uncovered a direct link between helicopter parenting and low self-efficacy.[66]

In ordinary language, this scientifically verifies that young adults who learn to over-rely on parents to step in and fix life problems for them tend to have a harder time staying motivated to set and achieve important personal goals on their own. For convenience and anxiety-reducing reasons, a parent might write a thank-you note in her son or daughter's name to a college administrator to maximize his or her chances of being accepted there; shop for clothes for an adult son to wear at a job interview, without his knowledge; unasked, put a call in to the mother of his or her teenage daughter's friend to help mediate a conflict; or be mobilized each morning to wake up a twenty-one-year-old stepdaughter to ensure she's on time for her internship. A pattern of these actions doesn't only undermine a young adult's capacity for self-directedness, it syphons time and energy away from parents carving out physical and emotional space to be a couple. It can make coupledom wither.

Leisure time together before children is often a spontaneous occurrence. With children, a couple needs to earmark it, be militant about setting aside time to pursue enjoyable time together. It is no easy feat. Windows of opportunity—taking into account parents' work schedules, children's extracurricular activities, and the availability of a sitter or family member whose judgment both parents can agree upon—seem rare. Gay and lesbian parents with adoptive children sometimes face the added burden of having to locate sitters approved by government entities overseeing the foster care system.

No matter, studies show strong correlations between the length of shared leisure time couples report and the probability of marriages dissolving. For example, one study revealed that when couples increase their shared leisure time from an average of 1.7 hours a week to 4.9 hours, the chances of their marriages dissolving were reduced by 50 percent.[67] There's even a metric for the ideal number of date nights couples should go on to reduce the probability of them separating or divorcing—once a month. Harry Benson from the Marriage Foundation and Steve McKay from the University of Lincoln, in England, teamed up. They tracked almost 10,000 couples with a young child for over a decade to determine what date-night habits were typical of couples who stayed together. They found that married couples who set aside time for date nights once a month had the highest odds of remaining together. These researchers concluded that scheduling date nights is not some drab, mechanical exercise, but a way for couples to mutually reinforce the importance of their relationship.[68]

In ending, it is essential to call attention to the deep personal rewards that can be derived from raising children, both for each individual parent, and indirectly for the strengthening of a couple's attachment.

To paraphrase the eminent social scientist Roy Baumeister, parenthood may be a faulty strategy to find happiness, but it is an exceptional one for achieving a meaningful life.[69] We are in the realm of the ancient Greek notion of *eudaimonia* here, or the profound sense of personal fulfillment arising later in life from knowing in certain respects you might have succeeded at your mission of raising children who embody elements of the very character virtues you yourself strove all your life to procure—determination; personal integrity; a capacity for self-reflection and assumption of personal responsibility; a life of the mind; compassion; fair-mindedness; family loyalty; an appreciation for humor, irony, and a sense of the absurd.

With these thoughts in mind, I take the very personal step of sharing with the reader an email my son, spontaneously and of his own accord, sent me several years ago on Father's Day. Feeling groggy, having woken early to go on a camping trip with my wife, not remembering it was Father's Day, I checked my emails and found this (the tattoo referred to is the coat of arms of Vergemoli, a village in Northern Italy where my grandfather was born, and where my father fought as a partisan against the Nazis in World War II):

> I love you so much dad. When I say that I am slowly becoming you it is not a bad thing. (Maybe, just the irritability is bad!). I am so lucky to have just half of the drive and work ethic that you possess. My tattoo on my side is not just for grandpa but rather to show my heritage. My tattoo is there as a reminder of your success, and your story.
>
> Whenever I don't want to work out, or whenever I don't want to do schoolwork, I look at my tattoo and am reminded of you. I feel a healthy burden that I cannot fail because you have set me up to succeed. I am so proud I have you as a father to emulate. My desire to go to law school is partly because of you. I want to further my education because you have made me realize how important it is to learn, and to be an intellectual. When I was younger I used to ridicule your intelligence, and rebel against it. Wow was I wrong.
>
> You have taught me more than that. As a father you have taught me strength, perseverance, independence, and

confidence (just waiting on style!). You have taught me to embrace my emotions as a man, and not to run away and hide them. You have taught me to embrace my insecurities. Most importantly, you have taught me the power of humor.

The older I get the more grateful I am. As a father I could only imagine what it must be like to have to be the "bad guy" in your son's eyes. However, with age, I realize you were not even close to the bad guy. Your constant effort does not go unnoticed. Have a great Father's Day. Smoke a couple of cigars on the camping trip for me!

Reading this, I wept, and wept, and wept, and felt a profound sense of satisfaction and appreciation. A word that is usually used in religious contexts came to mind—reverence; but in this case it reflected simple earned human admiration. I revered, or had deep respect for, the reasons why my son felt the desire to revere me as a father. Peculiarly, I thought of death. I told myself some version of "my job is done, now I can die." It was indisputable that my son loved me, and that I loved him. Once my wife Janet read this, I silently knew she loved me more because she had a husband and son whose love was ironclad.

CHAPTER 3

Doing conflict well

L et's begin with an embarrassing personal confession. During marital quarrels, I'm often a spiker. Once I feel aggrieved, I'm quick to become emotionally uncorked. Despite my good faith attempts to stay calm and composed, in unnerving unison my voice takes on a barking tone, my eyes bulge, my brow furrows, my jaw clenches, and my hands flail around. In no time at all, my sympathetic nervous system ratchets up and I can almost feel the rising cortisol levels surge through my veins, preparing me for fight-or-flight. I desperately want to believe that it's my words alone that matter. If I can just craft an argument that accurately captures what occurred to upset me, my dear wife Janet will finally see the light and recognize the error of her ways: "Can't you see what awful timing it is to call attention to following up with our friends to plan our next get-together right before bedtime when I'm half asleep and can't really do anything about it?"

At one level, I know that my accusatory tone will only leave Janet feeling scolded, itching to snap back, rendering any possibility of me getting the acknowledgment I thirst for, dead on arrival. Yet somehow, I ignore this enlightening glimpse and believe the words coming out of my mouth should be listened to, independent of my loudness.

Time and time again, I'm confronted with how the *intensity of my demeanor* compromises the *legitimacy of my grievance*, no matter how carefully worded. In the heat of conflict, I have learned to dial back my emotionality over the years. It has helped some: breathing deeply, trying not to interrupt when Janet's rebuttals seem to further mischaracterize me, admitting that my intensity is a bit much ("I know I'm coming on strong, but can you see why I'm upset?") and sucking it up, calling off the dogs, going along with her suggestion to revisit the issues when we are calmer. I'm slightly better at pulling myself together and striving to refrain from doing and saying things that just make matters worse—"damage control" (when I've had no more than one glass of wine and been visited by restful sleep the night before). But it never ceases to astonish me how rapidly a feeling of goodness of connection can devolve into a feeling of badness of connection when an argument flares up, all too often over the same mundane concerns.

It turns out that it's more common and normal than people think for happily married couples like my wife and me to get ensnared in the same arguments in similar ways in the long arc of their relationship. Having observed couples in his Love Lab at the University of Washington for decades, the marriage expert John Gottman claims that in almost 70 percent of cases the same conflicts perpetually reoccur: "if a couple has an ongoing clash over a particular issue—money, housework, and sex are common—they're likely to have the same conflict forever."[1] I'm reminded of the satirical *New Yorker* cartoon where a sleepy-eyed woman rebuffs her partner in bed with the caption: "I'm too tired to have sex but awake enough to argue about it for the next five hours."

In the National Survey of Marital Strengths, sampling over 20,000 married couples, three of the top ten issues cited as significant problems center on conflict resolution.[2] A hefty 78 percent of participants indicate: "Our differences never seem to get resolved." Findings from an Israeli study of couples married for at least 40 years "both attest to the difficulty of resolving conflict in all types of marriage, including vitalized ones, and make the ability to resolve conflicts a major determinant of the quality of enduring marriages."[3]

What about the fantasy that my conveyed irritability and loudness ought to be overridden by my wife, who should simply dial into the content of my speech? The available science proves that's indeed a fantasy.

Oxford University evolutionary psychologist, Robin Dunbar, conducted an experiment where she had participants listen to taped conversations see what is deduced from voice tones. In some cases, the speakers' words were purposely muffled. She discovered that participants who had heard the muffled conversations were able to determine the quality of the interaction (positive or negative) with 80 percent accuracy compared to those who were able to decipher the words. "It's really remarkable," Dunbar stated. "Most of the information we give each other about our relationships comes from these non-verbal cues. The verbal content is only adding a relatively small amount."[4]

Human dialogue seems designed for miscommunication and misunderstanding when we factor in all the non-verbal signals that need to be deciphered and synchronized lightening quick in real-time conversations: the impact of eye contact, matching or non-matching facial expressions, smiling, head nods, pace and volume of speech, voice tone, open or closed body posture, and subdued or animated reactions, to name but a few.

It's estimated that listeners' responses are emotionally attuned to what speakers say a mere 5 percent of the time, according to a study spearheaded by Graham Bodie in the Department of Communication Studies at Louisiana State University.[5] Given that the average length of silences in adult conversations is less than a tenth of a second,[6] it's virtually impossible to process all the interactional information at hand and offer a full understanding of what the other is communicating. The famous jazz trumpeter, Miles Davis, once acerbically quipped: "If you understood everything I said, you'd be me." Maybe he's onto something. All understanding derived from human conversations seems imperfect and incomplete, opening the door for confusion and disputes.

Add this all up and what can be said with any degree of confidence? It's a myth that happy couples don't argue or that when you love somebody harmonious communication comes easily. Those who have spent their professional lives studying these matters line up in assuring us that conflict in close intimate relationships is unavoidable. It's not the elimination of acrimony that should be front and center of loved ones' minds, but it's management. They point to the importance of learning to "pick your battles," or knowing when to step around an issue that is a guaranteed source of friction. One such voice is Amy Rauer, the director of the Relationships and Development Lab at the University of Tennessee at Knoxville. She says, "being able to successfully differentiate between issues that need to be resolved versus those that can be laid aside for now may be one of the keys to a long-lasting, happy relationship."[7]

Couples that go the distance somehow become privy to the hard-won realization I've acquired—in the heat of conflict, it may be out of reach emotionally to say and do things that remedy the situation, but you can resist the temptation to do and say things that will surely worsen matters. The philosopher Mike Martins sums this up best in his book, *Happiness and the Good Life*: "happy couples manage conflict better, not necessarily by fighting less but by fighting in ways that minimize hostile escalations and sweeping denigration."[8]

Perhaps the single most distinguishing feature of successful couples is how they proactively go about truce and repair after conflicts. This reflects an acquired emotional willingness to let go of being apoplectic mixed with skill at being apologetic. As we shall see, this involves moving away from prideful monologue toward humble dialogue. First, though, I'd like to address communication style mismatches in couples that, if seen as differences, rather than defects, become avoidable sources of strife.

Communication style mismatches

In one of his stand-up comedy routines, the British comedian Jon Richardson humorously unpacks a common interaction with his wife that fatefully leads to a falling out.[9] He divulges that they argue mostly while watching TV together. Richardson cheekily asserts that his wife's susceptibility to talk while the TV is on is the cause of their discontent: "I can only conclude it's because she doesn't watch TV correctly."

He watches TV to soak up information and experiences his wife's commentary as interfering with this. Wanting to be an attentive husband, he hits the pause button on the remote to inquire what she just said. His wife assumes he's being passive-aggressive: "If it's going to be that much of a bother, just turn the TV on again!" Richardson persists: "No, darling, I want to hear what you have to say." She eases up: "That looks like where we went on holiday." Confused, he replies: "Yes," thinking to himself, "Why would she make a statement I can only agree with?" Continuing with his fumbled attempt to be sensitive, he elaborates: "Yes… the tablecloths are green, just like the ones in the hotel where we stayed on holiday." He knows exactly when he says this that something is awry in his response. She storms off, in a huff.

What renders this scenario funny, yet vexing at the same time, is its playful handling of classic mismatches in gendered communication styles. Richardson embodies stereotypical masculine ways of communicating. For him, talk serves the purpose of exchanging information. It's transactional. When his wife interrupts his TV viewing, he assumes she is about to inform him of something important he needs to know, even take action on. For her, talk is sharing, for relationship-building purposes. It's interactional. When she interrupts Richardson's TV viewing, she assumes he will join with her in verbal sharing. These are stereotypical facets of feminine ways of communicating. Over thirty years ago, the sociolinguist Deborah Tannen captured these gendered communication differences by using the terms "report-talk" and "rapport-talk" in her best-selling book, *You Just Don't Understand: Women and Men in Conversation*.[10]

Within this gendered framework, conflict looms when men assume women should speak and listen in characteristic masculine ways, and women assume men should speak and listen in characteristic feminine ways. I say "gendered" to make room for people identifying as more masculine or feminine in their communication style, rather than presupposing these reflect biologically based essential male and female traits.

Tannen also offers compelling ideas why interrupting during conversations is not all bad. In their interactions with other women, many females engage in "cooperative overlaps," interrupting one another to offer affirmations ("Wow, do I know how you feel!"), eagerly chime in with similar troubling or joyful life stories, or ask questions aimed at more detailed elaboration of life events ("Did your uncle also fight in World War II?"). Being highly involved in a conversation might mean disallowing silences, because it seems rude to be quiet in response to someone's heartfelt disclosure. Not surprisingly, Tannen likens many women's preferred conversational modality to a "jam session."

Men, on the other hand, according to Tannen, gravitate toward a one-person-at-a-time speaking modality. Silence is taken as a sign of respectful listening. Interrupting by interjecting comments or asking questions is more likely to be off-putting because it is perceived to interfere with the detailed telling of a point of view.

Uncoupling these from gender, Tannen distinguishes between "high considerateness" and "high involvement" in conversational styles. The former is noteworthy for expectations of non-interruption and longer pauses between speaker–listener turn-taking. The latter for expectations of interruptions with likeminded ideas and shorter pauses while conversing. She maintains that unquestioning adoption of the interruption-is-rude model can unfairly malign people who embody the interruption-shows-involvement model: "Being blamed for interrupting when you know you didn't mean to is as frustrating as feeling interrupted. Nothing is more disappointing in a close relationship than being accused of bad intentions when you know your intentions were good."[11]

The interruption-shows-involvement model turns out to be good for long-term intimate relationships. In their 2000 journal article, "Don't interrupt! A good rule for a marriage?" Canadian psychologists Val Daigen and John Holmes present their research findings on seventy-eight cohabitating and married couples observed discussing a conflict of their own choosing.[12] At the two-year follow-up, couples who interrupted each other to express agreement ("It makes complete sense to me that you would want to go to bed early tonight") or gain clarification ("What do you mean by wanting me to back you up with the children?") were happier with their partners and more satisfied with their relationships than couples who interrupted to disagree ("That's not what I said!") or tangentially change the subject ("Wait, where did you put my shoes? They're not on the porch where I left them last night").

Another common source of conflict in intimate relationships revolves around disconnects in communicating love through what might be called "acts of service" as distinguished from "acts of sympathy." Take the following example:

> Roxanne: I'm so frustrated with my dad right now. He expects me to drop everything on a moment's notice and drive him to his medical appointments.
>
> Filipe: That's a no brainer. I'm free all week and can drive him.

Roxanne: I didn't ask you to take that on. Can you just listen!
Filipe: Why are you getting mad at me? I'm just trying to be helpful!

In my office, I have witnessed many a dispute between partners, one leaping into "fix-it" mode (more often than not a male) when the other prefers to be listened to with a sympathetic ear (more often than not a female). Sometimes these conflicts arise from clashes in what anthropologist-turned-marriage-counselor Gary Chapman labels different "love languages."[13] Some people are more predisposed to communicate and anticipate the expression of intimacy through words of affirmation, others through acts of service. Research has demonstrated that acts of service is the primary love language for most men, and words of affirmation is deemed more important to women than men.[14]

In my experience when working with couples who successfully navigate these seemingly discrepant ways of manifesting and anticipating affection, there's less acrimony due to the awareness that one's partner intends to act lovingly in the way they know how, even if it's off-cue as far as what the recipient really needs in the moment. Often, it's the timing of a displayed love language that matters. In the example above, if Filipe had prefaced his solution-oriented comment with, "I can see why you're frustrated. That seems so unfair," and given Roxanne a chance to feel her feelings, there's a good chance the conflict would have been averted.

No discussion of divergent conversational styles with gendered themes that threaten squabbles in intimate relationships would be complete without touching upon "mansplaining." Merriam-Webster defines this as "a man talks condescendingly to someone (especially a woman) about something he has incomplete knowledge of, with the mistaken assumption that he knows more about it than the person he's talking to does."[15]

Without any shadow of a doubt, clear-cut cases of mansplaining are proof positive of the legacy of patriarchy, of men verbally lording it over women, overconfidently expecting their mate to submit and concede they know more, know better, know how, and know when, regardless of the equal or superior competence of that mate. This form of male boorishness is represented in the following online depiction of explaining-while-male: "Hey, I'm just telling it like it is. Don't be mad at me because your lived experience contradicts my half-assed conjectures." Writer and comedian Jaime Lutz warns against showing "himpathy" (ill-suited sympathy shown to men who behave egregiously) with this behavior: "for the love of God, don't just smile and nod. However obligatory the gesture seems to you, it's just going to encourage him."[16]

All this said, women's justifiable outrage at systemic reinforcement of men's efforts to silence and one-up them has clouded the difference between what I like to call "hard-edged" versus "soft-edged" mansplaining. I've already explained the former (maybe even mansplained it). As for the latter, some men who do a deep dive into a topic of interest to them crave opportunities to articulate their procured knowledge. If, like most men in heterosexual couplings, they rely on their female partner as their main source of intimate social contact, that person becomes their favorite listener.

It may seem to their female partner they are *talking at*, rather than *talking with* them. However, their intention is not to dominate, condescend, or patronize. The combination of their complex grasp of a topic and their enthusiasm to masterfully articulate it means they need ample time and space to adequately break their knowledge down. They may not feel entitled to be listened to, though desire a degree of patience and interest in paying attention to their intricate ideas that makes their partner feel they are entitled to be listened to.

They may be swayed in the direction of using flowery language that is annoying, but since communication appropriates an aesthetic quality for them, they're trying hard to be creative, not tiresome. There may even be an evolutionary basis to this. John Locke, Professor of Linguistics at Lehman College, City University of New York, has written about the ancient reasons why men use their idiomatic creativity, or "verbal plumage" to impress, mostly other men, that is.[17] Natural selection seems to have favored a tendency for men to be "duelers," to cleverly brag in same-sex contexts about their conquests and adventures that put down competitors and enhance their tribal reputation and status. Problems emerge when they manifest their "verbal plumage" with women, who are inclined by natural selection to be "dueters," less given to use language to dazzle, more to join with, get along, and cement bonds.

There's a joke going around: "Many women don't fully understand what mansplaining is." If we factor in Locke's evolutionary bent, it's no longer a joke—for both women and men—because there may be biogenetic reasons that both sexes are unaware of that predispose many men to explain themselves with a degree of flair and detail that can be problematic in modern contexts where what is required socially deviates from what the male brain, designed in non-modern conditions, has to offer.

The takeaway from all that I've laid out above is that couples have to be charitable with one another where differences in communication style exist. The task is not to avoidantly condone or aggressively condemn speech and listening habits that seem to occur naturally to significant others, not intended to elicit annoyance. Rather, working with the frustration inherent in the otherness of how a partner talks and listens can be a veritable labor of love, keeping a partnership vital—when it's a joint endeavor. In the words of Deborah Tannen: "Mutual acceptance will at least prevent the pain of being told you are doing something wrong when you are only doing things your way."[18]

Less prideful monologue

I've often wondered whether intimate partnerships flourish or founder depending on how each person is able to be really present to the other during everyday conversations. Imagine my surprise when I discovered a dissertation on this very topic out of the University of Texas at Austin. Thankfully, the author was easy to locate.

Lisa Leit used the results of her study to start her own consultation practice assisting couples to build more fulfilling relationships: The Happy Whole Human Institute. Before interviewing her, I thoroughly acquainted myself with her work. Let me summarize it. The study tracked eighty-nine expectant couples over a seven-year period after they had initially been videotaped in their homes engaged in a series of discussions.[19] Leit analyzed the discussions for the presence of "support" and "shift" responses. She borrowed these terms from the influential sociologist Charles Derber whose work she told me she admired.[20] "Support responses" show conversational attentiveness and genuine interest in a person's disclosures:

> Carla: I'm so under water at work. I don't know if I'll ever be able to catch up.
>
> Jamal: Why is that? Do you have a greater work load that usual?

"Shift-responses" denote a habit of steering the conversation back to oneself:

> Carla: I'm so under water at work. I don't know if I'll ever be able to catch up.
>
> Jamal: Welcome to my world! This month has been the busiest of my career.

Derber concisely defined "conversational narcissism" as "preferential use of the shift-response and underutilization of the support-response." Leit discovered that a whopping 78 percent of the marriages she observed were characterized by elements of conversational narcissism and that this back-to-me habit of listening and talking predicated divorce at the seven-year mark.

When I eventually interviewed Leit over Zoom (it was during the Covid-19 pandemic), I was diligent in minding my use of shift-responses because, being male, and privy to another finding of hers—men were far more likely to exhibit conversational narcissism than women—I wanted to defy that stereotype. Leit called my attention to an even more acute statistic in her study. In 39 percent of the marriages, overt disrespect was commonly manifested. I pressed her for examples: "Manipulative comments like, 'I really expected much more from you than that,' or full-on gaslighting where one partner negates the other's reality: 'That's not true. What's wrong with you. You're making that up.'" The interview cemented my concern that in marriages heading for trouble, there's a good chance one or both spouses was pridefully self-involved.

Pervading Christopher Lasch's 1980 US National Book Award-winning *The Culture of Narcissism* is the notion that mainstream cultural norms in America subtly encourage hyper-individualism, whereby personal responsibility does not extend in any thoroughgoing way to the effects of one's actions on others.[21] The poster child for this egoistic attitude is none other than famed movie cowboy John Wayne. He's associated with the motto: "I'm only responsible for what I say, not for what you understand." This I-am-me and you-are-you mindset can animate and rationalize tactless displays of honest disclosure in relationships, not to mention exempt partners from showing consistent active interest in each other in everyday conversations.

I know I have to sit forward in my seat and marshal my mediator energies when one or both members of a couple I'm meeting with qualifies a cruel statement with "I'm just being honest" or "I was only venting." This occurred between Miguel and Brad, a gay couple I was treating whose arguments were often so fierce that Brad was in the habit of spitefully removing his wedding band in protest, sending Miguel into a downwards spiral of abandonment panic.

Having been raised in a family where emotions ran high, Brad mimicked his father's habit of being self-righteously rageful, resorting to accusatory, totalistic language: "Your time-management skills suck. I can never rely on you to be on time. When will you ever get over your selfish ways and put me first for once? If things don't change, I'm done with this marriage." Miguel retorted: "You can be so mean. I can't believe you talk to me this way. I've told you 1,000 times I have ADHD and time management is an issue." Brad reacted with the proverbial, "I'm just being honest."

It was not uncommon for Brad to wake up the night after a heated argument and be confused why Miguel was still fuming over what had transpired. Brad had "gotten a lot off his chest" and was "ready to move on." Miguel resented Brad's sense that he could rage with impunity, conveying sparse little remorse. Desperate to have Brad self-reflect and take ownership for the hurtful effects of his mean words, Miguel peppered him over and over with variations on a theme: "You know you have an anger problem, don't you? Every time you fly off the handle, I lose respect for you and am less attracted to you. Is it any wonder why I shun you when you want sex?"

The relentless pushback often propelled Brad to deliver self-serving excuses ("I'm angry because I don't get the eight hours' sleep I need. When you stop snoring, I'll start sleeping better!"), trade insults ("Maybe it's the weight you've put on that makes you feel less sexual"), or pile it on by bringing up old hurts ("Talk about losing respect. I lost respect for you when you got fired from your last job for being tardy and I had to support you for three months").

There are homespun names for Brad and Miguel's cyclical warring argumentativeness—emotional mudslinging, playing tit-for-tat, flipping the script—and there are clinical ones—non-repentant wrongdoer debate mode, blame reversing, criticism-deflection sequence, attack-mode mentality—that's because the tendency to get stuck righting a wrong by wronging a right seems to be a quotidian aspect of what it means to be human. A large-scale example of this would be the nation-wide dueling monologues that dominated the airwaves during the Trump presidency. A more humorous one is the popular David Sipress cartoon with a husband standing over his wife who is seated, arms crossed on a couch, both in a fit of rage, with the caption: "Well, if it doesn't matter who's right and who's wrong, why don't I be right and you be wrong?"[22] This funny caption captures a not-so-funny human predisposition to respond with self-righteous indignation when one's pride is injured.

Rather than show our soft underbelly and plead for mercy due to feeling rejected, ashamed, envious, embarrassed, unloved, or any other of this family of hurtful emotions, pride wins out. We go on the offensive. We engage in a rat-a-tat-tat of verbiage with the basic plot line: "I'm not the one in the wrong, you are." We pour gasoline on the fire with knee-jerk "whataboutisms"—"what about the time when you left your keys in the car; you're far from perfect." Paraphrasing the late Helen Lewis, a pioneer psychoanalytic writer on pride and shame dynamics, most of us would rather turn the world upside down than turn ourselves inside out.[23]

A recent study of newly romantically involved heterosexual couples attests to this. They were given a digital audio recorder to use over a two-week period to turn on when they were hanging out at home. Analysis of the video data revealed that when couples argued, criticisms were handled by turning the tables on the other person, or masking hurt by reacting to shame through counter-reactive shaming (shaming the shamer/blaming the blamer) over 61 percent of the time.[24]

In my mind, the preeminent experts on pride and shame dynamics in marital arguments are Suzanne Retzinger and Thomas Scheff, married faculty members at the University of California Santa Barbara. Their investigations boil the causes of radioactive conflicts down to three ingredients: shaming or disparaging comments, lack of acknowledgment by the sufferer that these comments have inflicted shame, resulting in felt estrangement from a partner who is lovingly relied upon, yet is the source of the shame.[25]

Neither Brad nor Miguel in the descriptions above acknowledge feeling ashamed by the other's derisive comments. The mutual shaming that ensues causes a sudden rupture in their relationship such that their reliance on each other for needed closeness is jeopardized. They are pridefully emboldened to lash out at each other because, in the moment, the mutual shaming has broken their loving bond—ally has become adversary. They feel justified to put each other down because they're "cut off" from each other as well as any willingness to admit the shame the other's actions has caused.

Need I remind the reader how terribly painful it is to encounter a counted upon loved one who counters us in shame-inducing ways, severing a needed connection when it matters most? Ensnared in shoot-first die-last prideful exchanges, Brad and Miguel's tragic predicament reminds me of several lines from a favorite book of mine, *Traumatic Narcissism*: "Each becomes locked in the conviction that they are the victim of the other, each feeling they must negate the other, or be negated."[26]

Miguel's sense that it was maddeningly unjust for Brad to feel no remorse in the wake of his verbal attacks, making him push back unrelentingly in the hope that Brad would take some ownership, is a common occurrence in heated disputes. Often, when we feel offended, we are energized to let the person know about their offensiveness. If the offender is perceived to lack adequate contrition, there's a strong impulse to plead our case more emphatically. Marriage guru John Gottman cleverly labels this "summarizing yourself syndrome."[27]

This state of mind is familiar to me because I've been on that boat going nowhere a thousand times with my wife over the years. Flooded, irate, and obsessed, I act somewhat like a disgruntled prosecutor cross-examining an unrepentant criminal, spinning the same argument with different phraseology, delusionally convinced that she will eventually cop to the lion's share of the responsibility for hurt caused: "Maybe I didn't make myself clear enough. It feels to me like you staying angry with me like you are is so much worse than the hurt I caused you by accusing you of being indecisive around our garage upgrade plans.

Don't you see?" "Okay, let me try it another way. When you had a hard time making up your mind about our garage upgrade plans and I mentioned the word 'indecisive,' clearly, I hurt your feelings. But you've been telling me for the last fifteen minutes or so how insensitive that was. To me, that outdoes any hurt I caused you. Do you get it?" It starts to become obvious that "summarizing yourself syndrome" may be the very definition of prideful monologue.

Pridefully using totalistic language, leaning in with the second-personal pronoun, "you," is a tried-and-true way of peeling away any shred of personal dignity a loved one might possess: "You're never on time"; "You always think of yourself"; "Can't you for once remember what I told you to pick up from the grocery store?"; "You always forget my birthday"; "I'm completely convinced all the time you put your friends before me." Absolutist wording in everyday conversations with non-inflammatory intent between intimates like "you never get the mail out on time," or "you always forget to put empty bottles in the recycle trashcan" can be a hasty generalization, a lazy way of attending to the evidence, an improper assumption—something objectively untrue that's easily corrected: "Hey, that's not accurate. I remember putting the mail out on the days I didn't need to leave early for work this week," or "Wait a minute. Maybe you didn't see me dump our empty bottles in the trash can in the garage this week."

When injured pride enters the picture, totalistic expressions, prefaced with you-statements, are usually designed to hurt. Take the bitter exchange between Neve and her curmudgeonly husband Edwyn in Gwendoline Riley's novel *First Love*:

> Edwyn: "Get behind the project or get out!" (Implying "*you need to get behind the project…*")
> Neve: "What's 'the project?'"
> Edwyn: "The project is not winding me up. The project is not trying to get into my head and make me feel like shit all the time!"[28]

By languaging his contemptuous complaint in terms of Neve being the sole cause of his upset, Edwyn pretty much guarantees that Neve will not respond with the sort of contrition he demands. That's because, as Harriet Lerner puts it in her 2017 book, *Why Won't You Apologize?*,

"If one's identity as a person is equated with one's worst acts, it can be impossible to access genuine feelings of sorrow or remorse. To do so would be to destroy whatever remnant of self-worth a person has left."[29] Prideful monologues prefaced with "you-statements" and absolutist language do nothing but unmoor significant others from a belief in their inner-goodness, which only puts them on the defensive. Who wants to admit they make their beloved feel like shit all the time without collapsing in unbearable shame?

The perennial concerns for disaffected couples cautiously bent on reconnecting are fairly predictable: How do we undo harm done? How do we take back things said we regret? How do I get her to see how her mean words make me love her less? What will it take for him to be less explosive in the way he's upset with me? The seemingly hopeless trek from the apoplectic urge for revenge to the apologetic desire for reconnection, or from prideful monologue to humble dialogue, is not unlike the hedgehog's dilemma illustrated later in the book: Ouch, that hurt, but it's best to let it go.

Would I rather be right and argue back, or ignore the comment and have half-a-chance at being happy to have my teddy-bear-boy back? Wouldn't it be best if I divulged how hurt I am, inviting sympathy; that way my sweet pea will let me in closer, and we can get back to a good place? I'm hesitant to apologize because I'm afraid he'll turn on me worse, but I do really want to make things better. Allow me to elaborate.

More humble dialogue

The best definition of real dialogue I've come across is that supplied by the British psychotherapist Emmy van Deurzen: "A dialogue is when two people genuinely attend and listen to each other, not for what they want to hear the other say, but for what is actually being said, and also to what is only being hinted at. It involves a dual openness to the other and also to oneself."[30]

Without a doubt, before any semblance of real dialogue can occur, there needs to be a lowering of emotions. Getting from fight-or-flight mode to tend-and-befriend mode is no easy feat. I'm guessing a type of professional who is even more equipped than a couples therapist to inform us on calmer ways of resolving conflicts is a hostage negotiator.

Gary Noesner, former chief of the FBI's Crisis Negotiation Unit, has a great deal to say about how best to lower the emotional temperature and tease out root causes of people's grievances during bitter disputes.

In his highly entertaining talk at the 2017 Welcome Conference, he alluded to how his superiors often took issue with his negotiating team's unassertive stance. He justified it by claiming, "we are engaged in dynamic inactivity."[31] He fleshed out what he meant by this seemingly impertinent but incredibly effective stance in a later interview with *New York Times* journalist Jancee Dunn: "Resist the urge to fill any silences. A few judiciously placed pauses can help pacify an emotionally over-wrought subject."[32]

This is wise counsel. Rule number one when emerging out of flooded emotional exchanges is to remind oneself that what you don't say or do is often more important than what you do say or do. Since emotions are by their very nature contagious, self-calming induces other-calming. Ratcheting down one's intensity by breathing, and lessening loud, fast-paced speech, interrupting to disagree, overtalking, offering advice, or inserting unrequested little corrections, and *hearing out* the other, become dialogical prerequisites. Sometimes the best utterances we can muster to show we are listening are so-called "backchannel-responses," "Uh-huh," "hmm," "Yeah," or succinct affirmations, "Okay, I see…" "I get it now…" "Fair point…"

Manifesting *curiosity* about a person's experience is key. Noesner told Dunn: "Begin with an exploratory phrase, like 'You seem as though…' or 'I'm sensing that…' " He added, "Use open-ended questions like 'Can you tell me more about that?' or 'I didn't understand what you just said, could you help me understand by explaining that further?' rather than ones that start with 'Why?' which may come across as judgmental."[33]

In a magazine article, "Negotiating with terrorists," Noesner asserts that hostage negotiations aren't "synonymous with capitulation or acquiescence" but a means to keep dialogue open.[34] This idea has its parallel in the marital conflict resolution literature. A standard phrase couples therapists like myself use is "acknowledging is not the same as agreeing." Paraphrasing, or reiterating, someone's point of view to clarify and recognize it can be a powerful way of understanding their grievance and putting them at ease all at once: "If I'm following you correctly, you are mad at me because you had to remind me three times to turn the volume down on the TV and you thought I was ignoring you?" Once they feel relaxingly understood, there might be an opening to add: "I see where you're coming from, but I have a different take on what occurred."

Alan Fruzetti, who works with high-conflict couples out of Harvard Medical School, endorses notching up the type of acknowledgment partners need to strive for, expressing it more affirmatively. He calls it "finding the 'of course'": "of course your partner would feel that way or want that or do that. Just about anybody would. It makes perfect sense."[35]

Another key ingredient of healthy dialogue is replacing totalistic language with more measured word choices and switching out "you-statements" with "I-statements." Examples will help: Rather than, "You're always screaming at me. That's a surefire way of getting me to not listen!" "I'm feeling frustrated right now at you screaming at me because I'm doing my best to listen to you." Or instead of, "You never help out around the house," "I wish you would do more to help out around the house." It may even be that the high-water mark of pronoun usage during marital squabbles involves "we-statements."

Some research reveals[36] that older couples in long-term happy marriages that argue less and repair faster often use we-words, reflecting a collaborative spirit and shared stake in the outcome: "We're better than this. What can we do to put this issue to rest?" or "I know we can work this out. Here's what I'm willing to do…" Being older, and perhaps more palpably aware of their mortality, there's the background sense of dread when contemplating the death of a cherished spouse or life partner that fuels a desire to work as a team and be dialogically sensitive.

In a journal article I recently wrote for fellow mental health professionals, I challenged the notion that the only existential anxiety we face is our own mortality—driving us to live our lives more deliberately and purposely in the present, as far as our personal "bucket list" goes.[37] I call attention to the more other-directed existential anxiety concerning contemplating the death of a cherished spouse or life partner, the vanishing of an indispensable source of trusted love, and how that type of noise-in-your-head proactively spurs the desire to be more overtly grateful, appreciative, and conversationally sensitive with them.

Of course, every so often using no statements at all—zipping it—helps arrive at a truce. We forget how benignly ignoring a provocative remark from a loved one can be a choice, a dignified expression of personal agency, rather than a non-dignified expression of acquiescence. Before she died, the resilient Supreme Court justice Ruth Bader Ginsburg was asked for some good advice to pass along to students at Stanford University who had amassed to hear her deliver a speech. She chose a nugget handed down by her mother-in-law on her wedding day: "In every good marriage it helps sometimes to be a little deaf."[38]

This bit of sage counsel seems to have served her well in her fifty-six-year-long marriage, which she honored at her Supreme Court confirmation hearing: "I have had the good fortune to share a life with a partner truly extraordinary for his generation, a man who believed at age 18 when we met, and who believes today, that a woman's work, whether at home or on the job, is as important as a man's."[39] More than occasionally, judicious deafness helps love endure.

Confrontational conversations can become cooperative ones when couples fully comprehend another aphorism bandied around by couples therapists: "complaining is not asking." There's a world of a difference between saying "I wish you wouldn't leave your dishes on the table after dinner, expecting me to clean up after you" and "Could I please get you to carry your dishes from the table to the sink?"

It never ceases to amaze me in my work with couples how the texture of their relationship can become altered from one of ill-will to good-will when they start to appreciate how love must always be tethered to common decency. It's not pollyannaish, but upstanding, to encourage couples to say "please," "thank you," "That was nice of you…" or "It would mean a lot to me if…" That said, the whole enterprise of coaching couples to mind their word choices, and change their tone and delivery, is an artificial exercise absent the fostering of genuine motivation on the part of each member to be a more considerate, fair, just, appreciative, forgiving person.

The movement from prideful monologue to humble dialogue is not a word game. It's about language of the heart. It's about verbalized emotional awareness. More specifically, it's about the offending party being humility sensitized and able to make full use of healthy guilt. Ezra T. Benson, a former president of the Mormon Church, once discerningly wrote: "Pride is concerned with who is right. Humility with what is right."[40]

Taking notice of our guilt and humbling ourselves in the eyes of a loved one to admit wrongdoing in the midst of a festering argument is as close to a virtuous act of courage as I can think of. Guilt has gotten a bad name. Just size up the proverb: "A clear conscience is usually a sign of a bad memory." Neurotic guilt aside ("I'm innocent, but why do I feel so guilty?"), it's important to reckon with the fact that guilt is one of the primary social emotions that keeps people socially aware and appropriately self-conscious. It signals us when we have acted badly and need to make amends to get our relationships back on track.

In the plainspoken words of the philosopher Herant Katchadourian in his mesmerizing book, *Guilt: The Bite of Conscience*: "guilt makes us feel bad to make things better." It realigns the power imbalance that has occurred in relationships due to hurtful actions through the "redistribution of distress."[41] Knowing that the person who has hurt us feels bad about his or her actions, and desires to make amends, makes the hurt he or she has caused us more bearable. Their guilt results in the distress in the relationship being more evenly distributed. It's not just me feeling bad when she acted badly. She also feels bad for having acted badly. The pain is shared. In a sense, we feel better by the transgressor feeling worse. The transgressor's guilt is the emotional catalyst for them to desire to make amends. Knowing that the pain is shared makes us receptive to their reparative gestures.

All this was borne out in a recent consultation I had with a divorced couple who were determined to be the best parents they could be for their eight-year-old son, James, even though as marriage partners they both knew they were incompatible. Liz owned her own jewelry design company that took off after the divorce, while Scott's job in marketing was on and off. Because of her rapid rise in standard of living, Liz decided to up-scale and move to a wealthy area of Los Angeles, partly governed by her new husband, who worked closer to that area.

She orchestrated this move, as well as researching local school options, without telling Scott, who had gone overboard to cultivate connections with the current neighborhood school. He had become adept at checking in with teachers about pending homework assignments and setting up play dates with James and other kids in the neighborhood. When Scott found out about Liz's plans and realized all that he had established could be undone overnight if she insisted on moving James to a new school, he felt terribly betrayed. That's when I got the distress call and scheduled an emergency meeting.

I knew early on during the session that Liz was starting to regret her actions. It helped that Scott recognized she wanted a bigger house closer to her work: "I totally get it, you are doing well financially, need the mortgage tax break, and want a bigger house that's less of a drive to work. But don't you see how I can quickly become irrelevant as an involved dad if James settles into a school with new friends that's an hour's drive away?" Angrily interjecting: "What were you thinking!"

Liz replied: "I know… I know… you have been such a good dad… but my new house puts me a twenty-minute drive from my office, instead of an hour-and-a-half, with traffic, which has made it virtually impossible to do school drop-offs or pick-ups. You've been so involved in James' school life and that's great, but I've been missing in action and I feel horrible." Tearing up, Liz confessed, "It reminds me of when I had post-partum depression after James was born and was so checked out."

Scott softened. "Those were rough years. Had you told me about the move in advance, I would have worked with you. I want the best for James, just like you do, but this time around I think you just completely dropped the ball."

Liz plaintively conceded, "You're right. If I could rewind the clock, I would have informed you of and involved you in my plans. I'm so sorry. It won't happen again."

Even though the air was cleared for them, and the wheels were in motion to broker a mutually agreeable plan, it took an almighty amount of emotional self-discipline for me not to collapse and shed tributary tears devoid of any power of speech. I was supposed to be the therapist in the room, after all.

I pulled myself together and earnestly said, "It's remarkable to me that the two of you can set aside whatever unhappiness you caused each other as husband and wife and access so much goodwill for each other as parents. That takes humility and courage. It's a privilege for to me to witness." I found myself thinking Liz and Scott might not be a couple who lasted as marriage partners, but there was every indication they would last as co-parents.

The compassionate interaction between Liz and Scott is the high-water mark of the sort of contrition–apology–forgiveness–reconciliation undertaking that perpetuates goodwill in relationships. Her willingness to humble herself, admit wrongdoing, convey remorse, and apologize are unmistakable. Her apology is not a pseudo-apology. There's no prideful "but" tag-on, as in "Okay, I apologize, but I had good reason to move across town." There's no prideful blame reversing as in, "I apologize. But you need to apologize too because you haven't made it easy on me to stay involved in James' school life." Nor is there the insincere, "I'm sorry you feel that way." Or the go-to of those given to haughtiness: "I apologize, but nobody's perfect."

Based on Harriet Lerner's definition of a true apology in her book *Why Won't You Apologize?*, Liz is spot on: "Part of a true apology is staying deeply curious about the hurt person's experience rather than hijacking it with your own emotionality."[42] Liz's heartfelt apology leaves an opening for Scott to tamp down his justifiable resentment.

He has every reason to strike back in anger because Liz is not *entitled to be forgiven*. Her betrayal of trust is incontrovertible. Scott could hold a grudge, but he doesn't. Instead, he dials into Liz's remorse and accepts her contrition perhaps as conciliatory gestures rendering her *deserving of forgiveness*. Clearly, Scott has compassion for Liz. He keeps his focus on the badness of the deed while still appreciating the goodness of the doer-of-the-deed, his ex-wife, the mother of their son.

The forgiveness scholar Frank Fincham might opine that Scott is giving Liz "an altruistic gift,"[43] starting the process of forgiveness. Not a single declaration of intent that wipes the slate clean, but the initiation of "a difficult process that involves conquering negative feelings and acting with goodwill toward someone who has done us harm."[44] Fincham espouses the idea that true forgiveness doesn't involve a "forgive and forget" mindset, but an "accept and remember" one.

Scott accepts that Liz was in the wrong but chooses to forgive her, regardless of this. Presumably, the sequence of events and its reconciliatory outcome will live on in their dim memory as a touchstone of their capacity to face and resolve breaches of trust.

In a moral-religious context, forgiveness on the part of a wounded person is often experienced as obligatory and expressed as a one-time declaratory statement, improving one's moral footing in the eyes of God. It's a notion of forgiveness frequently associated with a forgive and forget approach to human transgressions. There's some assurance that forgiving a transgressor will bring you closer to God, but not necessarily the flesh-and-blood intimate who hurt you.

Psychologically speaking, this moral-religious conceptualization can minimize the wrongdoing and the relational benefits obtained from thoroughly facing it and working it through. It can short-circuit fuller expressions of anger and sadness brought about by rejection, deceit, and betrayal at the hands of a supposed lover. It can whitewash the guilt that needs to stay flickering which motivates making amends. It can leave emotional scar tissue that tugs and pulls in the deep recesses of one's mind. Everett Worthington, Professor Emeritus of Psychology at Virginia Commonwealth University, poetically sums this up: "The calluses of the soul may be thick and hard after years of hurting without confession, repentance, or forgiveness."[45]

Forgiveness comes easier for couples when there's a preexisting reservoir of gratitude in their relationship funneled with an abundant flow of small, everyday kind acts. Unpleasant events tend to have a more tenacious psychological effect than pleasant ones and if they fail to be regularly undone by a steady stream of pleasant ones, an attitude of unforgiveness can seep into a relationship. There's even a metric for this, according to findings out of Gottman's Love Lab: five kind acts or utterances to nullify each single unkind act or utterance.[46]

So-called "emotional capital" can accrue from abundant expressions of Derber's "support responses," like the one I just texted my wife before writing this sentence. She texted me a picture of a black-headed grosbeak (in the cardinal family of birds) which she spotted on our property. I know she's thrilled with the new birdfeeders we installed in the front and back yards. I texted back: "OMG! Front or back yard?" She typed in return: "Back yard." Emotional capital might accrue with "big ticket" items like a surprise, all-expenses-paid trip to a partner's dream vacation location, but it's the in-the-trenches, boots-on-the-ground, under-the-radar small gestures baked into everyday life that really matter: putting the toilet seat up or down; tiptoeing to the bathroom in the middle of the night so as not to rouse a sleeping mate; taking out the trash; replacing the batteries to the TV remote; picking up your wet towel from the bathroom floor; replenishing postal stamps (and so on and so forth) unasked, or without attitude, when asked.

Shared run-of-the mill moments—laughing together at the same joke, sticking to enjoyable after-work rituals, cuddling in bed in the morning to stay warm—add up and maximize each partner's openness and willingness to respond benevolently when the inevitable clashes erupt.

The acclaimed French novelist Marcel Proust once wrote, "Love is reciprocal torture." That's surely true when couples are ensnared in dueling prideful monologues. When vicious cycles of spiteful behavior—shaming the shamer and blaming the blamer—predominate during disagreements. John Wayne's rugged-individual cowboy ethics are operating. Dueling beliefs of the "I'm only responsible for what I say not what you understand" variety are a recipe for agonizing gridlock.

Somehow, in fits of prideful rage, we lose the capacity to feel responsible for the effects of our behavior. More insidiously, we rationalize and concoct notions that we shouldn't be responsible for the effects of our behavior: "If you're choosing to sulk just because I forgot today was our wedding anniversary, that's your problem." There's a mutual stopping of caring to care, a collapse of ethical responsiveness to and responsibility for each other. Martin Buber, the philosopher of dialogue, and author of the agelessly profound text, *I and Thou*, would remark that this is an *I-it* conversational space—*self* treating the *other* as a depersonalized being, thing-like, just there to vent on.[47]

Repersonalizing the loved one you have depersonalized entails the bedrock realization: you can't hurt someone and feel *entitled to* not get hurt in return. An emotional reset is required, imploring a restoration of caring to care. The person on the other end of your tirade is not just a flesh-and-blood person, any person, but *your* person. Being considerate of their feelings is the only real way to invite them to consider your feelings. There's an inescapable connection between responsibility to the self and responsibility for the other. Yes, it's important to be honest with what we feel (responsibility to self), but without tact, we lose sight of the existential imperative of being responsible for the other.

This is a Buberian ethic, "I'm always responsible for what I say and how it contributes to what you understand," not a cowboy one. Buber penned the pithy phrase: "Love is the responsibility of an I for a Thou."[48]

The relevance of this maxim for conflict resolution involves grasping how inner guilt can signal we have hurt someone special to us—*we* have wronged them—and the best way to right a wrong is to show contrition and apologize. That conveys responsibility *for* and *to* their hurt. Humbling ourselves in this way opens the potential for forgiveness and reconnection.

Where there's lot of "emotional capital," and couples know in their bones what good times feel like, there's keenness to get back on track. That's probably the idea behind the quote from the prominent American journalist Robert Quillen: "A happy marriage is the union of two good forgivers."[49]

CHAPTER 4

Humor me

The celebrated American novelist John Updike once said of marriage that it was "a million mundane moments shared."[1] Had he lived long enough to witness the cloistering couples faced throughout the Covid-19 pandemic, he would have had to recalculate that number upwards. Out of the blue, couples were cooped up at home, devoid of the everyday routines that availed them with time apart: commuting to work; dropping the kids off at school; heading out to the gym; sneaking time at the coffee shop; stopping by a friend's house. The pandemic became a giant social experiment on how couples cope stuck under the same roof with one another, mired in domesticity.

One couple that satisfied our collective fascination with married life under Covid-19 conditions was actor and singer Mandy Patinkin and Kathryn Grody, an Obie Award-winning actress and writer. They turned into a social media sensation when their thirty-four-year-old son, Gideon, posted videotapes of their unvarnished interactions holed up together in a cabin in upstate New York waiting out the pandemic.

In a segment titled "True Love," Gideon queried them on what contributed to the success of their forty-year marriage: "Wouldn't you agree that part of your secret to success has been spending a fair amount of time apart?" They both replied with a resounding, "Yes!" and spoke of the challenges of spending so much uninterrupted time together.[2]

Yet, if you binge watch the various scenes from their marriage readily accessible online, like I did, what becomes patently clear is that the enduring fondness they have for each other is better explained by the rampant humor in their lives. Joined at the hip due to the pandemic, humor saturates their displays of affection and is smoothly employed to step around and bounce back from squabbles.

The examples are plentiful. When asked by Gideon, "If your relationship was a dog, what breed would it be?" Kathryn giggles and responds, "Definitely a mutt," which prompts Mandy to amusingly and lovingly liken Kathryn to their dog, Becky: "You're a tall, leggy blonde; maybe you have a little Lab mix!"[3]

In another segment, Mandy is glued to his laptop, determined to erase 38,000 unread emails from Kathryn's account. Kathryn jests that she has planted them in her computer on purpose to keep Mandy out of her hair, a comment that he ignores, earnestly claiming: "I've deleted about 28,000 so far!" With a good dose of irony, Kathryn remarks: "Oh my God, you're doing it too fast, honey. You gotta do a little less!"[4]

In a clip that is actually a very sophisticated depiction of how humor enables couples to non-threateningly discuss a sore topic, Gideon seeks his father's perspective on why his mother gets irritable and short-tempered. With mild sarcasm, Mandy jokes that he's never noticed how irritable Kathryn gets, then adds: "My nose is growing. I just broke the screen door." Mandy then, tongue-in-cheek, alludes to the fact that he must be the cause of Kathryn's ire: "I think it's me. It has to be me," which has everyone cracking up.[5]

Humor scholars would submit that Kathryn and Mandy display gobs of affiliative and self-enhancing humor in their everyday interactions. The former involves amusing others to keep things positive and lively in ways that sustain and enrich a relational bond. The latter reflects an ability to poke fun at yourself in a good-natured way, or to see the humor in unfavorable life events. According to a Belgian study comparing married and divorced men and women, a surefire way to be satisfied in your relationship and lessen the risk of divorce is to liberally indulge one's propensity to use affiliative and self-enhancing humor. Kathryn and Mandy embody this scientific finding.[6]

Lots of shared laughter is a bellwether for how alike partners are and how close they feel to each other. Summing up some research findings on this topic, Sara Algoe at the University of North Carolina at Chapel Hill concluded: "People who spent more time laughing with their partner felt they were more similar to their partner. They had this overlapping sense of self with the other person."[7] Algoe's study was limited to people in their twenties and thirties who had been romantically involved for an average of just over four years. Other studies of younger couples testify to the significance of humor and laughter for relationship success.

Several years ago, a *CBS News* poll discovered that a sense of humor was five times more important than sex when it comes to building a successful marriage.[8] A 2017 study out of Romania looking at twenty-somethings romantically involved for one to five years revealed that a sense of humor outranked physical attractiveness, ambition, earning potential, and an exciting personality when evaluating mates.[9]

Over the long arc of a relationship, humorous exchanges and shared laughter take on added importance. It has been shown that compared to middle-aged couples married at least fifteen years, older ones—married at least thirty-five years—rely more heavily on humor to convey tenderness and lessen friction.[10] This prompted a headline in *Science Daily* encouraging partners to stay the course: "Honeymoon long over? Hang in there. A new University of California, Berkeley, study shows those prickly disagreements that can mark the early and middle years of marriage mellow with age as conflicts give way to humor and acceptance."[11] As couples age, *snickering often replaces bickering* in the joint venture to make one's dwindling years less friction filled and more joyful.

That's certainly true in my marriage. Just the other day, over breakfast, my wife Janet gingerly mentioned that she had a lousy night's sleep because of my snoring. Wide awake and irritated, she had audiotaped my snoring on her smartphone as incontrovertible proof. Listening to it together at the breakfast table, I quipped, "Wow, that's quite melodic. How can we know with any certainty that's me?" We shared a laugh and Janet segued into kindly requesting that I go back to rinsing with a saline solution before bedtime to curb my snoring. A decade ago, a conversation like this would have gone sideways fast with me defensively referencing her snoring.

The comedian Sinbad is less sanguine in a skit of his on snoring. Bantering with a woman in the audience who complained of her husband's snoring—which she insisted was non-existent before their marriage—Sinbad launches into a riotous tirade: "You sucked the life out of him. He's got no oxygen. He's just trying to survive the night. He ain't snoring, he's dying. A little bit each night. Y'all call it sleep apnea, we call it marriage."[12]

Common knowledge, backed up by scientific evidence, underscores that men and women like their partners to have a "good sense of humor." Digging deeper into the research, we learn that they mean different things by this: men often strive hard to be funny and prefer women who respond to their wit (humor production), while women tend to develop a fondness for men who make them laugh (humor appreciation).

In a clever experiment by Liana Hone, a psychology postdoc at the University of Missouri, participants were supplied with an imaginary budget to "spend" on an important quality they desired in their mate—either a flair for telling jokes, or an openness to appreciate them. She discovered that women spent just $1.91 on a mate who laughs at their jokes, whereas men shelled out $3.03.[13]

Gil Greengross, a Welsh evolutionary psychologist, reviewed this study and suggested that men like being in the presence of a girlfriend or wife who makes them laugh: "But for men, that's more of a luxury than a necessity."[14]

Those endorsing an evolutionary psychology perspective would maintain that being funny is a "fitness" indicator for males, an ancient way to signal to potential mates their intelligence, friendliness, social confidence, and knack for bonding in positive, affectionate ways. Given that natural selection pressures females to be more choosy when it comes to mate selection and retention, to maximize the chances that she will have a loyal, dependable, competent mate to co-raise offspring, laughter in response to the humor of a mate cements a loving bond with an upstanding prospect. In this scenario, a happy wife—someone who smiles and laughs a lot in response to her husband's on-target humor—indicates a happy life for both: there's regular good-hearted give-and-take of displayed and cherished amusement that greases the wheel of happiness in a marriage.

In fact, a 2014 study in the journal *Evolutionary Psychology* found that women who are partnered with humorous males initiate sex more often and enjoy more and stronger orgasms.[15] Apparently, being with a man who is witty and amusing is sexy. It may be that humor is a form of loving attentiveness that has sexual arousal benefits for women. To understand what another person finds funny, you have to put yourself in their shoes. There's attentiveness and attunement involved. In some sense, a female partner may feel cheerfully tended to and cared for when her male partner engages her with levity and funny repartee. It frees her up to playfully flirt, feel sexually enticed and enticing, really let go. In those moments, from a male perspective, a happy wife is definitely a happy life.

Of course, we can't overstate the gender breakdown here. The average women, or person who identifies as female, may not be as caught up eliciting laughter as the average man, or person who identifies as male. Getting a laugh is important no matter one's gender, or gender identification. Time will tell if the tired old motto, "happy wife, happy life," will be replaced with "happy spouse, happy house."

A twelve-year-long study by the Gottman team at the University of Washington on gay and lesbian couples highlights how they have much to offer straight couples as regards the use of humor to enrich relationship well-being.[16] Same-sex couples are more apt to remain upbeat during conflicts as well as use humor to sidestep and quickly resolve disagreements. Gottman chalked this up to gay and lesbian partners being more adept at being subjected to negativity without taking it too personally. It's possible that humor is honed by LGBTQ individuals as a means to cope with homophobia and heterosexism. Knowing how to deflect a mean comment, see the humor in it, to preserve one's dignity in the face of undignified behavior, becomes a survival skill. Internalized homophobia among gay and lesbian partners can lead to humorous exchanges that to a naïve observer seem harsh, but to those involved are a more hard-boiled way of venting frustration and moving on.

We see this depicted in the movie *Uncle Frank*, which chronicles a road trip a gay couple takes from Manhattan to Creekville, North Carolina, to attend the funeral of the family patriarch, whose moralistic homophobia has emotionally scarred Frank, the son, and rendered

Walid, Frank's life partner, persona non grata. As tensions mount because Walid insists on attending the funeral, Frank erupts: "Are you the stupidest man alive?" The insult is swiftly neutralized by Walid: "Obviously, look at who I'm with."[17]

Using humor to channel friendly intent, deflect potential insults, confess one's shortcomings in lovable ways, and preserve positivity during disagreements is not laborious. It involves an attitude of levity and nonseriousness that is sincere without being serious. It flies in the face of the advice so many self-help gurus direct at struggling couples around the theme of "working on the relationship." Inspirational quotes like the following are commonplace: "A relationship is like a job. You have to work hard to get in it and have to work even harder to stay in it."

Deborah Cabaniss, Professor of Clinical Psychiatry at Columbia University, captures this same onerous spirit in her *Huffington Post* contribution: "Good relationships take hard work. Sustaining a relationship over the years is not for the faint of heart. You can't be lazy about it or dial it in. Doing well at your career takes work. So does staying in shape. Why shouldn't having a good relationship take work too?"[18]

It's not the concrete guidance experts like Dr. Cabaniss offer disheartened couples that I take issue with—edit what you say, think about the other person first, be nice—it's the rhetoric of seriousness and hard work. In my estimation, this rhetoric strikes fear in the heart of people contemplating long-term monogamous relationships. It associates marriage and romantic cohabitation with thankless drudgery. Perhaps that's one reason why living with a romantic partner is falling out of favor.

According to the General Social Survey, in 2018, 51 percent of Americans were cohabitating with a partner or spouse, up from 33 percent in 2004.[19] The lexicon of *effortful hard work* in long-term partnerships has its place—being intentional in how we speak and act with one another in ways that may not come naturally that are essential for goodwill and harmony: aspiring to be kind, appreciative, inclusive, decent, tactful, and generous. But if we are to reignite interest in what long-term intimate commitments might offer those jaded by modern romance, we have to emphasize the lexicon of *effortless play*—the emotional payoff approaching the myriad mundane aspects of matrimonial life with an attitude of levity and nonseriousness.

We would do well to heed the wisdom of the Irish playwright Oscar Wilde, who had every reason to be cynical—imprisoned for his consensual gay relationship with the son of a Scottish nobleman, Lord Alfred Douglas—but who managed to be more charitable in his outlook: "Life is far too important to be taken seriously."[20]

Love's grand absurdities and petty grievances

In a letter to a friend in 1822, the English poet Samuel Taylor Coleridge wrote: "To be happy in Married Life … you must have a Soul-mate."[21] This is the first recorded use of this widely popular term. Coleridge heralded the belief that marriage was meant for two people who were made for each other, a perfect union of souls, destined to be together for life. Reading the poem, "The Kiss," penned for his soon-to-be wife, Sarah Fricker, one assumes he had found his soul mate:

> Too well those lovely lips disclose
> The triumphs of the opening rose,
> O fair! O graceful! I bid them prove
> As passive to the breath of Love.[22]

In October 1795, the newly wedded poet wrote: "On Sunday I was married … united to the woman whom I love best of all created Beings."[23] There's a backstory that's not so charming. At the time of his marriage to Sarah, Coleridge was still secretly in love with Mary Evans, the older sister of a college classmate.[24] There's also a grim postscript. By 1804, Samuel and Sarah had separated and thereafter had an on-again off-again relationship, residing together for only about six of the forty years they were married. By then, Coleridge was deeply in love with Sara Hutchinson, the sister of (fellow Romantic Age poet) William Wordsworth's wife.[25] We know all we need to know about the downturn in Coleridge's marriage from two lines in his 1802 verse, "Dejection: An Ode": "I may not hope from outward forms to win; The passion and the life, whose fountains are within."[26]

It's ironic that the very person who authored the term soulmate fell prey to the inescapable disappointing effects of taking it seriously. The legacy of Coleridge's married life tells us that belief in a soulmate—for every person there's a single romantic match; when we first meet that match, we will "just know it" and have instant and lasting compatibility; when we find The One, he or she will meet our highest ideals—may be an enchanting proposition, though no less a set-up for being let down. It primes people to opt out, rather than dig in, when a partner is less than perfect.

Research backs up this sober conclusion. In a 1998 landmark study, Raymond Knee, a social psychologist at the University of Houston, divided up college students' relationship attitudes in two ways: destiny beliefs (I am destined to be with one partner who I will be endlessly compatible with) or growth beliefs (Success in relationships involves facing and resolving the inevitable challenges that occur). Those with destiny beliefs were far more likely to avoid proactively dealing with relationship problems that arose as well as abruptly end romantic involvements.[27]

In a similar study published in 2014, aptly titled, "Framing love: When it hurts to think we were made for each other," Canadian psychologists found that people who expect love to be a "perfect match between two individuals meant to be together" are more distressed when conflicts arise than those who see romantic partnership as "a journey with ups and downs."[28] We would do well to heed the sage advice of the ever-provocative love scholar, Alain de Botton, who turns the notion of a soulmate upside down: "Compatibility is an achievement of love; it must not be its precondition."[29]

Mystical belief in finding a soulmate as a ticket to lasting love has remarkable staying power, despite the abundant folk wisdom and science that ought to disabuse us of it. In 2017, a Marist poll revealed that 73 percent of Americans believe in soulmates.[30] Even those older than forty-five—who should know better because they've spent more time on the planet to be bruised by love—endorse a belief in soulmates in hefty numbers (69 percent).

Embedded in the idea of a soulmate is the implication that each person is destined to be innately and endlessly compatible with their "other half," making it uncomplicated to use that time-honored line in one's marriage vows: *Till death do us part.* When we zoom out and incorporate an historical perspective on life expectancy and marriage length, past and present, confident utterance of an altar-to-grave nuptial pledge becomes more complicated.

In 1549, when the phrase "till death us depart [sic]" first cropped up as facet of official marriage vows in the *Book of Common Prayer* written by Thomas Cranmer, Archbishop of Canterbury,[31] life expectancy in Europe and the Americas hovered around thirty-five, slightly longer than the 32.5 years hunter-gatherers lived, on average, thousands of years previously.[32]

Until advances in modern medicine in the late nineteenth century, it was not uncommon for marriages and intimate partnerships to last in the range of fifteen years, cut short by early death. Nowadays, the median age of first marriage in the US is twenty-seven for women and twenty-nine for men.[33] Assuming these newlyweds live into their mid-eighties, and bullishly aspire to a life-long commitment, this would put their projected marriage length close to the sixty-year range—nearly four times longer than what the majority of humans have experienced for most of human history.

From an evolutionary perspective, humans are scrappily designed to navigate long-term intimate partnerships of the sort we currently contemplate. The talented comedian Wanda Sykes puts it less academically: "Till death do you part. That's biblical times. Moses wrote that. That's the Old Testament. They had no problem saying till death do you part back then because they didn't live that long. They had good plagues. Soon as that guy got on your nerves, here come some locusts to eat his ass up for you."[34]

Marrying your soulmate—you're everything, you're perfect match—should inoculate a person from being nostalgic for past lovers, or desirous of new ones. Yet it's estimated that almost 50 percent of people maintain contact with ex-spouses between two and ten years after splitting up.[35] Nearly a quarter of people wish they could preserve a sexual relationship with an ex-partner as an aspect of their post-dating relationship.[36]

A robust survey by the leading sex toy retailer, LoveHoney, on people's favorite masturbatory fantasies revealed a data point that soulmate fans will surely find favorable: the number one fantasy across all genders and sexual orientations turned to by people when they self-pleasure is replaying in their mind's eye a steamy sexual encounter with their current partner.[37] However, devoted mates will be chagrined by the second most popular fantasy: imagining hot sex with an ex-lover. In their private thoughts, most people are less loyal to their primary love interest than is presumed.

Work by leading evolutionary psychologist David Buss has shown that males and females alike secretly cultivate an average of three "back-up mates," real or imagined replacements for their current partner, should the relationship prove unacceptable or end.[38] This lends scientific credence to the cheeky Mae West wisecrack: "Save a boyfriend for a rainy day—and another, in case it doesn't rain."

There's a centuries-old proverb linked to the English playwright John Lyly that contains more than a grain of truth: "Marriages are made in Heaven and consummated on Earth."[39] It's the consummated on earth part most people get hung up on. The domestication process that enables loving couples simply to co-exist under the same roof for extended periods of time. More people who tie the knot would do well to incorporate into their wedding ceremony a custom from the Southern States, "jumping the broom" (leaping over a broom hand in hand), embracing their entrance into domestic life together.

Without a charitable, humorous attitude, the potential for trivial issues to mushroom into emotional showdowns is habitually hotwired: whether the toilet seat should be left up or down; mail left sitting, or immediately opened; tin foil placed in the recycle bin, or regular trash; dirty dishes left in the sink overnight, or cleaned off and stacked in the dishwasher before bedtime; windows in the bedroom cranked open at night, or sealed shut; bathroom towel used to wipe off lips after teeth brushing, or not; pictures of the in-laws hung in the living room or dining room; the use of subtitles during TV shows, or not. The list is endless. I'll bestow attention on one issue that is mercilessly mundane and vexing for most couples: arriving at a mutually satisfactory room temperature.

In one of the few studies of its kind, analyzing the daily diary entries of partners from 112 households in Ohio on joint decision making around household temperature settings, it was discovered that women are losing the "thermostat wars."[40] When disagreements occur between couples over preferred household temperature, women tend to don additional layers of clothes as opposed to standing their ground and insist on adjusting the thermostat. Few people are privy to the fact that, compared to men, women have a lower metabolic rate, reducing their heat production, as well as a larger ratio of body surface to body mass, resulting in more heat loss.[41] Women deserve to win the "thermostat wars."

This brings to mind a story told me by an endearing married couple I recently interviewed for this book. Like many senior couples, Bill and Mary had long since staked out their favorite side of the bed to sleep on. The trouble was that the air-conditioning vent sat above Bill's side of the bed, blowing heat on him when on. Foolishly, rather than break with tradition and switch to the cooler side of the bed, Bill pleaded for the heat to be turned down. To keep the peace, Mary acquiesced and often slept wrapped in multiple layers of clothing, even pulling a woolen beany over her head. During a woman's support group Mary attended, several of the older members disclosed they often slept naked with their male part-ners. Up in years, there was less chance of unwanted erections prompt-ing occasions for sex, interfering with sleep. The women spoke glowingly of bedtime skin-on-skin contact comfort that had become much to their liking. Intrigued, one Saturday morning Mary woke early, stripped naked, and climbed into bed with Bill. When he awoke to Mary's nudity, he exclaimed, "Good morning, Mr. Sunshine. There is a God!" They snuggled in the buff and thereafter the thermostat was no longer under Bill's jurisdiction. Mary had finally won the temperature wars.

There's a maddening gap between the extravagant expectations people place on intimate coupledom and what can be realistically obtained. So many upbeat relationship ideals strain common sense to uphold. Added to this is the ever-certain tedium of shared domestic life that somehow needs to be coped with. Humorous expressions frequently tap a cultural nerve, such as *Washington Post* feature writer Monica Hesse's remark: "Is marriage just two people taking turns mashing the trash down in the hopes the other folds first and empties the bin?"[42] Partners can get so habituated to each other's petty grievances, accumu-lated minor acts of retaliatory neglect, and ignorance of the need to be decent and appreciative that their bond becomes unnecessarily spoiled.

It may sound preposterous, but many struggling couples "make the worst out of a good situation" (rather than the classic "best of a bad situation"). This was deduced from observations out of the Love Lab at the University of Washington. John Gottman and his colleagues wit-nessed a systematic trend for unhappily married couples to overlook their partner's kind and appreciative gestures 50 percent of the time.[43] This finding legitimizes the theme of the old Irving Berlin song, "After You Get What You Want, You Don't Want It."

Relational boredom can arise when a person's marital or cohabitating situation goes through longer than expected phases of being unexciting and monotonous, while also seeming extraordinarily inconvenient to end. Battling the fear of missing out, taking flight, obsessively thinking about reinventing oneself, and going on a perennial odyssey to find one's true soulmate are classic ways vulnerable people respond to ordinary relational boredom. No matter, realistically minded, conscientious, caring individuals do not abdicate intimate ties so impetuously. Having it in our toolkit to somehow find a way to accept and adapt to the humdrum aspects of domestic life with significant others is imperative.

If we are to avoid the ugly pitfalls of resignation and bitterness that can kick in when a mostly beloved partner once again picks his nose or spits in public; walks ahead of her at a noticeably long distance; annoyingly asks every morning how he slept that night; tells and retells that story about the time he caught a 5 lb. rainbow trout with sparkly Power bait; nods off when the movie has just begun; is overly enthusiastic in praising a granddaughter for finishing a hike in the woods without complaining; goes on that same old tirade about the time she was most qualified for the job, but was passed over for a less experienced nincompoop; empties the dishwasher before coffee is brewed and all are fully awake; schedules golf, not thinking to check the family calendar indicating that on that same day, our son was playing in a club soccer final; fails to reposition the shopping cart where the sign says it should go; leaves residue of cooked meat on a pan that was supposed to be properly washed; says she'll be home from work in thirty minutes and walks in the door an hour later; stomps through the bedroom in the wee hours of the morning to pee; undertips the waiter; treads on her delicate succulents in the front yard; leaves a new toilet roll sitting above the cardboard cylinder of the old one, without inserting it in the retractable bar; leaves her toenail clippings scattered on the bathroom floor; forgets to pick up milk on the way home; walks across the living room arguing with a co-worker on his phone, oblivious to the fact that our son is taking his Algebra mid-term via the internet due to the Covid-19 pandemic in that same areas of the house; takes an unusually long time to cater to her pre-bedtime ritual before agreed-upon sex—we need to seriously embrace a nonserious attitude of lightheartedness, jocularity, and mirthful acceptance.

Leveraging levity

My wife and I have always been avid campers. In 1992, a year or so before we were married, we spent two fabulous weeks tent camping at Succor Creek State National Area in Eastern Oregon, known as a "remote haven for rock hounds and wild life watchers." En route back to Seattle, we spent the night in a cowboy-kitsch hotel in Pendelton, Oregon. Having been off the grid for what seemed like a lifetime, we were eager to watch television and settle in for the night.

We spun the dial on the black-and-white set and happened upon a 1972 zany horror film called *Night of the Cobra Woman*.[44] The lead male character, Stan Duff, falls under the spell of Lena, a "serpentine seductress," who transmogrifies back and forth from gorgeous woman to venomous cobra. Lena uses her charms to literally suck the life out of Stan, piercing and poisoning him with her fangs, to ensure eternal life for herself. The far-fetched and garbled plot, weird eroticism, off-cue musical score, and groovy clothes worn by the actors, all watched on a black-and-white TV no less, in a room with faux cowboy memorabilia, had Janet and me laughing hysterically.

From that day onwards, "duff" (Stan's last name that was embroidered on the shirt he wore throughout the movie) became mine and Janet's favorite term of endearment. On any given day, we use it dozens of times. That is, when we are feeling particularly close and playful. We both know when we address each other by our birth names that something weighty is about to go down.

So much is unconsciously packed into our constant use of that one pet name, "duff." No doubt, we are reliving a precious historical moment of closeness in some miniscule way; a reminder that what we had then can be what we have now; gently signaling each other never to forget the value of levity, laughter, and the absurd dimensions of life. This fits with what Leslie Baxter, Professor Emeritus in the Department of Communication Studies, University of Iowa, has written about terms of endearment (TOE): "couples create TOE early in the relationship to create and reinforce their nascent bond, while their later use of TOE reminds lovers of their history as well as buttresses their continuing relationship."[45]

It should come as no surprise that couples who use affectionate idioms with each other on a regular basis are more satisfied with their relationship. That was the conclusion reached in a 1993 research article aptly titled: "'Sweet pea' and 'pussy cat': An examination of idiom use and marital satisfaction over the life cycle."[46]

There's intimacy built into the exclusivity of using our pet name, "duff." I doubt Janet has, nor will, use this term of endearment with anyone else. I know I have not, nor will. It has become a sort of relationship signature. It's unique to us. Couples who are adept at being amusingly loving and lovingly amusing not only use terms of endearment, but also phrases and lines that have distinctive consensual meaning for them.

A lesbian middle-aged couple I once worked with told me of an entertaining moment that had cemented their joint attraction when they first started dating. Joanna had off-handedly made the comment, "Do you like my hat?" pointing to a sun hat she was wearing. Quickly picking up on the double meaning—one being the reference to a scene in the P. D. Eastman children's book, *Go, Dog. Go!*—Monica chuckled and in a singing voice replied, "I do not!" Joanna was completely smitten by Monica because she had instantly sourced the connection between Joanna's comment and the *Go, Dog. Go!* scene where the pink poodle asks the blue one if he likes her hat.

This amusing moment can be thought of as Joanna and Monica creating an intimate mini-culture between themselves, a shared background knowledge that generates a feeling of oneness. For years thereafter, when Joanna wore a woolen beanie in bed, a baseball cap to the farmer's market, or a sun hat outdoors, they merrily replayed this tender moment: "Do you like my hat?" "I do not!"

The use and reuse of ritualized sayings, secret puns, and insider jokes not only reinforces the uniqueness of a couple's bond, it also keeps everyday interactions lively and positive. It never ceases to amaze me how often my wife and I recycle the same funny quips over and over. They never seem to get old. They're gifts that keep on giving.

One expression we resort to was plucked from the comedy show, *Little Britain*. Dressed as a woman, David Walliams plays the role of an overworked, stone-faced, rude receptionist who always seems to get customers' information wrong when inputting it in her computer. In a clip of this sort, a mother checking her six-year-old daughter into the hospital requests that the receptionist look into the erroneous computer-generated detail indicating the girl is on schedule to get a double-hip replacement: "There must be some kind of mistake. She's here to get her tonsils removed." After a few clicks on her keyboard and a glance at the computer screen, the receptionist curtly responds: "Computer says no!"[47]

Since watching these skits over a decade ago, not a week goes by without Janet or me playfully using this expression in a thick Cockney accent when responding to a domestic request that we end up fully complying with: "Can you turn the lights off before you come upstairs to bed… can you make sure the back door is locked… can you put your sweaty clothes in the hamper outside?" "Computer says no!"

Puns and clever use of words are a way to signal partners we want them to collaborate in keeping things breezy and light. Veteran linguist Jennifer Coates would say they help establish a conversational "play frame," or interactional space that is not unlike group musical activity, specifically jazz.[48] Mutual banter and repartee, where couples spontaneously feed off each other's witticisms, taps a similar improvisational spirit found in jazz music.

In life, just as in non-improvisational music, there are rules, traditions, and conventions to follow that can become wearisome. Joking around, just like jazz riffing, temporarily frees those involved from the stresses and strains of having to deliver results, be "on" all the time, in control, vigilant, serious. It's like getting a reprieve to be a carefree child, in an adult body that only knows how to be careful. Hence the commonality between the quote by social critic Terry Eagleton, "joking is a brief vacation from the mild oppressiveness of everyday meaning,"[49] and that of legendary jazz drummer Art Blakey, "jazz washes away the dust of everyday life."[50]

A couple I see is well acquainted with the liberating effects of playful banter. Christine, a fifty-year-old surgeon, sheepishly confessed during the intake session that she never knows if her fifty-three-year-old former ambulance driver husband, Alan, will be "Pooh Bear" or "grizzly bear" when he awakes in the morning. When Alan is Pooh Bear, he's a hoot. On one occasion they made me aware of, Alan came into the kitchen saying "9:50" aloud repeatedly, to remind himself when to switch the clothes from the washing machine to the dryer. Christine misheard him, thinking he was saying, "I'm fifty." She started dancing around singing, "I'm fifty! I'm fifty!" Alan joined with her in singing this and they waltzed together arm in arm across the kitchen floor.

On another occasion, Christine came into the living room holding a cup of popcorn to hand to Alan. They both had been trying to lose weight. Because of this, Alan expressed his surprise that Christine was delivering a full cup. At the same time, he noticed that Christine was not wearing a bra and her nipples were erect. Alan giggled and played with the double-entendre, "full cup": "I changed my mind. I'll have the full cup." Christine played right along: "I'm happy to give you the full cup, if it's the full cup you desire." They laughed so hard that Christine flatulated loudly, which made them crack up even more.

Accessing a comedic state of mind can be all-important in dampening the shame felt around embarrassing accidents, compromising exposures, and silly oversights, especially with the passage of time. Hence the philosophical adage by television personality Steve Allen, "tragedy plus time equals comedy."[51]

In my late thirties, as my days as a competitive soccer player were dwindling, I had the good fortune to play in an exhibition game at the famed Colosseum stadium in Los Angeles. Realizing this was a once-in-a-lifetime opportunity, I impressed upon my wife the importance of videotaping the match for posterity. When the day came around, she unwittingly forgot to put a blank tape in the video recorder. I was crestfallen. She was profoundly apologetic. After a while, I used some self-deprecatory black humor: "I'm glad that match didn't get taped. My performance was pathetic!"

These days, reference to the incident is simply a lighthearted, tongue-in-cheek reminder not to forget to do something, engendering smiles: "Can you double-check to see if we are taping the just-released Ernest Hemingway documentary, we don't want another Colosseum moment."

Minor nuisances can be deftly handled with lightheartedness. When my brother-in-law cannot find kitchenware where he last left it, he is fond of saying to my sister-in-law things like: "If you were a spatula, where would you be?" The wife of one of my best friends is in the habit of addressing his spaciness with comments like: "Did you mean to leave the burner on?" An overtalking friend usually punctuates his long-winded expressions with droll comments like, "…to make a long story longer," and jokingly prefaces delivery of his new ideas with a phrase that seems brash, but isn't because of his jolly tone, "…back to me," which oddly makes it much easier to listen to him longer.

In the first book of its kind, *Conversational Joking*, analyzing common humorous exchanges between people, Neal Norrick discusses a class of humor involving "questions we deem too obvious to deserve a serious reply."[52] Occasionally, I find myself in this predicament with my wife. Well-intentioned, and wanting to converse and connect with me, she'll say things like, "How are you going to cook that?" I'll reply, "Well, I'm going to take out the pan, put it on the burner, turn up the heat, dump in the pork chop…" Her stock response is a half-irritated, half-amused, "Oh, stop!"

After watching Stanley Tucci in his *Searching for Italy* series, discovering that we were both born in November 1960, I wanted to look shiny bald just like him. I fanatically researched head shavers, which I thought my wife was privy to. When my AidallsWellup Men's 5–1 Electric Shaver for Bald Men (with 1,111 customers giving it a 4.5 rating on Amazon) arrived in the mail, I excitedly extracted it from the box. Seeing a conversational moment, Janet queried me, "Is it made to shave heads?" She was not particularly enthralled by my response, but it did help me whistle through the interaction without my head exploding: "No, I bought it to shave my legs!"

It's imperative that each member of a couple adapt to what can be realistically obtained from the other if a loving bond is to flourish over time. As Andre, a character in Tayari Jones's novel, *An American Marriage*, muses: "You have to work with the love you are given, with all the complications clanging behind it like tin cans tied to a bridal sedan."[53]

When a relationship plentifully meets our essential needs and is mostly good, what makes it chug along rather than keep sputtering out is a mindset of mirthful acceptance in the face of a mate's negative traits. An openness to humorously shrugging off the myriad inescapable sources of potential irritation surrounding sharing a life with a fellow flawed human being.

Wittiness ethics

Central to any understanding of human ethics is the viewpoint that people should do what is within their means to reduce suffering and promote happiness in the world. On a small scale, when we apply this to any given intimate relationship, it quickly becomes apparent how a humorous habit of mind has much to offer in minimizing emotional harm, as well as maximizing happiness, among loved ones.

The ability to laugh at oneself isn't just a fun experience, it's an ethical achievement; that's because when we nurture the ability to refrain from taking ourselves too seriously—lightheartedly accepting our own shortcomings—we can't then, in good conscience, be heavy-hearted and overly serious with the ones we love. This is a win–win in relationships because, not only is there a reduction in intra-personal suffering, but also interpersonal suffering. We do an end run around the cynical mindset contained in the line by humorist, Gregg Eisenberg: "I'm not doing much to alleviate the suffering of humanity, other than transferring some of mine onto you."[54] We become more relaxed in the way we handle our own limitations, quirks, and insecurities and it feels more natural to approach our loved one's limitations, quirks, and insecurities with the same degree of levity.

On the subject of wit promoting happiness, none other than the philosophical heavy-weight Aristotle had skin in the game. In *Nicomachean Ethics*, he is both plainspoken and profound in suggesting that ready-wittedness is a virtue because it enables people to relax and enjoy being together. Being fun to be around involves being tactful and tasteful in one's witty displays. Present company always applies. You need to know how to read a social situation well, know what's appropriate or not to say, discern where the line is. As with all of Aristotle's virtues, moderation applies.

Carrying humor too far is buffoonery. It's cluelessness. It's tactless and tasteless. It's not knowing when sincerity is called for and a cavalier attitude ruins the moment. Often it includes mean-spiritedness. Several years ago, during a couples therapy session, the husband groused about his wife's lack of sexual availability: "You'd think she'd been brought up in a convent the way she treats me." That's not funny. That's mean. Aristotle would classify that as unvirtuous.

On the other end is overseriousness and dullness. Not seeing a joke, not getting a joke, not wanting to be jocular. That's unfun. That's counterproductive to Aristotle's sense of the good life.

On a different note, there's ethical significance to rising above personal concerns to appreciate the interests of others. In our most mature moments, we can get our mind around the notion that accepting a spouse for who they are, not who we need them to be, is emblematic of genuine love. But that level of maturity often eludes most humans. Perhaps there's a fundamental ambivalence at the heart of practicing true love: needing an other's otherness to conform to our selfness, while knowing only too well love is supposed to hinge on a deep appreciation for their otherness.

This ambivalence is the stuff of countless jokes: "I love you no matter what you do, but do you have to do so much of it"; "If you were just a little different, you wouldn't need to change at all." Years ago, when my wife and I were much less skilled at love, we engaged in wordplay that reflects this ambivalence. We toyed with the sonoric resemblance between the words "love" and "loathe": "I looothvvve you!" Perhaps one of the most ethical ways to act lovingly is to keep our sense of humor about how difficult—though necessary—it is to relate to a loved one on his or her terms.

In the grander scheme, the mundane matters otherwise compatible couples squabble over are ludicrously absurd: whether to repaint the bathroom blue gray or arctic gray; order sparkling or regular water at dinner; take the train or bus to work; serve pancakes or bacon on Christmas morning; listen to country rock or hip hop on the ride home; access the freeway or side streets to visit Grandma; put jeans in the washer with pastels or darks; sign the kids up for swimming or tennis lessons. Sometimes these squabbles signify deep cracks in a marriage, where each other's yearnings to be loved right have been long since calcified. More often than not, they're on the order of not picking at a scab. It's a scab that shouldn't be picked at, because life is short.

It's dreadful to consider—but soberingly important—that death is a fact of life. Existentialist thinkers underscore the motivational benefits of contemplating our own mortality. Knowing death can visit an individual at any time inspires him or her to live more fully in the present, pursue cherished dreams and goals more vigorously.

The Swedish philosopher, Martin Hagglund, proposes that the death of our beloved is far more harrowing "not least because it is a death you have to survive."[55] Religious faith has value, but it can lend slender solace. Hagglund cites the agonizing tale of C. S. Lewis, told in *A Grief Observed*, whose stalwart faith instructed him to believe he would see his wife in heaven; however, he desperately desired her back on earth.

The background awareness that time is always slipping away, that we have a finite spell on this planet with our mate, that he or she could be stolen from us by material death, or slow soul death due to dementia, somehow needs to be an ethical call not just to live and love well now, but to live and love better now. If we don't want our beloved to haunt us from the grave, we'd better not be insufferably boring or boorish, but sufferlessly funny.

CHAPTER 5

Lust is a must

Twenty-six years into her marriage, Caroline knew the implications of what she agonizingly revealed to me during an emergency therapy session:

Michael has been my best friend for eons, but the romantic spark is gone. Truth be told, it never really was there from the beginning. We were friends in college and after being emotionally bruised by so many jerks his compassion and loyalty won out. He looked so good on paper and was such a nice guy. I made the rational choice and agreed to marry him. I always believed that some erotic energy would emerge in time, but it didn't. The sex was passable, but not what I would characterize as lovemaking by a long stretch. I know he loves me—and I have love for him—but I'm not *in love* with him. That's such a cliché, but it's true. The prospect of asking for a separation, knowing it will crush him, feels awful; after all, I still care for him a great deal. I feel incredibly guilty and selfish for wanting out, but I can't keep living a lie.

Caroline's predicament recalls the pithy phrase by the Scottish-born philosopher John Armstrong: "Love is friendship plus sex."[1] Not just sex like friends might have—mutual respect and niceness mitigating any real possibility for sustained, or even periodic, eroticism. Sex like people in love have—lustful letting go, sensual enjoyment, carnal expressions of loving desire—sufficiently, and with more than a flicker of intensity, in the long arc of a committed relationship.

We don't often ponder whether our marriage or long-term partnership will survive if our significant other stops ranking close to the top of our friendship list for a lengthy period of time; but we do if good sex with him or her hits a long dry spell. Perhaps that's because there's no greater way for spouses or partners to make obvious and tangible the love they possess for each other than to be willing and eager to have sex.

These days, established couplehood is trending in the direction of "love is friendship, low on sex." About fifteen years ago, scientific findings by Paul Taylor and colleagues at the Pew Research Center in Washington, DC, showed that 70 percent of people in the US viewed a satisfying sexual relationship as very important for a successful relationship, compared to 46 percent who emphasized "having shared interests."[2] Fast forward to the present. The prioritization of shared interests for the well-being of American couples outranks a satisfying sex life—64 percent endorsing the former, 61 percent the latter—according to the most recent data out of the Pew Research Center.[3]

What parameters can we use to address the delicate issue of how much sex keeps a relationship vital over the long haul? British farmers are on the more ambitious end—over 33 percent mentioning that they have sex at least once a day.[4] The coital kinetics of the Mangaians in Polynesia are equally as impressive.[5] By their late twenties, it is expected that males put to good use the sexual mentoring they have received by adult females in the group to do the deed in ways that bring themselves and their partners to orgasm five to six times a week. It's both eye-rolling and eye-raising to learn that around the world, a whopping 40 percent of couples age eighteen to fifty-five and older have sex three to four times a week. Based on this data point, the authors of the *Normal Bar* study—collecting information on the sexual practices and attitudes of 70,000 individuals across the globe—are unapologetic in their conclusion: "Are couples who have sex frequently happier over the years than couples who don't have sex as often? Yes, they really are. Three to four times a week is the magic frequency."[6]

Before the undersexed reader weaponizes these data with his or her less lusty partner, an important caveat is in order. Surveys of over 30,000 North Americans conducted over four decades suggest that more sex doesn't always equal more relationship happiness. Summing up years of sexual frequency research, Amy Muise, Research Chair in Relationships and Sexuality at York University in Canada offers a less quixotic viewpoint: "Although more frequent sex is associated with greater happiness, this link was no longer significant at a frequency of more than once a week."[7] She even goes so far as to propose that the emotional rewards for couples being amorous weekly, rather than just monthly, was equivalent to those gained by lifestyle benefits yielded from an annual salary bump of $50,000!

Let's assume that getting between the sheets at least once a week is important to sustain an erotic bond in a committed relationship; what percentage of couples are being thusly romantically diligent? The numbers vary but are low and getting lower. One of the most comprehensive surveys of its kind conducted by sex therapist David Schnarch, through his website, found that a mere 26 percent of married and non-married couples have sex once or twice a week.[8] Recent data yielded by the American Family Survey show that about 64 percent of married Americans engage in sex weekly, down from 72 percent in 2016, a reduction that is head-scratching given all the extra time at home during the Covid-19 pandemic.[9] In Great Britain, fewer than half of men and women in the sixteen to forty-four age bracket engage in lovemaking once a week or more, with the steepest reductions occurring among married and cohabitating couples.[10] Be that as it may, close to half of women and two-thirds of men in this National Surveys of Sexual Attitudes and Lifestyles study wished they were having sex more frequently.

From a health standpoint alone, when it comes to sex, we should walk the talk. Males reporting more frequent orgasms tend to have improved cardiac health[11] and lower prostate cancer risk.[12] Women who are sexually active are at lower risk of starting menopause early.[13] People who enjoy one to three orgasms weekly lower their susceptibility to depression and experience an immune system boost that leaves them less vulnerable to colds and other viruses.[14] A few years ago, results like these prompted the National Health Service in Great Britain to promote more sex for its citizenry for health reasons: "Weekly sex might help fend off illness."[15] Apparently, too many were undermining their own health by taking the old refrain too literally: "No sex please, we're British."

Remarkably, what the French call "la petite mort," or "the little death," in reference to post-orgasmic tranquility, may even stave off death itself. In a decade-long study of middle-aged Australian men, those who reported the most orgasms had half the premature death rate of their less orgasmic peers.[16] Findings from the Longevity Project, delving into the health outcomes of people first recruited as far back as the 1920s as part of the famous Terman study out of Stanford University showed that female participants with greater lifetime frequency of orgasmic sex tended to live longer than their less gratified female counterparts.[17]

An active sex life also reduces the risk of "death by infidelity" of a marriage or established partnership. Infidelity remains the number one reason why intimate relationships dissolve. Regular enjoyable sex at home can lessen—though not eliminate, as the myth holds—the chances that one's mate will stray both in fantasy and reality. In the *Normal Bar* study cited above, one in four of those who claimed they were extremely satisfied with their sex lives believed "there was someone out there who would be even better for me than my current partner,"[18] as opposed to three out of four who were sexually dissatisfied in their relationships. Whereas 18 percent of men and 14 percent of women who were sexually satisfied at home admitted to having sex outside the relationship, 46 percent of men and 35 percent women who were domestically sexually dissatisfied confessed to doing the deed with a paramour.[19]

Despite the rather obvious health and bonding benefits of regular, loving sex, it is estimated that less than a third of couples actually make sex a priority in their busy lives.[20] Nearly three-quarters of people in long-term intimate partnerships have never embarked on a romantic vacation.[21] Even more disconcerting is how little time intimates set aside for lovemaking of a quality where both men and woman reach orgasm. It's common knowledge that women need more sexy time to orgasm. Mae West, the trailblazing sex symbol, once put it in alluring, unclinical terms: "A guy what takes his time, I'll go for any time,

I'm a fast moving gal, I likes some slow." Said in unsexy, clinical terms, if we start the clock with foreplay, on average it takes a straight woman almost fourteen minutes to orgasm—according to a reliable international study by sexual health experts in India.[22] Of course, that's just the first orgasm, which often takes a bit more tender loving care. To experience multi-orgasmic sex, some science supports that anything less than thirty minutes of bedroom antics leaves a female sweetheart short changed.[23] This doesn't even account for luxuriating around afterwards, engaging in the sort of post-coital kissing, cuddling, and caressing—creating the so-called "sexual afterglow"—that some researchers tell us is even more important than time dedicated to foreplay and sex itself for sexual and relationship satisfaction for both men and women.

Sadly, survey data by the sexual tracking app, Lovely, uncovers that the average duration of sexual intercourse for American couples is twelve minutes.[24] This time allotment rivals mundane tasks like taking a shower (eight minutes),[25] doing one's business in the latrine (fourteen minutes),[26] walking the dog (ten to fifteen minutes)[27] and stealing a smoke break (ten minutes).[28] It far exceeds the duration of sought-after indulgences like time with one's feet up in the pedicure chair[29] or flat on one's back enjoying a massage (forty-five to ninety minutes).[30]

Many couples seem to have slipped into a mindset about the role of sex in formal and common-law marriages that is an age-old one, with its roots in organized religion: sex for pleasurable bonding is optional; not essential; not a must. Providence dictates that if you are with your true soulmate, he or she will lovingly overlook the extra weight you've put on, your disinterest in looking sexy or handsome, or your flagging energy to be more sensual or mix things up in bed. After all, as the popular online poster submits, a soulmate is "someone that wants to undress your conscience and make love to your thoughts." Sex for procreation—having babies—allows souls to love bodies. After that, any sustained eagerness to accentuate the body and mate for the sake of mating—recreational sex—is somewhat of an indulgence. As if upkeep of the body is independent of upkeep of the soul. As if a person's attractiveness and desirability aren't types of "embodied character," or cumulative life choices they make to remain as fit and healthy as possible, strive to act smart and stylish, as well as be kind and considerate in their actions, not just their words.

As we shall see, past and present moralizing of sex by organized religion hinders full cultural acceptance of sex-positive attitudes that might breathe new life into erotically compromised relationships. If the sex lives of more couples are to flourish, not just limp along, there needs to be less focus on sexual morals in the religious sense and more on sexual ethics in the humanistic sense—keeping up your appearance not for vanity reasons but because the best way to be desired is to make oneself desirable; not wanting to repeatedly sexually disappoint because that would be uncaring with someone who genuinely cares for you; due regard to the reciprocal giving and receiving of sensual pleasure out of love for your flesh-and-blood partner, not as "duty sex" mandated by a religiously inspired conjugal contract.

De-moralizing sex

The flagship product of the largest e-commerce sex toy business in the US, Adam and Eve, is a fun-size device called the Wild G-Spot Vibrator. Its "triple-prong teaser," "curved tip," and "spinning metal beads" are designed to maximize women's orgasmic pleasure: "A slice of Heaven you didn't know existed."[31] From a marketing standpoint, it's savvy of "America's most trusted source of adult products" to go by the name Adam and Eve and imply that women deserve the sort of orgasmic delight that ecstatically unites them with the gods, a brief transcendent crossover from earth to heaven that historically has been the purview of men. The latter is embedded in the double meaning of the word "ejaculation"—a brief aspirational prayer, like "Hallelujah!" or "Amen!" and the moment when men excitedly splooge, maybe even exclaim, "Oh, God, I'm coming."

Normalizing female pleasure with Judeo-Christian themes helps push back against standards of sexual purity pushed on women over the millennia by mainstream religions, in all likelihood attracting customers. More than we want to admit, our current cultural climate informing us on female sexuality retains a strong flavor of what Professor M. L. Holbrook righteously announced before the New Haven Medical Society over a century and a half ago: "the Almighty, in creating the female sex, took the uterus and built a woman around it."[32] It's light on what the Wild G-Spot Vibrator serves up: "Every fiber of your being is caught up in the key of Wild G."[33]

Even though fewer Americans belong to organized churches than several decades ago, Judeo-Christian, and to a lesser extent Muslim, values remain the preeminent arbiter of sexual conduct in our society. Who you have sex with, when, how, and why comes under moral scrutiny in the minds of religious people far more than other moral issues, like lying, stealing, and cheating. Across six experiments involving almost 4,000 participants looking at what distinguishes a truly religious person, Liana Hone at the University of Miami and a handful of researchers concluded: "Conservative stances towards sex and reproduction are quite close to the core of what it means to be a religious person."[34] This is hardly surprising, at least in the Christian tradition, which has an asexual savior (Jesus) and asexual founder (Paul). Saying nothing of how: "When the queen of heaven is a virgin, the animal nature of mortal women is bound to give rise to concern."[35]

In vast numbers, Americans check in with their theological conscience before any clothes come off and sex parts get touched. In a survey sponsored by the advertising agency Euro RSCG Worldwide on sex, religion, and infidelity, 39 percent of Americans agreed with the statement: "My religious beliefs factor into my sexual behavior."[36] The US had the dubious distinction of beating out Great Britain, France, Germany, and China in this category.

Natural sex in most mainline religious traditions is procreative sex—penis in vagina, culminating in male ejaculation, preferably in the missionary position, ONLY in the context of marriage. Unnatural sex is everything else: oral sex, anal sex, masturbation of self or of another, that the Roman Catholic lay theologian and author of *The Catechism of Catholic Ethics* insists "are intrinsically evil and always gravely immoral because these acts are not unitive and procreative."[37] Don't be chagrined if you're unfamiliar with the term unitive. It involves the sublime state of fixating your thoughts on God and off carnal desires. An evangelical protestant minister once similarly advanced the cause of church-approved sex: "We're the Moral Majority and we know what's RIGHT/We'll come to your bedroom to check every night/We'll let you have sex on just one condition/it's done with your wife in the missionary position."[38]

The problem with what various religious denominations categorize as normal sex is that it ignores female pleasure. In her every-sexually-active-person-must-read-book, *Becoming Cliterate*, leading sexologist

Laurie Mintz presents highly plausible data underscoring how only about 4 percent of woman reliably reach orgasm with penile thrusting alone and that 77 percent of women need either direct clitoral stimulation or intercourse with direct clitoral stimulation if they are to get their goodies.[39] For legions of women, the missionary position is really the "missing-it position." Mintz puts it more bluntly: "Our cultural overfocus on the importance of putting a penis into a vagina is screwing with women's orgasms."[40]

All the religious enthusiasm around the uterus and copulation for procreation has taken the focus off the clitoris, literally "the key" to women's pleasure. And it shows. A well-regarded study discovered that one in four men are unable to locate the clitoris when provided with a diagram of female sexual anatomy.[41] We should consider that shameful. Instead, shame is encoded in the very language used to identify the vulva, where the clitoris lies: pudendum, in Latin, "thing to be ashamed of."

Women need what organized religion deems unnatural sex acts to get off—oral sex and/or digital masturbation. No matter, clerics give no quarter. Fr. Hugh Barbour, O. Praem, Chaplain at Norbertine of St. Michael's Abbey in Silverado, California, advises those tempted to provide oral pleasure: "they should train their hearts to prefer face to face (not face to groin) communication in the expression of their love and should prefer that use of their genitals that is directly related to human procreation, not some kind of elaborate acrobatics that ludicrously overemphasizes the pleasure of one or the other."[42] Raised Catholic myself—and full disclosure, I was so deep in, I studied to be a Catholic priest in my teens—it has always been a source of consternation to me why priests who take a vow of chastity are looked to as authorities on best sexual practices. Shouldn't we all pay heed to the quote by French poet and novelist Remy de Gourmont: "Chastity is the most unnatural of the sexual perversions."[43]

It's not surprising that guilt is baked into many women's sexual experiences, since they are more apt than men to participate spiritually and socially in religious communities. Women gravitate toward being teachers and keepers of the faith and carry the responsibility for tamping down male sexual arousal. They pivot on the double-edged sword of having to be desirable, but not too desiring, lest their desire mixed with that of their mate is a volatile combination. Guilt can arise when the religious messages about proper sex floating around in their heads interfere with their body telling them to go off script and crave more than plain penis in vagina intercourse. A recent University of Toronto study sampling over 1,600 sexually active heterosexual adults in committed relationships indicates that women who see themselves as religious struggle more than male believers relaxing and enjoying sex with their partners.[44]

Masturbation guilt is also prominent for women, setting them up to self-pleasure less than men and self-reproach when they do. National Survey of Sexual Health and Behavior data show that three times as many men as women aged thirty to fifty masturbate two to three times a week.[45] About a third of women report feeling remorseful about engaging in autoerotic acts.[46] Guilt is encoded in the very word masturbation. It combines the Latin "manus," meaning "hand," with "stuprare," "to defile," to produce the literal translation, "self-defilement with the hand."

Turns out, masturbation guilt is bad for long-term intimate partnerships, insofar as it inhibits generous amounts of self-diddling. Research shows that women who masturbate tend to have greater interest in partnered sex such that self-pleasuring *complements*, or "primes the pump," augmenting what they already get between the sheets. They are more likely to know what brings them to orgasm and guide their partners accordingly in bed. For men, masturbation often serves the purpose of *compensating* for the amount and variety of sex they obtain with their mate, frequently making the unbalanced sexual bank account tolerable.[47]

Within most religious contexts, for people in gay and lesbian relationships, the best sex is no sex. Insofar as non-procreative sex has been considered neither here nor there, homosexuality has been demonized at worst, suspect at best. Sam Allbery, author of *Is God Anti-Gay?* engages in vigorous mental gymnastics to self-identify as someone who is not gay, per se, but prone to "same-sex attraction." He admits the distinction is "clunky" but swears by it because framing things this way allows him to treat his gayness as an appetite to be suppressed in loving service to God, not a sexual identity that screams for gratification. Curiously, Allbery, without even a hint of awareness of the sexual innuendo involved, offers an analogy: "Take another kind of appetite. I love meat. But my love for meat does not mean I would want someone to think that 'carnivore' was the primary category through which to understand me."[48]

On a more somber note, the gay Catholic political commentator Andrew Sullivan has gone on record about the psychological damage caused by his religious upbringing: "My childhood and adolescence were difficult to the point of agony, an agony my own church told me was my just deserts ... Forcing gay people into molds they do not fit helps no one. It robs them of dignity and self-worth and the capacity for healthy relationships."[49]

Lesbian couples who decide to have children, or who bring children into a marriage from an earlier heterosexual coupling, face a peculiar marginalization in religions that revere motherhood as the sine qua non for women's existence and sexuality. If we stick with the ecclesiastical logic, lesbian relationships should be modular since, as Mary Hunt, cofounder of Women's Alliance for Theology, Ethics, and Ritual in Silver Springs, Maryland, smartly deduces: "if one mother is great, why aren't two mothers greater?"[50]

We are at an inflection point in our culture where the debate needs to shift from sex negativity to sex positivity in guiding people's attitudes towards optimal sexual practices. Faith-based communities have a role to play in this, since, as Elizabeth Boskey who works with transgendered children and youth at Boston Children's Hospital mentions: "Religion is not inherently inimical to healthy sexuality."[51] Martha Schick, the self-identified queer Youth and Young Adult Ministries Leader at the Old South Church in Boston notes: "sex positivity means approaching sex and sexuality without judgment; valuing communication, consent, and safety; and pushing for education and laws that empower people to make healthy sexual decisions." She adds, "churches and faith communities try to teach their young people how to live by the Biblical ideals of love, forgiveness, and peace—why would they not teach these lessons when it comes to interpersonal sexual relationships?"[52] When consensual and mutual pleasure is accorded a front and center role in sexual activity it can even be argued, as the theologian Christine Gudorf does, that subverting it is a "violation of the Christian obligation to love thy neighbor."[53]

We need to bring body and soul together in our thoughts about good sex. "Yada" in the Jewish tradition captures this well. It's the Hebrew word for knowledge, while also used in reference to sexual intercourse. Becoming deeply intimate with someone entails gaining knowledge of him/her/them derived from how they expose their true character physically and emotionally while making love. Yada even recognizes orgasm equality between the sexes! As far back as the thirteenth century, the *Iggeret Hakodesh*, an authoritative rabbinic text, instructed husbands to hold off ejaculating until their wives had orgasmed.[54]

Sex-friendly passages in ancient Muslim texts also exist. On matters of how best to please your wife, Asbag, a pupil of Imam Malik, a leading cleric of the Maliki school of law, remarked many centuries ago: "He is allowed to lick her vagina with the tongue."[55] Imam ar-Ragib, another leading Muslim scholar, in an ancient text wrote, "Oh Allah, strengthen my penis for therein lies the satisfaction of my wife" and "the most shameless sex is the best."[56]

Change may soon be on the horizon in the Roman Catholic tradition, at least as it pertains to heterosexual sexual pleasure in the context of marriage. Pope Francis recently bemoaned the over-moralizing of sex in the church during an interview with the Italian writer, Carlo Petrini, as "having caused enormous harm which can still be felt strongly today." Encouragingly, he identified sex as a "gift from God" and added: "sexual pleasure is there to make love more beautiful and guarantee the perpetuation of the species."[57]

One wonders if the Pontifex Maximus had finally gotten around to giving the Song of Solomon in the Old Testament a thorough read. This long poem is a celebration of erotic love between a young man and woman ("O loved one, delectable maiden/May your breasts be like clusters on the vine/Let us go into the fields/There I will give you my love")[58] that would definitely be a reassuring addition to any sex education curriculum sanctioned by the church.

Though, it can't be emphasized enough, to lessen the occurrence of demoralizing sex brought about by the over-moralizing of sex, it's better that people don't feel answerable to church elders. Matt Groening, creator of *The Simpsons*, advises caution: "When authorities warn you of the sinfulness of sex, there is an important lesson to be learned. Do not have sex with the authorities."[59] In all seriousness, people are better off feeling answerable to what they themselves yearn for sexually; what each individual and his or her partner feel they deserve and are worthy of in bed; or on the couch, or on the kitchen counter-top, of course, when the kids are well-asleep.

Unsynched libidos

Veronica and Miguel, a middle-aged Latinex couple who had married in their early twenties, sought out therapy with me to deal with their sagging sex life, which they hoped would have gathered steam now that their two daughters were in high school. Veronica acknowledged that she was so underwater juggling all that was involved running a household, taking care of her aging parents, and keeping her part-time event planning business afloat that sex was low on the list. Miguel resented this because in his mind, he "carried his weight," driving their daughters to school, helping them with their homework, and making dinners several nights a week. This was light years ahead of his father, who had few misgivings about his domestic contribution.

Because Miguel had to awaken early to consult with clients overseas, he went to bed sooner than Veronica. He was in the habit of reaching over to cuddle with her in a semi-somnolent state in the morning, half testing to see if she might want to get it on. He treasured these moments in bed when they would cuddle, draping his body over hers, whether it resulted in sex or not. She found herself being increasingly perturbed by this because it woke her up prematurely and she required all the sleep necessary to be rested and get through the day ahead. At the same time, Veronica appreciated how sex was important both to her and for their relationship.

Finding the time and ensuring that she would be in the mood were embarrassing challenges for her. She often felt a mixture of guilt and irritation fending off Miguel's sexual advances, not craving sex as much as he did. She didn't mind his spontaneous tender hugs and kisses. She did mind his habit of suddenly grabbing her tush from behind, or reaching around to squeeze her breasts.

Veronica tried not to succumb to all the petty things that Miguel did that annoyed her and turned her off sexually, like wiping his mouth on their shared towel leaving toothpaste stains, and his habit of waiting to take the trash out at the last minute. She hated that this made her just like her mother, who nitpicked constantly about things her father did wrong. Miguel was also so busy being a good dad and consolidating his position at the new accounting firm he was hired at that his preoccupations got in the way of Veronica's romantic gestures. Once, on a planned date night, he called her, having forgotten, asking her permission to umpire the softball match after the one their daughter had played in, because the next volunteer had failed to show.

The main issue for Miguel was that Veronica let all these things get to her. Why couldn't she tune all this out and just want to have sex? After almost twenty years being married to Veronica, he remained physically attracted to her. He found her dark, soft skin still hard to resist. Whenever she showed any interest in sex, he was ready, willing, and able. Listening to Miguel talk, sex appeared to him to be the only show in town to make him feel pleasurably excited, undefended, appreciated, connected, and at peace, all wrapped up in one.

The mismatched libidos Veronica and Miguel worried about touch upon the dual definitions of the word libido itself. "Libido" is commonly accepted as the Latin word for "sensual passion, or lust." It first showed up in the work of pioneer German sexologist Krafft-Ebing's landmark 1886 text, *Psychopathia Sexualis*, then was adopted and popularized through Sigmund Freud's writings.[60] Putting it crassly, Freud's concept of libido involved a spontaneous upswelling of horny sexual energy that needed an outlet, without which over time a person would develop a bad case of the anxious jitters. It was an idea that caught on. It still exists in the popular vernacular when people talk of "being hot and bothered, needing to get their rocks off."

The Latin word "libere" also feeds into the meaning of libido. It roughly translates as "to be frank, open, pleasing." I call attention to these idiomatic distinctions because they have a bearing on how we think of sexual desire discrepancies in men and women.

Up until the past several decades, academics bought into Freud's notion of libido. It shaped Masters and Johnson's notions of the linear build-up to sexual activity: sexual desire springs up, leading to arousal, culminating in orgasm. It was a model that was thought to apply equally to men and women, which, as we're learning, has been very unfair to women. Taking this model at face value, women just don't fantasize about sex enough, which is the main gateway to sexual arousal.

In one of the only studies of its kind, Terri Fisher had a duo of students in her Psychology of Human Sexuality class at Ohio State University pass out golf tally clickers to about 300 willing undergrads to monitor their rates of spontaneous sexual fantasies. They discovered that the typical man thinks about sex once or twice an hour, about double the rate of women.[61]

Another study uncovered that women in long-term relationships experience spontaneous sexual thoughts at a frequency of once a month, or less.[62]

A 2019 article in *Archives of Sexual Behavior* published results from two longitudinal studies of heterosexual couples' fluctuating sexual desire over the span of three to five years. Newlyweds reported moderate to high levels of desire on average, though husbands' levels were higher than wives'. Over the course of the study, women's sexual desire declined steeply, while men's was relatively unaltered.[63]

Results like these play into corny gender-based jokes around sexual desire discrepancies: "I have sex with my wife almost every day! Almost on Monday, almost on Tuesday, almost on Wednesday." "My wife is a sex object—every time I ask for sex, she objects."

It turns out that measuring women's libido in quasi-internal-combustion-engine ways, as an energy level, fueled by sexual fantasy, misses the point. The other meaning of libido is relevant here. Many women need their partner to be "frank, open, and pleasing" *in order to* activate sexual desire. A team of Israeli and American social scientists best sum up the latest position on female libido: "for many women, particularly those involved in long-term relationships, the willingness to experience sexual arousal and subsequent desire is regulated more by intimacy needs than by spontaneous urges."[64] Feeling listened to, special, and supported—partner responsiveness—is a prominent sexual driver for many women. Thoughtful gestures and caring listening go a long way in making them feel desired, and therefore more desirous.

Deeper into committed relationships, especially in midlife when women are peri- or post-menopausal, desire is less likely to pop up on its own and often occurs *in the act* of feeling aroused, not the other way around. Fifty-three-year old Elana describes this perfectly normal aspect of many women's sexual desire process: "I think when I was younger I used to feel it really genitally. I used to feel sexually engorged, and now it's more as if I can become sexually engorged as we're starting to have sex, but it's not as much beforehand."[65]

The Australian-born journalist Belinda Luscombe humorously says of sexual desire in women as relationships progress: "It arrives after the party has started."[66] Frequently, getting the party started in the first place is not the electric spontaneous occurrence it is during the romantic phase of a marriage or long-term partnership. Many couples spend years quarreling over the lack of spontaneous sex in their relationships, as if relinquishing this sounds the death knell for sex itself.

I once had a male client in couples therapy who badgered his middle-aged wife ceaselessly for not initiating sex with him more, like greeting him after work at the door with nothing on but the ruby-red raincoat he had purchased for her. He had no clue that his being kinder, more attentive and decent, and collaborative in planning and setting aside time for sex was the only way his wife would ever don that ruby-red raincoat nude.

Sex therapist Michael Aron shares this perspective: "The truth is that sex loses spontaneity for most very early in the relationship. It has to be prioritized, planned, and sometimes even choreographed to make it feel spontaneous. Those couples waiting to have sex for the right opportunity to feel spontaneous often find themselves waiting a very long time."[67]

The responsive nature of many women's sexual arousal and desire process is cause for buoyancy, not impatience. Collaborating on and communicating about preferred time of the day, what sets the mood, cologne or no cologne, best hygiene practices, making sure the favorite sex toys are ready at hand, and perhaps the shivering anticipation of passionate kissing and oral sex!

In a sample of over 38,000 cohabiting and married men and women who had been together for at least three years, about one in three reported their sex life to be as passionate as it was in the beginning. What differentiated them from their less satisfied cohort? More collaboration around mood setting, sexual communication, switching up sex positions, and receiving oral sex.[68]

In the *Normal Bar* study, mutual passionate kissing was one of the main sexual practices that kept desire strong for couples high in sexual satisfaction. Men seem to be late to the party when it comes to realizing the orgasmic advantages of cunnilingus for their female partners. In the twenty to twenty-four age range, estimates show that only 55 percent of men have given oral sex to a female significant other in the preceding year. That number jumps to 69 percent in men aged 30 to 39.[69]

Low sexual desire is not the exclusive terrain of women. Epidemiological studies show that anywhere between approximately

12 to 18 percent of men in Western countries lose interest in sex for a significant period of time.[70] One of the most highly regarded studies on this topic was conducted by Bob Berkowitz and Susan Yager-Berkowitz and documented in their book, *When Men Stop Having Sex*.[71] When polled, 68 percent of the heterosexual wives of sexually disinterested husbands claimed, "He lost interest and I don't know why," while only 28 percent of their husbands answered, "I lost interest and I don't know why."

The authors surmised: "Either the men aren't talking or the women aren't listening." The age sample of the reticent husbands is pertinent. The mean age of the males was fifty-five, and that of the females forty-eight, and the couples had been married an average of fifteen years. For most men as they age, sexual desire flags, as does arousal. They need more erotic stimulation to get and stay erect, while pride and awkwardness hinder them from communicating this. In heterosexual partnerships, they wish their women enjoyed sex more but miss the cues telling them what sensual actions they could adopt to make this happen; hence the old adage, "Silence doesn't mean your sexual performance left her speechless."

When a little kind persistence, sweet talk, and playful flirtation might make the difference between a sexless or a sexy afternoon, many men are too focused on being spurned by their mate that they fail to hang in, making it a lose–lose for both parties, and no party. Amy Muise at the University of Toronto offers evidence to suggest that in established intimate relationships, most men don't see subtle sexual signals where they exist, or "underperceive their romantic partner's sexual desire."[72]

Study after study confirms that men rely more heavily on visual cues to help invigorate their erotic life. Weight gain and sexual disinterest go hand in hand. Of people who are sexually unhappy, a sizable 83 percent say they're too heavy, according to the *Normal Bar* study.[73] The problem is particularly sensitive to keep alive male romantic interest. In a 2011 MSNBC-reported poll of 70,000 people, almost 50 percent of the men said they'd end a relationship with a partner who gained weight, contrasted with a mere 20 percent of women who might do the same.[74] Yet men seem peculiarly unconcerned about their own weight gain, especially higher-income men who seem to feel entitled to let it all go while at the same time expecting their partners to stay trim and fit, based on numerous studies out of the Open University, the United Kingdom's main public research institution.[75]

Men don't seem to get it that balancing careers and family obligations leaves most women with little time to eke out the discipline to eat right and exercise. When coming home *from work* is nothing more than a prelude to coming home *to work*, who has the time? That's not to let women off the hook. In my decades of clinical practice, as a man I feel like I have both hands tied behind my back and a sock in my mouth dare I ever comment during a couples therapy session on how a girlfriend's or wife's weight gain might have sexual dampening effects on a relationship, no matter my considerate word choices. On this sensitive matter, all sensitivity, every way around, goes out the window. Let me quote some science that doesn't exist in the real world, but that still strikes fear in the hearts of many men: a recent study found out that women who have a little weight gain live longer than the men who mention it.

Things that might seem inconsequential, like a woman's hair length, turn out to be consequential for many men's sexuality. A recent poll by the *Daily Mail Reporter* of 3,000 men found that 80 percent of them would absolutely notice if a woman altered her hair length.[76] This brings to mind a couple I saw in treatment years ago where the live-in girlfriend had unilaterally, and without warning, cropped her long dark hair in tandem with being disinterested in sex. Henry took Perla's haircut and rebuff extremely personally, as if he was suddenly bereft of a life source.

He had just exited a fruitless five-year relationship and reconnected with Perla, his ex-girlfriend, who had always been his one true love. Sparks flew and Perla left friends, family, and a meaningful career to head from New Orleans to Seattle to move in with Henry. In the months that followed, Perla's sexual openness allowed Henry to gratifyingly make up for years of stimulating but asensual sex with his previous girlfriend, as well as offset the sensual hunger he carried inside, having been raised in a large Catholic family with a mother whose religiosity made her caregiving somewhat ascetic. Cutting her hair and pulling back from sex had not occurred in a vacuum for Perla. She found the intensity of Henry's desire invasive. This, mixed with the loss of self she underestimated, leaving friends, career, and family behind, propelled her to take drastic measures for self-preservation reasons.

In her timeless book *Bonds of Love*, Jessica Benjamin eloquently captures Perla's existential predicament: "Insofar as a woman's desire pulls her toward surrender and self-denial, she often chooses to curb it all together."[77] The suffering on Henry's end was no less palpable. It disallowed his needed erotic tie to Perla. Esther Perel equally eloquently captures Henry's existential predicament: "Through sex, men can recapture the pure pleasure of connection without having to compress their hard-to-articulate needs into the prison of words."[78] In the world of heterosexual romance, sometimes hair is not just hair, and sex not just sex.

Academics and experts who have dedicated their entire professional lives to studying human sexual behavior more or less agree with Amy Muse at York University when she states: "Satisfying sexual encounters are important for the quality of couples' relationships, but maintaining sexual desire and connection over time in a relationship is challenging."[79] Mismatched erotic needs are a constant once couples get beyond the romantically bonding stage of a relationship. As many as 80 percent of individuals on any given month experience a desire mismatch with their partner.[80] It's not only a one-way street, with males feeling deprived and females being the depriver. One study discovered that in 60 percent of cases in straight couples, the women is ready to go when the man isn't.[81] We're entering unchartered terrain now that women's earning potential is on an upwards swing, as is their easy access to birth control and pregnancy prevention measures, both of which embolden their sexual agency, leaving them less economically dependent on men and with more than one eye on having pleasurable sex, the fear of an unwanted pregnancy eliminated.

In a heterosexual context, whether they like it or not, men need to show love outside of the ways they both need and prefer to receive it, with due consideration to how their female partners need and prefer it. The same applies to women. Michelle Weiner-Davis, the relationship expert, offers some catching wisdom: "If you continue to look at the differences in your levels of sexual desire as your spouse's problems rather than as a couple's problem, you are courting disaster."[82] Lovingly committed partners simply need to pull out all the stops to reach sexual compromises that please both partners. More often than we feel comfortable admitting, in heterosexual couples that means men being supportive out of the bedroom.

In the 2016 journal article, "Skip the dishes? Not so fast! Sex and housework revisited," a team of Canadian scholars showed how more frequent and satisfactory sex occurred in relationships where men made a fair contribution to domestic chores.[83] Men should not be dismayed when they ask their female mates: "Do you still fantasize about me?" Leaving her to respond, "Yes, doing your fair share of the dishes and laundry." On the other hand, women may need to perk up as to why for years around the globe one of men's favorite porn categories to visit online is MILF (Mothers I'd Like to Fuck). It's probably not due to unearthing murderous/lascivious Freudian urges to eliminate their fathers, seduce their mothers, and reign supreme; although we shouldn't completely rule that out. In all probability, it's because as woman age, they are less self-conscious about their bodies, care more about their own needs for sexual pleasure, and show more sexual agency—all of which is a huge turn-on for the average male. Sexiness for most men has less to do with the pure physical beauty of a woman, and more to do with their genuine interest in and eagerness for good sex.

The takeaway is that unsynched libidos need not be a cause for panic in established partnerships. Even in the most vibrant heterosexual relationships, where both partners are extremely satisfied with their sexual relationships, a key study shows that only about 42 percent of couples agree their needs for sex are equally matched.[84] Let's not forget the sage advice of Peggy Kleinplatz, director of couples therapy training at the University of Ottawa: "Perhaps low desire only shifts when we help couples create sex worth having."[85]

Getting it on, not just over with

Going back several years, two of the world's foremost relationship experts threw the gauntlet down over whether good sex in long-term partnerships ought to involve cuddling or not. On one side was Susan Johnson, the Canadian psychologist best known for having founded Emotional Focused Couples Therapy, a popular approach to helping the relationally troubled based on ideas about human attachment. On the other side was Esther Perel, whose international bestseller, *Mating in Captivity*, established her as the leading contemporary voice on erotic intelligence.

Johnson defined good sex as "synchrony sex … when emotional openness and responsiveness, tender touch, and erotic exploration come together. This is the way sex is supposed to be. This is sex that fulfills, satisfies, and connects."[86] Cuddling, and the hormones it releases—oxytocin and vasopressin—fortifies the close, safe bond that couples need to stay erotically connected.

Perel cheekily challenged these notions by underscoring how too much cuddling can actually kill off erotic desire. If sex is relied upon to feel close, tender, secure, safe, and connected, a host of other needs in the bedroom conducive to erotic vitality might wither away—mystery, risk, danger, adventure, and forcefulness. Too much cuddling can deprive a sex life of the naughtiness needed for it to be exciting.[87]

It was as if Johnson hadn't read the erotic poetry of Pablo Neruda: "I want to eat your skin like a whole almond,"[88] or of Michael Faudet: "I never understood desire until I felt your hands around my throat."[89]

Or Perel the erotic poetry of Molly Fish: "Carry me down to that liquid place again where we meet without talking, even though sometimes we're talking, where we laugh without making a sound … My hands will wrap around the tendons of your wrists to hold you here, lowered over me like clouds before a storm, the enormous thunder and then the rain."[90]

John Gottman, Professor Emeritus of Psychology at the University of Washington, weighed in and gave Perel the thumbs down based on his 40 years of researching couples' intimate lives. He quoted a finding in the *Normal Bar* study indicating that a mere 6 percent of non-cuddlers were happy with their sex life.[91]

Needless to say, the cuddle debate was more about competing paradigms on how to think about sustaining passionate sex in long-term relationships, not the act of snuggling up itself. It would be folly to disregard Perel's basic premise that "sexual desire and good citizenship don't play by the same rule."[92] What she means here is a healthy dose of boldness and selfishness is necessary for many couples to enjoy sex. In the act of lovemaking, it takes a certain amount of self-assuredness to flit between depersonalizing your mate—fixating on enjoying his or her body—while also staying empathically connected to him or her as a person. Being careful and oversolicitous in the ways you attend to your partner's perceived sexual needs can put you out of touch with your own erotic cravings—which he or she needs to stay erotically charged up.

In moment-to-moment lovemaking, good sex partners know how and when to mutually respect each other's needs to tune in to their own pleasurable inner sensations, without leaving the other feeling ignored. Like Perel, Michael Aaron in *Modern Marriage* echoes the sense that strong personal sexual agency lends itself to mutually satisfying lovemaking: "Sex is not for the timid … good sex occurs when both partners are focused on getting their needs met."[93] He highlights the "virtuous cycle" of partners sensing each other deriving pleasure from their own and other's action. Each taking advantage of the other for the advantage of each other. Of me-desiring-you making you-desire-me, intensifying the eroticism of the exchange.

One sex therapist sees this as the very definition of fucking: "the subjective experience of doing each other and being done simultaneously."[94] In *Love Worth Making*, Stephen Snyder cautions: "we can become too focused on *giving* pleasure instead of *taking* it. Sexual generosity that's not accompanied by a certain kind of selfishness just isn't very erotic."[95]

Let's bring it back to cuddling and the need for tender touch, caressing, melting into each other's eyes, bonding, and feeling as one. These are core features of good sex, whether they dominate to keep passion ablaze, or whether during intimate sex they yield back and forth to momentary urges to put fingers, tongues, and other body parts where they ordinarily don't belong—turning your sexual subject into a sexual object in mutually pleasurable ways.

Desires for emotional merger—especially for people deprived of them as infants denied caregivers eager to respond to their hungry needs to be held, gazed at, and touched in loving ways—can be dangerous. They threaten to open up what you didn't get sensually when you were supposed to and what you're always entitled to have more of. Hungry needs for sexual merger, if met in the right way by an unperturbed lover, can be utterly life affirming. It's intoxicating to have a sexual partner who doesn't just tolerate, but invites, your strong ache to erotically possess him or her, all the while secure in their own selfhood. Person-to-person, or subject-to-subject love making is anticipating that when one gazes longingly, touches eagerly, or groans in delight, the yearnings expressed are far from off-putting; sometimes tolerated; but mostly invited.

In heterosexual long-term relationships, many women need to feel they are the object of their mate's desire in order to amplify their own.

Swiss author Madame de Stael succinctly captures this: "The desire of the man is for the women; the desire of the woman is for the desire of the man."[96] That said, women need to also feel they are sexual subjects. The difference between a woman feeling desired, rather than just sexually used, is this optimal blend. It's the feeling of being libidinously gazed at, caressed, fondled, and even grabbed, in consensually pleasurable ways, for the special and unique woman her mate experiences her to be.

In *Bonds of Love*, Jessica Benjamin says of female sexuality that there's the omnipresent threat of being so caught up desiring being desired, women lose touch with their own sexual needs—denial of self. She says of male sexuality that there's the omnipresent threat of men overemphasizing their own pleasure in ways which leave them oblivious to that of their partner—denial of the other.

Mediocre sex can be the result of men being too sexually self-absorbed and women not being self-absorbed enough. Among straight couples undergoing a downturn in the quality of their sex lives, frequently the bedroom dynamic is one of men moving too fast in the direction of genital stimulation, getting what they need to become and stay erect, and giving the bare minimum to arouse their partner. Foreplay is approached as if it is *an onerous step to prepare the vagina for penetration*. There's little appreciation for the non-genital ways women get aroused.

Veteran sex therapist Bernard Apfelbaum reminds us that "seduction begins with a compliment,"[97] and this is especially true for women. Several years ago, the mass media company iVillage conducted a survey of married couples and concluded that women "lust after sentiments" because almost half of their female sample reported their partner saying kind and appreciative things to them as a "fire starter," or sexual turn-on.[98] Which is not to say that feeling positively connected to a mate is sufficient to enhance the average woman's arousal. In this same survey, over one in four women wished their partner would make foreplay last longer and almost that same fraction craved more oral sex from their man.

Often, the stage is set for humdrum sex when women somehow feel they have no choice but to capitulate to these conditions, skimp on foreplay, and undervalue the sexual implications of being treated with kindness and goodwill for the person they are. Being a less-than-enthusiastic sex partner and nullifying any need for regular or semi-regular orgasms becomes a lose–lose proposition for both members of the couple. Many men draw emotional sustenance from the love they offer and receive communicated in the act of sex such that they are left feeling unloved when their mate seems to be just going through the motions.

Episodically, or for short or extended periods of time, the vast majority of long-term partners will experience sex as awkward, passable, not great. In otherwise loving couples, more often than we'd like to admit, this is due to a perfect storm of mundane events. It's a wonder any of us can override the everyday forces conspiring against anything resembling a luscious sex life: mismatched bedtimes, bedroom temperature preferences, and time taken to complete pre-hanky-panky grooming needs; kids in the next room, or prudish neighbors upstairs, making dirty talk or loud groans and moans a non-starter; lights on or lights off; blankets or no blankets, pets or no pets on the bed; disagreements over best time of the day to do the deed; invasive thoughts about perceived ugly body parts; fears around not being lubricated or hard enough to enjoy sex; off-putting smells, sounds, or glances; sex toy power glitches; lubricant spills; anticipation of a hellish workday; nagging guilt around unfinished household chores, or any number of ordinary life stressors. The synchrony of well-timed eye contact, gentle or forceful switching of sex positions, and rough or tender touch can be very delicate—turn-ons rapidly turning into turn-offs. All of this can be aggravated by well-known causes of poor sexual functioning: medical conditions, like diabetes and heart disease; antidepressant drug side effects; or a history of sexual trauma.

When the optimal conditions are off, sex can become a veritable "hedgehog's dilemma." These spiny mammals need to huddle to stay warm and join bodies to procreate, but their quills threaten to disallow this. They position and reposition themselves to find the ideal amount of contact that allows for closeness and mating with minimal injury. Analogously, among humans when conditions are unconducive to great sex, if decently good sex—rather than no sex—is to happen, partners are best advised to ignore, *not indulge*, fleeting turn-offs, misattunements, grievances, and annoyances. Benign ignoring, mixed with intentionally focusing on the most favorable image of our mate—tuning out the turn-offs and tuning in to the turn-ons—can make or break a sex life during trying times.

This brings to mind an example recently told to me by a married couple I was counseling. Taking advantage of a kid-free afternoon, they got naked and climbed into their backyard pool. In the midst of heavy petting, Clarissa blurted out that she observed fungus growing on some of the tiles surrounding the pool that "really needed cleaning." Colin resisted letting this off-cue remark ruin the mood, amusingly rolled his eyes, and went on kissing and caressing Clarissa, who managed to refocus on lovemaking. They hedgehogged their way to some decent pool sex that afternoon.

In the long arc of a marriage or intimate partnership, if a vital sex life is to be preserved and enhanced, each member of the couple steadily accepts that eroticism is not a given, but requires intentional cultivation. Mutual attentiveness in everyday life; date nights; romantic getaways; respect for each other's likes and dislikes; setting aside bountiful time to settle into reconnecting emotionally and physically; being playful, lighthearted, and forgiving in the face of inevitable sexual mishaps—all take on added importance. The couples that last are those that mature into realizing that one's own pleasure is intrinsically linked to that of one's partners. It's reassuring to know that when you derive pleasure from giving pleasure, you'll be pleased back in pleasurable ways.

When we listen to older couples who still have memorable sex, we discover this *ethic of fairness*. In a Canadian study involving men and women over the age of sixty across heterosexual and LGBTQ married couples who had been together for over twenty-five years,[99] optimal sexual experiences were characterized by the reciprocal giving and receiving of pleasure based on what each other needs and prefers, in nonjudgmental, playful ways. There was more of a focus on sex for pleasure and enjoyment—kissing, cuddling, fondling, genital stimulation—than for orgasm, although the former often led to the latter. Gone were the days of needing to perform or implement new sex positions and skills in a quasi-desperate way to keep your love life interesting.

Older women were less concerned about their body image and felt freed up sexually. Older men were more apt to communicate about sexual preferences. There was a mutual desire to be creative in bed with fuller acceptance of what works, rather than hanging on to unrealistic fantasies about what should work. Both sexes had finally aligned in highlighting the mutual importance of being in the moment, feeling connected, genuinely wanting to show and receive pleasure, and keeping channels of communication open in non-critical ways. These marital veterans reported that their current sex lives were superior to that of their younger years. The takeaway lesson is that when couples take joint responsibility for making lust a must, as time marches on, sex can become a mutually desired, and deserved, pleasurable bonding experience.

CHAPTER 6

Wrangling with roving desires

A s a rule, wearing a wedding band is considered a way to announce to the world that the love of your life has been found and there's a desire to remain faithful and committed to that person. The tradition of placing a ring made of precious or semi-precious metal on the fourth finger of the left hand was officially sanctioned by King Edward VI in the sixteenth century. It was believed that this particular finger contained an artery—vena amoris (lover's vein)—where blood flowed directly to the heart. Keeping a wedding band on lets others know you are "taken," "off limits," "out of the mating scene." Romantically speaking, it's meant to signify that the love you have for your spouse forecloses amorous or sexual feelings towards anyone else. That's a shaky premise.

In one of the only surveys of its kind, the UK law firm Slater and Gordon polled 2,000 heterosexual British couples and discovered that one in five spouses routinely removes their wedding ring, mainly to draw attention from the opposite sex.[1] This adds credence to the punchy comment by sex educators Janet Hardy and Dossie Easton: "a ring around the finger does not cause a nerve block to the genitals."[2] Put more solemnly, the Scottish philosopher John Armstrong clarifies for

us the normalcy of roving desires: "Even if we are emotionally committed to one person, our sexual instincts will continue to behave as if
in ignorance of this commitment. It is as if the erogenous parts of our
bodies just don't know very much about our current emotional lives."[3]
Science backs this up.

Developing a crush on someone other than one's long-term partner
is more common than we want to believe. In a study spearheaded by
Margo Mullinax at the HIV Center for Clinical and Behavioral Studies at Columbia University, involving mostly heterosexually identified
women in long-term relationships, findings revealed that 70 percent of
them experienced an outside crush at some point along the way. Many of
the women incorporated fantasies about the person they were crushing
on into their masturbation habits and to rev up sex with their current
partner. For example, one woman wrote: "I indulge in some daydream-
ing, sometimes use the visualization during sex with my husband and
then it's fulfilled its useful purpose and it's gone." Curiously, over one in
five of the women identified an old boyfriend as the person they secretly
lusted after.[4]

Unloving an old love to commit more fully to a current one can
be a real predicament for many people. This is especially true, nowadays, with ready access to smartphones and social network sites. Old
flames can be followed on Facebook or other electronic communication
platforms, tempting contact and stoking romantic reunion fantasies.
Former lovers represent one of the main categories of "back burner"
individuals that are looked to by people in committed relationships in
order to keep their options open should that bond dissolve.

It may surprise the reader to learn that most people in long-term
committed relationships—about 62 percent in one study—have at
least one "back burner" love interest, someone who occupies romantic
real estate in their mind as a possible fallback in the event that they
leave, or are left by, their current partner. Of that number, half cite
an ex-boyfriend or ex-girlfriend as the most desirable "back burner"
partner. Summing up their findings, John Banas in the Department
of Communications at the University of Oklahoma and his colleagues
conclude: "Back burners are commonplace in the modern romantic
landscape [and] ex-partners represent a kind of back burner for whom
the fiery limbo smolders."[5]

You might think it's taboo for people to lust after their partner's friends. The vast majority of people tend to deny this when asked directly, but when indirectly probed, nearly half of married men and a quarter of married women admit to being attracted to friends of their partners and are even tempted to act on it—according to one of the most comprehensive research projects on long-term intimate relationships available.[6]

Ex-paramours and known acquaintances may seem like convenient sources of sexual fantasies and dalliances, but the accessibility and anonymity afforded by internet-based extramarital romantic adventures takes convenience to a whole new level. Data supplied by Ashley Madison, the online dating service marketed to married and partnered people, show that it has upwards of 70 million members worldwide and facilitates one million affairs every month.[7] The website's motto is "Life is short. Have an affair," and the company's experts unabashedly exclaim: "Over time, sexual energy changes in a relationship, and what was once hot and heavy has now become boring, bland, and unfulfilling. Looking for new energy, a fix, outside of the relationship is not that uncommon."[8]

Adhering to a strict moral code doesn't even offer married folks uniform immunity against going online to look for fresh romance. A 2014 survey by Ashley Madison showed that 24 percent of male and 32 percent of female subscribers say they pray regularly.[9] Founder Noel Biderman told the *Daily News* that year: "You can go and pray every Sunday, or Saturday, or three times a day, and it may not make a difference in how monogamous you are."[10]

The Ashley Madison phenomenon capitalizes on what psychologists call the "intimacy–eroticism" paradox—over time, the more comfortable, close, and settled people feel with their significant other, the greater potential their sex lives will take a nosedive. A Canadian study investigating relationship problems reported by couples over the long arc of their partnership showed that by the ten-year mark, they were three times more likely to bemoan the lack of physical affection or sex between them compared to the first few years of their relationship.[11]

There's a growing sense that since sex is destined to taper off in long-term intimate relationships, it should be more culturally acceptable for lustier partners to outsource their sexual needs. I don't want to overstate this. The numbers shifting the norms are small and there are huge generational differences. YouGov's latest statistics show 9 percent of thirty- to forty-four-year-olds in America are "OK with their romantic partner engaging in sexual activities with someone else" compared with 4 percent of forty-five- to sixty-four-year-olds, and 3 percent of those sixty-five years and older.[12] Of course, that's just the numbers involving romantically stepping outside of an established relationship *with consent.* Estimates of affairs among Americans range from 26 to 70 percent for women and 33 to 75 percent for men, the vast majority of which are conducted *without consent.*[13]

There's also keener cultural interest surrounding the idea that monogamy subverts people's needs for sexual variety and that for partners who desire something kinkier than their mate allows, alternatives outside the relationship might be fair game. Opening up an intimate partnership in consensual ways to meet people's needs for sexual novelty and variety is more common in the LGBTQ community than among heterosexuals (24 percent versus 5 percent). In fact, it's estimated that 32 percent of gay male couples consensually spice up their sex lives with outside partners.[14]

Males, whether gay or straight, often complain they're sexually deprived. A Relationships in America survey of people in long-term relationships indicates that 52 percent of straight men and 49 percent of gay men are unhappy with the amount of sex they get.[15] There may be something to the old saw that the male brain is wired for sexual variety. Evolutionists argue that the impetus for men to seek multiple sexual partners is rooted in the fact that for over 99 percent of human history, this would have increased their potential offspring. Continuing with this logic, men have evolved powerful urges to desire a variety of sexual partners because, historically, it enhanced their reproductive success. This evolved preference for sexual variety may gear the male brain towards becoming less sexually satisfied with one particular intimate partner. In cold biological terms, men whose sexual interest in a current mate lessened over time might be tempted to sexually pursue a variety of women, thereby leaving more descendants.

Evolutionary explanations for men's strong sexual variety urges may seem antiquated and controversial, but short of other persuasive explanations, they can't be easily sidelined. David Buss, an evolutionary psychology pioneer, proposes that the meteoric rise in internet pornography "owes its success largely to hijacking men's evolved sexual psychology."[16] Research backs this up. A classic study of male arousal, using both self-reports and measures of blood flow to the penis, found that men get less and less turned on when the same erotic images are presented and re-presented. Yet, when intermittently shown images of different erotic images of women, these same men become readily re-aroused.[17] Compared to women, men are far more likely to gravitate to pornography to satisfy needs for sexual variety. A 2017 article in the *Journal of Couple and Relationship Therapy* found that engaged (20.3 percent) and married men (19.6 percent) were six times more likely to report using pornography at least weekly than engaged (3 percent) and married women (2.9 percent).[18]

That said, other surveys suggest an uptick in women's use of pornography as they take more agency over their sexual likes and dislikes. A *Marie Claire* study, conducted by contributing editor Amanda De Cadenet, polling over 3,000 women revealed that 10 percent watched pornography daily, and 31 percent weekly. Close to half the sample watched lesbian pornography and a sizable percentage gravitated toward erotic stories.[19] So-called "romance literature" with steamy sex scenes is big business.

Lea Singh, lawyer and blogger for *Culture Witness*, estimates that close to 70 percent of American women purchase at least one romance novel a year as a form of "literary pornography." She smartly mentions: "Our culture considers romance novels to be a harmless hobby, almost like scrapbooking."[20] A report by eBay Australia during the early lockdowns imposed by the Covid-19 pandemic uncovered a spike of 423 percent in erotic fiction sales compared to the year before.[21] For legions of men, a laptop never says no and for legions of women, a paperback always says yes, en route to some sexual relief.

Where does all this leave loving couples who seek to build a life together, maybe birth and raise children, pursue financial security, weather the unavoidable flagging of sexual interest, survive the encroaching effects of steal-away romance, have each other's back through the inevitable medical and family crises that life brings, create memories that can be told and retold?

Author of inspirational quotes Donna Lynn Hope wisely states: "People will sometimes find themselves attracted to others, that's just who they are. It's what they do with that attraction that defines them."[22] Despite the moral voices in our heads telling us that if our partners have crushes, grow tired of us and secretly compose an online dating profile, enact a sexual or emotional affair, ogle over pornographic images, or get swept away by erotic stories, it automatically means they have fallen out of love with us, wanderlust is less of a threat to the survival of our loving bond with our main squeeze than in our darkest moments we allow ourselves to accept.

Returning to some of the research above, authors of the 2019 article "Roving eyes: Predictors of crushes in ongoing romantic relationships and implications for relationship quality" conclude: "Crushes were fairly common and seemed to have few negative implications for those in established relationships."[23] Pooling together survey data from members, Ashley Madison's chief strategy officer, Paul Keable, deduces: "Most of our members love their partners or spouses … they are not looking to leave their relationship, just to fulfill a need that's been missing."[24] Close to a third believed the excitement of dabbling on the website indicated their main relationship "somewhat improved" or "improved a great deal."[25] Contrary to the popular belief that people who engage in extramarital affairs no longer love their spouses, statistics show that 56 percent of men and 34 percent of women who stray rate their marriages as happy or very happy.[26]

As we shall see, if committed love is to endure, we have to find a way to neither automatically condone nor condemn wayward expression of our innate intimacy needs and sexual enticements. More curiosity about what constitutes normal kink will help couples with discrepant sexual tastes. Mutual consent to open up a marriage, with transparency and honest communication about sexual preferences and jealous feelings, is considered the high-water mark of ethicality with couples who are eager to stretch what they can psychologically obtain from outside erotic attachments. But ethics also come into play when nonconsensual affairs are conducted. As slippery a slope as it sounds, arguably, there's still lighter shades of betrayal with partners who engage in one-time, opportunistic dalliances with others than with those who settle into long-term outside romantic attachments; choose strangers over close friends; use a neutral location, not the family home, as a love nest; engage in passive denial ("I love you, honey. I'm busier than I want to be at work right now"), rather than hard-edged gaslighting ("You're crazy. I was away fly fishing with my best friend. What's wrong with you?"); are careful not to jeopardize the financial security of their marriage or established partnership by spending lavishly on their new mister or mistress; and continue to be physically affectionate with their spouse or significant other, whom they still love, rather than channel all such needs to their paramour.

Kinky vanilla sex

Not long ago, I happened upon the following blog excerpt posted anonymously on AskMen.com by a woman who was concerned about her boyfriend's sexual predilections: "I recently started seeing a new guy and he occasionally asks me to bite him or scratch him during sex/foreplay—I've started doing this on my own initiative and he really seems to like it, even though I know I might be hurting him … I just wondered if this is normal?" A reassuring person had this to offer: "Seems to me this is more about intensity. Your nail marks or bites show that you really care and it is important to you."[27] This constitutes sage advice since it dovetails what is contained in the *Kama Sutra*—the ancient Indian Hindu sex manual—pertaining to how sexual pleasure can be intensified with more roughness: "nothing seems to increase love so much as the effects of marking with the nails, and biting."[28]

The idea that hot sex is mutually consensual and pleasurable rough sex seems to be catching on. Or, given that the *Kama Sutra* was written in the second century BC, perhaps it's a classic case of the more things change, the more they stay the same. Seventy-nine percent of couples in a recent study report incorporating "rough sex" (choking, hair-pulling, and spanking) into their intimate lives.[29] A few years ago, an article in the *Archives of Sexual Behavior*, investigating the sex lives of over 1,000 individuals, revealed that upwards of 70 percent found one of the following gestures desirable (while half of the participants found three such gestures desirable): ties me; handcuffs me; pulls my hair; bites me; slaps me; spits on me; talks dirty to me. The authors concluded: "aggressive and humiliating sexual play constitutes a normal variation in sexual desire."[30] Is it any wonder the comedian Joan Rivers can joke, guilt-free: "It's been so long since I had sex I've forgotten who ties up whom"?[31]

Historically, getting kinky in these ways, or enjoying BDSM sex play (bondage, discipline, submission/sadism, masochism), was frowned upon and pathologized because it was associated with the sexual habits of gay, lesbian, and bisexual people. The cultural shift toward sexual minority inclusiveness has freed up those members of the LGBTQ community who are given to BDSM sex play to be vocal about its intimacy-enhancing potential.

Frankly speaking, as someone who struggles to get his mind around how the infliction of pain during sex can enhance intimacy, I was all ears during my participation on a panel at a fall 2021 virtual conference, "Open Hearts… Bigger Beds? Monogamy, Polyamory and Psychoanalysis." My fellow panelists were Cadyn Cathers, a transgender male psychologist who is the executive director at The Affirmative Couch (an agency offering mental health services to the LGBTQ community) and Maria Two-Strap, a Los Angeles-based intimacy coordinator and sex educator.

On the subject of rough sex, Maria mentioned: "When you're pulling someone's hair, it's not like you're scalping them! It doesn't cause injury. It's all about consensually seeing how far you can go to mix pleasure and pain without hurting someone." Cadyn chimed in: "People don't show playful aggression with just anybody. Aggression can be a connecting emotion. Then there's the after-care, bringing the person back to reality, dealing with whatever emotions come up around how the sex went down. There are tears, love, tenderness. That's what healthy kink is all about."

BDSM sex may not be my cup of tea, but Maria and Cadyn's viewpoints call attention to the phenomenon of people *desiring pain* to enhance pleasure. Someone who writes a great deal about this is Leigh Cowart, author of *Hurts So Good*, a book that unpacks the heightened joy that can be obtained from those who *actively choose* to seek pain in pleasure situations. In her estimation, people who seek to mix pain with their pleasurable sexual activities do so because "it creates a contrasting sensation that intensifies pleasure. All pleasure all the time sure sounds nice, but a little pain mixed in can really boost the experience of both, the way people add salt to syrupy-sweet caramel."[32]

Touching upon the exhilaration that comes from pushing the limits of what the body can endure, Cowart adds: "There are vast similarities among getting spanked for pleasure, eating spicy foods, jumping into cold lakes, and running a marathon."[33]

Another reason given for the appeal of BDSM sex is that the whole aura surrounding exercising or submitting to control keeps partners in a state of delightful suspense, instantly clearing the mind of all the "mad monkey" thoughts that often derail being present in the moment. If you're half-gritting your teeth waiting to be lightly flogged, you're not thinking about having forgotten to pay the gardener that day.

All this said, because of the abundant aggressive sexual content on pornography websites widening the goalposts regarding what passes for normal, we have to be mindful of how fuzzy the line can be between BDSM sex positivity and unwanted sexual aggression. This may be especially pertinent among the Gen Z and Millennial generations. A 2019 study out of the United Kingdom surveying women between the ages of eighteen and thirty-nine discovered that 38 percent of them had undergone unwanted "slapping, choking, gagging, or spitting during consensual sex."[34] We also have to be careful not to assume that spicing up a sex life *requires* replacing what often is disparagingly called "vanilla sex"—tender, sensual, comfortable, missionary position—with kinkiness.

Prominent sex educator Justin Hancock reminds us: "There's this idea that you're either staring into each other's eyes in the missionary position and it's gentle and everyone magically comes at the same time, or it's rough and violent, involving bruising someone's butt and making them cry. But it's kind of a false binary."[35]

A vanilla sex life can go from mild to wild and back again when partners find a way to seductively indulge smidgens of aggressive urges—pinching and lightly slapping thighs and buttocks, tugging on hair, lightly scratching and biting, inserting fingers in mouths and anuses—during moments of elevated passion, switching sexual positions all the while. That can be hotter-than-hot vanilla sex. You don't have to suit up in a latex French maid servant baby doll uniform and reach for the butt plugs to prove to each other that you're committing to having hotter sex. Actually, rather than turn toward BDSM sex play to spice up their sex lives, the average couple is probably better off getting over their inhibitions engaging in bedroom oldies but goodies and other not-so-risqué practices that are a surefire way to attain sexual fulfillment.

Let's start with oral sex. As recently as 1994, it was considered relatively taboo, with a mere 27 percent of men and 19 percent of women claiming in a *Slate* survey that they had received oral sex in the past year.[36] Nowadays, going down on a partner is widely accepted as a facet of standard foreplay, or a way to use "mouth music" to bring someone to orgasm. Men get giddy at the prospect of having their partner approach them with eager lips. The supreme pleasure men obtain from oral sex by a lover finessed in that fine art is fancifully described by one AskMen.com interviewee: "It feels like having your favorite four-thousand nerve endings dipped in the warm spring that comes from God's own garden."[37]

Yet, in a heterosexual context, a surprising number of women are reluctant givers. The 10,000 strong Esquire Survey of the American Woman found that only 30 percent of the fairer sex love giving oral sex, the remaining 70 percent indicating either, "I like it because he likes it," "I'll do it, but I don't like it," or "I won't do it."[38] For too many men, that sucks.

In this same survey, when asked how they feel about receiving oral sex, a whopping 54 percent of women stated either "I don't like it" or "It's nice every once in a while." This is perplexing, given that we know women who typically always orgasm are three times more likely to receive oral sex from their partners than women who rarely orgasm.[39] It's hard to decipher how much of this is due to women being outside of their comfort zone permitting a partner to venture south of the border, or partner ineptitude or squeamishness.

Among heterosexuals, the upcoming generation of men do seem to be manning up. Professor Debby Herbenick at Indiana University tracks emerging trends in sexual behavior and extrapolates from her research, "the vast majority of young men are really into cunnilingus."[40] Young men who are able and willing, and older men who may be less able and willing, would do well to heed the advice of Sarah Sloane, host of the Social Intercourse Podcast, who likens tonguing a woman to licking an ice cream cone: "Start like you're trying to lick all the ice cream in July. Think long, soft licks, as opposed to pokey bird-like pecks."[41] This "I scream, we all scream, for ice cream" approach to cunnilingus might just edge women into an orgasmic comfort zone.

A saucy joke that's making the round these days goes as follows: "What do you call the act of turning over in bed to switch from missionary position to doggy style? A sexual revolution." Millennials and boomers may quarrel over work-life, home-life balance; whether to rent or own; treating a pet as a quasi-child or a just a four-legged companion; however, on matters related to their preferred go-to sex position, they line up—doggy style. Respondents to this survey commented on this sex move's greater stimulation of the prostate and g-spot derived from deeper penetration, as well as the enticing opportunities to derive sexual pleasure from primal expressions of dominance and submission.

Among heterosexuals, the man is the two-legged canine—entering from behind—the woman the two-legged canine being entered. Unless a strap-on dildo is being used by the woman to be top dog. The dirty secret is that many women prefer doggy style because they can furtively get themselves off by fingering their clitoris while their male partner is obliviously thrusting himself to orgasm, playing master and commander from behind. The sex toy permutations surrounding back-door sex with lesbian and bisexual women can be left up to the imagination.

Of course, gay male couples are used to having their hind quarters in the air, switching off entering, and being entered, doggy style, just involving a different orifice. That different orifice, the anus, one of Freud's erogenous zones, happens to be an anatomical venue where a great number of people, regardless of their sexual orientation, itch to put their tongue, finger, or a sex toy in during moments of sexual passion—upwards of 40 percent in a survey conducted by Evan Goldstein, CEO of Bespoke Surgical, a medical practice optimizing gay men's sexual health and wellness.[41] A tongue, a finger, or a sex toy is one thing, a penis another.

Speaking strictly, concerning heterosexual intimacy where women are the recipients of anal sex, science shows the hullabaloo around its hotness is misguided. It may be periodically enticing—about 13 percent of women report recent anal intercourse and 36 percent having tried it over the course of their sexual history—but it's not a regular go-to desire to take it in the butt for the vast majority of women.[42]

Getting back to the use of sex toys, like vibrators and dildos for women, their usage does not necessarily make sex mechanical or impersonal. For women, the simple act of telling a mate she wants to purchase a vibrator or dildo can be a sexually awakening experience. Indiana University sexologist Debra Herbenick surveyed woman young and old and found that over half reported using a vibrator in one of three scenarios: masturbating alone, reaching for it during foreplay/sex play, or incorporating it during intercourse.[43]

Joan Price, who has much to say about sex among the aging, quips: "It's not a choice between him or it. Make it a threesome: the two of you using a vibrator together."[44] However, there's a buyer beware clause. Overreliance can make achieving orgasm too easy and desensitize the clitoris. In partnered sex, this can make achieving orgasm an uphill battle. Sex therapist Vanessa Marin cautions women: "If all you've ever know is vibrational stimulation, you're going to have a tough time teaching a partner how to get you off with his or her fingers, because you won't know how to do it yourself."[45] That said, for women who need something extra to arrive at orgasmic sex, and still want intimacy, use of a sex toy mixed with rough and tender touch, and hungry eye gazing, may send them over the edge.

The long and short of it is, over the long haul, most couples will hit the skids in their intimate sexual lives and be tempted to step outside their partnership to feel emotionally and carnally desired in the ways they convince themselves they're deprived of. Sometimes the answer is to courageously push the boundaries of the drab sex they have fallen into to add some kink to their otherwise vanilla sex lives. This need not be overly performative, characterized by frenetic eroticism. Often, it involves an openness to blend the kink with the vanilla. After all, as New York City psychologist and relationship expert Laurel Steinberg declares: "even though people use the term 'vanilla sex' to mean unin-spired, unacrobatic, or formulaic sex, vanilla is actually known by the culinary world to be an extremely complex flavor."[46]

Ethical nonmonogamy

Three months into therapy, forty-three-year-old Brian plucked up the courage to disclose aspects of his sex life with his same-aged wife, Kristen. He had held back, based on the fear that I'd deem his secret desires wayward or perverse, like a previous therapist had. I smiled and reassured him that in my long career, I had heard everything and was more open-minded than he might think. Brian shyly revealed a strong inclination to open up his marriage, which his wife was well aware of, though less enthusiastic about the prospect than he.

They had met in high school and remained romantically attached ever since, each being the other's first and only sex partner. Brian was a successful real estate agent, Kristen a kindergarten teacher, beloved by her students. They had two pre-teen daughters, the younger afflicted with a variety of learning issues related to being born prematurely. Brian adored his daughters and felt grateful that as a self-employed real estate agent, he could orchestrate his schedule to be readily available to them, chauffeuring them to doctor's appointments, soccer practice, and other events. Twice a year, he surprised each of them with a fun-filled father–daughter day off school. Even though their family and career lives were hectic, Brian and Kristen had a trio of babysitters, which allowed them to have regular "date nights," even the occasional romantic weekend away.

Brian was clear that Kristen was his life partner. He adored her and the vibrant family life they had constructed over the years. His polyamorous leanings in no way reflected deep dissatisfaction with Kristen or the marriage. Her anxiety wore on him at times—catastrophizing over small things and overthinking decisions—and he wished she was more sexually available and freed up in bed, but he mostly enjoyed sex with Kristen when it occurred, typically on a weekly basis.

Brian's sexual restlessness was more existential in nature. Entering midlife, it rattled him to project into the future and think he could go to the grave without having savored sex with anyone else. His pornography usage hinted at what that might feel like. Pursuing an affair without Kristen's knowledge was unthinkable to him. He was not a good liar. Besides, he knew in his heart of hearts that illicitly crossing the flesh line with someone else would aggravate Kristen's anxiety and abandonment fears. Hurting her in this way was off the table.

Instead, Brian suggested Kristen read books and listen to polyamory podcasts to expose her to what sexual adventures might be consensually possible without jeopardizing their marriage. They encouraged each other to have crushes. Brian lusted over his hairstylist, a sensuous, busty, tattooed woman. He reported back to Kristen when he returned from haircuts, most of which were an excuse just to indulge his crush.

Kristen egged Brian on, pulling for tantalizing visions about what Brian might do with the hairstylist if she indulged his crush.

Kristen lusted over the principal at the elementary school she worked at, a tall, bespectacled man who wore a suit every day. A favorite fantasy of Brian's was to imagine sitting in the corner of the bedroom, watching Kristen be ravished by the principal. She indulged Brian's fantasy by providing him with lewd details. Sometimes they swapped these fantasies in bed and called each other by the names of the hairstylist and principal while making love, both giggling and swooning like lecherous teenagers.

Brian and Kristen are seriously flirting with the thorny question posed by relationship guru, Esther Perel: "do we expect our partner's erotic selves to belong entirely to us?"[47] They are what is officially labeled "polycurious," pondering what it might be like to seek outside lovers while not ready or willing to convert fantasy into action. The latest data indicate that about a third of people in established monogamous relationships report that being in a sexually open relationship is "part of their favorite fantasy of all time."[48]

It's noteworthy that neither Brian nor Kristen seem to feel jealous over their respective crushes. At some level, they appear to accept—as is the case in polyamory culture—that a single person, no matter how securely bonded and devoted we are to them, can't meet all our needs. Perhaps because their lustful longings remain at a fantasy level, are mutually and consensually encouraged, as well as openly and honestly shared, the green-eyed monster of jealousy is defanged. In fact, we can go further and opine that their jealousy is eroticized. They use it—tantalizingly—to turn each other on. Playfully exposing each other to imaginal attractions keeps them on their toes (*I could lose the love of my life to someone else; I simply have to love my beloved better*), without losing their footing (*It's highly unlikely this person who loves me so much will ever leave me*).

Brian seems to experience what in the polyamory community is named "compersion," the opposite of jealousy—"a feeling of well-being, joy, or pleasure that is derived from having a partner experience pleasure with someone else." Granted, there's a world of a difference between fantasizing watching your wife being ravished by a tall, handsome man, and actually witnessing it.

When fantasy crosses the flesh line into reality, "careful what you wish for" often applies. I once treated a couple where the husband badgered his wife to attend a swingers' club. Mostly to please him, she agreed. She consented to a "fishbowl" experience where he and other attendees stood around observing her having sex with a hunky man. For months thereafter, the husband couldn't "unsee" this. He bitterly complained in therapy that she was more eager, excited, and vivacious during sex with the hunky stranger than she ever was with him in bed. That's the opposite of compersion—a feeling of reduced well-being, anguish, or unpleasantness witnessing a partner experience pleasure with someone else—or jealousy. This couple divorced within the year, not simply because of the "fishbowl" experience but because of the pernicious dynamic in the relationship involving him unselfconsciously treating her unlovingly, yet still expecting her to respond romantically.

Management of jealous feelings is pivotal with committed couples who actively and consensually pursue nonmonogamy. A shared covenant is agreed upon to strive to override the primal sense that any outside romantic prospect need be a rival, an upgrade, someone who will steal your love away. Certified sex therapist Martha Kauppi explains: "Maybe your partner can love and choose you, and also love and choose someone else, without taking anything away from you. It's very possible to have a securely attached open relationship."[49]

One couple in my practice that strives to enact this covenant is fifty-year-old Tanya and thirty-five-year-old Lorena, women who self-identify as sexually fluid. Tanya has two sons from a previous marriage and shares custody with her ex-husband, allowing her to have every other weekend child-free with Lorena. Periodically, throughout the year, they act on this window of time to have romantic interludes with several bisexual couples they have cultivated relationships with. They speak openly about preventing falling prey to the "the lesbian deathbed," or any steep drop in their mutual sexual attraction. Pursuing a polyamorous lifestyle is one way they mutually agree might help. Their set-up is not to separately identify and pursue individuals open for romantic involvement, but couples they can approach and engage with jointly. They prefer bisexual couples where one is male, since they both retain an attraction to men, and think some "male sexual energy" is good for their own sexual well-being. At the same time, these outside dalliances are not solely about sex. Both Tanya and Lorena subscribe to polyamorous life philosophy where eroticism can strengthen and add vitality to friendships that in turn make those involved more interesting and dimensional as people.

Tanya and Lorena's polyamory adventures are often an emotional work in progress, two steps forward, one step back. Tanya fears that because Lorena is much younger, she will fall in love with one of their paramours, and leave her, like her ex-husband did. Lorena fears that Tanya, deep down, really prefers men and will one day leave her for a man. Intense arguments can erupt over boundaries: the importance of acting extra-lovingly with each other in the presence of their outside romantic partners, for reassuring purposes; making sure each of them go to the other first with important or exciting news, rather than to their lovers; being transparent when there's contact of any sort with outside romantic partners and willingly offering synopses on the nature of that contact; when jealous feelings arise, strive to affectionately reassure each other that they are lovable and loved.

The energy Tanya and Lorena exert in showing ethical integrity around being honest and transparent with each other to minimize any potential for rejection and betrayal of trust is impressive. At times, they admit their polyamorous lifestyle is more trouble than it's worth. Mostly, though, they agree it's the "cherry on top," and "they get to have their cake and eat it too," meaning they can draw nurturance and security from their strong bond with each other and have outside relationships that add excitement and meaning to their lives.

Consensual nonmonogamy is considered the most ethical way people can go about satisfying needs for romantic novelty and variety because there's a shared commitment to be honest and transparent about one's sextracurricular pursuits. Current rates of partnered people in open relationships vary between 4 and 9 percent.[50] Diverse rates exist depending on sexual identity. Roughly 32 percent of gay men, 5 percent of lesbian women, 22 percent of bisexual persons, and 14 percent of those who list their sexualities as "other" adopt mutually agreed-upon open relationships. For heterosexual individuals, the numbers are small—2 percent.[51] That means the vast majority of straight people who step outside their marriages or established partnerships fall in the nonconsensual nonmonogamy camp. Or, in the vernacular, are cheaters, adulterers, philanderers, or any number of other dishonorable terms.

Taking such a hard moral stance, viewing infidelity as indicative of characterological defectiveness, may reflect society's need to see it as unforgivably forbidden because it's so compellingly alluring. It's virtually impossible to get accurate numbers on the percentage of married people who stray because, not only do people disagree on what qualifies as sex—oral, anal, vaginal, kissing passionately, heavy petting, cuddling, spooning, sleeping in the same bed, masturbating during live cybersex, masturbating alone to pornographic images—they are confused about the boundary between having a close friend and engaging in an emotional affair: routinely preferring to confide with that special someone other than one's main partner; valuing spending time with him or her other than you; turning to that "close" friend after fighting with you; and denying and becoming defensive if you question the intensity of their attachment to this special someone. Ironically, these definitions of an emotional affair are not off the mark for clients who have a transformative relationship with their psychotherapists!

If we settle on a loose definition, "having sexual relations outside the primary relationship," about 33 percent of men and 19 percent of women are unfaithful in a marriage, even though 90 percent of Americans still believe infidelity is immoral.[52] The word infidelity derives from the word infidel, a heretic who turns away from God. For many people—even those of faith—the real issue is not letting God down when indulging an outside love interest. It's trying to navigate the agony arising from deriving life-affirming pleasure from an affair that simultaneously poses to cause agony for a cherished partner—if the affair is discovered.

I think it's a mistake to assume a black-and-white ethical stance when people are unfaithful. We're in the realm of moral relativism here. Loyalty and honesty are not always compatible human virtues. It's possible to be loyal—stay largely committed to a partner, be emotionally and financially supportive, be attentive and affectionate—yet be dishonest about having a fleeting sexual or emotional affair.

Former columnist for the *San Francisco Chronicle* Charles McCabe famously wrote: "Honesty has ruined more marriages than infidelity."[53] I surmise what he meant by this is that plenty of strayers are psychologically incapable of containing the guilt they feel over the sexual enjoyment or emotional fulfillment obtained from a new sweetheart. There's also the guilt incurred over betraying their spouse or partner. It's all too much.

What amounted to a brief, torrid romance that posed no substantial threat to a solid marriage becomes an unkeepable secret. They confess in a state of emotional implosion. They overshare salacious details of the affair. The confession is more that of an emotionally tortured person trying to purge him or herself of guilt, rather than prudently disclosing relevant information with due regard for its potential to cause enduring psychic pain. Does an aging wife need to hear from an errant husband that his fling was young, beautiful, voluptuous, and therefore irresistible? Does an emotionally constricted, sexually unadventurous husband need to hear from an errant wife that her lothario offered her bountiful emotional depth and made her quiver like she was sixteen all over again?

Sometimes people cheat because they feel cheated by life. The sensual and emotional hunger that haunts them due to neglect in their early upbringing creates unmet needs of a magnitude that no single partner seems able to satisfy. They walk through life craving affection as well as affirmation of their lovability that sensual sex provides. This renders them vulnerable to an affair when someone enters their life who seems exquisitely capable of meeting these insatiable longings, revitalizing their self-worth.

The affair may be good for them as an individual—an ethic of enhancing one's personal happiness. Mostly satisfied in their marriage, motivation for the affair has little to do with a rejection of their spouse, even though if he or she found out, deep rejection is inevitable. Transparency and wished-for consent seem absurdly cruel. Who has the psychological fortitude to hear the unadulterated truth? "Darling, I met a man whose eyes I get lost in. When I look at him with hungry eyes, he smiles beguilingly, as if he can inhale my neediness and breathe it back to me, unperturbed, making me shiver with desire. His lips are round and juicy and when we kiss, I feel like sucking his soul into mine. When he envelopes me with his robust hairy body, I feel so protected. Wild dogs could show up in the room and I wouldn't flinch." Creating a firewall to preserve such a sublime, life-affirming experience so that a mostly loved spouse isn't hurt by its discovery becomes an ethical quandary. It raises an awkward question: To preserve a good marriage, while at the same time drawing primal satisfaction from a love affair that fortuitously dropped into your life, do you have to lovingly deceive? What does it even mean to lovingly deceive?

Let me explore this issue in the context of a male heterosexual client I worked with several years ago whose wife—his sworn life partner—suddenly declared she was disinterested in sex, which set the wheels in motion for him to be existentially unmoored.

Peter, a fifty-five-year-old architect, originally sought out therapy with me because he was burned out at work. For years, he poured all his energy into advancing his career. He had grown up in relative poverty and was determined to create a comfortable life for himself, his fifty-nine-year-old wife, Julia, and their twenty-year-old daughter, Blair, who the previous fall had been launched to college on the East Coast.

Peter was a strikingly attractive late-middle-aged man. He worked out daily and could pass for a James Bond stand-in: tall, muscular, chiseled facial features, suave, fashionably dressed. Living a life of duty and meeting all his personal and professional responsibilities was programmed into him. He was raised Catholic and imbibed the self-sacrificing values served up by his Scottish-Irish immigrant parents, and the nuns and priests who shepherded his education throughout elementary, middle, and high school in Montana.

Sexually repressed and inexperienced as a young man, he found Julia's libertine style intoxicating when he met her for the first time as a blind date arranged by a mutual friend. It was like a moth to a flame. He the awkward, fumbling one. She the straight-talking, I-know-what-I-want-and-will-get-it type. For years, they had an energetic sex life, even throughout Blair's childhood. Peter relished that Julia was a beautiful woman who turned heads when they were out in public together. She admitted to him that she used her charms to advance her career, often flirting with clients and colleagues to her advantage.

Fast forward five years. Julia made an abrupt unilateral decision to retire from her career as a graphic artist without conferring with Peter whether this might adversely impact the family finances, or square with their joint life plans. Despite being annoyed, Peter was given to pleasing Julia and went along with the plan. They purchased beach-side property out of state. Julia moved there full-time and took great delight in redesigning the property, tending to the garden, taking up quilting, and bonding with the two poodles she relied on for company.

Peter finished out his architectural career in Montana, leasing an apartment there and visiting Julia when able. Gradually, Julia took to wearing sweatpants every day, not shaving her legs, having groceries delivered, taking long naps, and spending hours on Facebook, reliving her past by following the lives of old friends. Out of nowhere, she announced to Peter she was no longer interested in sex. Menopausal changes caused vaginal dryness and pain during sex, which made it very unpleasant. She didn't want to endure the hassles and possible medical complications associated with hormone replacement. Besides, as an attractive woman who for years had to deal both with the allure and oppression of being subjected to the "male gaze," she found it immensely liberating to just shut her sexuality down.

Peter was torn between wanting to support the woman he loved in her phase of life struggle and push back against Julia due to her disregard of his intimacy needs. Periodically, as the months unfolded, he broached the subject, suggesting they might explore alternatives to vaginal sex, but she was disinclined to have this conversation.

I explored with him whether Julia might be experiencing a sudden awakening about feeling turned off, rather than turned on, by his standard sexual repertoire. Or whether he was insufficiently caring and attentive enough in his everyday habits in ways that flatlined Julia's romantic availability. Little seemed to make sense on Peter's end as regards underlying ways he might be disappointing Julia in and out of the bedroom. One thought he had was that sexual traumas in Julia's past had resurfaced. However, he couldn't muster a tactful way to bring this up without Julia experiencing this as him being dismissive of her newfound liberation from the oppressiveness attributable to keeping up her appearance and catering to male desire throughout her life. There was also the matter of her being prescribed Lexapro for mild depression, which may have dampened her libido. That felt to Peter like a no-go zone also because Julia had taken this medication for years and relied on it.

Just as is the case for most men, sex was a core way Peter felt bonded to Julia. It helped that they continued to snuggle in bed and affectionately kiss each other on the fly. But that was not enough. As the months unfolded, Peter told me in therapy that the prospect of never having sex with Julia—or anyone for that matter—for the rest of his life was harrowing. He felt fit, attractive, and on his game. He found Julia desirable. At a time in his life when he felt especially deserving of being desired, he badly wanted Julia to find him desirable. He confessed to me that while he remained very attracted to Julia, he was losing respect for her because her definition of liberation—retreating from the world and letting her appearance go—in his mind was tantamount to surrendering to aging and death.

Usually oblivious to female attention, he began noticing women checking him out at the gym. He was not a natural flirt but began smiling back and starting up conversations with several of them. Paraphrasing the Christian quote, I joked with him in therapy: "Temptation comes through a door that's been left open." He fired back: "Julia's the one that closed my door." I think we both knew it was just a matter of time before Peter would indulge his desires further.

Barbara, a female consultant his architectural firm had hired to do monthly audits, caught his eye. Tall, slender, and poised, she reminded him of Julia. It was Barbara who made the first move, suggesting they have coffee before work. Peter learned that Barbara had just ended a relationship with an abusive boyfriend, had no children, and lived alone in a small townhouse she had purchased. He found their conversation riveting, and she had a quick wit. A decade younger than him, Barbara prided herself on looking even younger. Peter was mesmerized. Within weeks, he was sleeping over at her townhouse two or three times a week. He felt he was the luckiest man on the planet being with Barbara because her sexual appetite seemed unquenchable. As the months progressed, they occasionally ventured out in public together, going to restaurants and attending music events, but never in locations where they were likely to encounter anyone they knew.

In his conversations with me, Peter was surprised by how little guilt he felt. Given Julia's hard line around sex, he thought this was a form of "involuntarily celibacy" he had not signed on for. He comprised a list in his head of all the potential harmful ramifications of the affair and checked off the boxes. Barbara was single and childless, so on her end there was no collateral damage to a husband, boyfriend, or offspring. She was an outside consultant and did not directly report to him at work, so this ruled out possible allegations of exploitation or workplace drama. He had made it clear to Barbara from the beginning that he loved his wife and had no intention of leaving her. They frequently reassured each other they were on a wonderful journey together that would be mutually rewarding while it lasted. Barbara told Peter that his attentiveness, wit, genuine attraction to her, and tenderness in bed restored her hope in intimate relationships, having come out of an abusive one. Peter told Barbara that it was incredibly revitalizing to be with a woman who desired him with kindness and fervor, making him feel like he was an endearing, youthful, vigorous person all over again. It appeared to Peter that Barbara was mature and boundaried, not someone who would vengefully call Julia and spill the beans about the affair. They both were adamant about being discreet, keeping the affair as private as possible.

Two topics cropped up in my work with Peter. Based on previous experiences with clients facing similar circumstances, I highlighted the harm that can stem from casting a spouse in too negative a light to justify an affair. Magnifying dislikable aspects of their behavior to lessen guilt and feel convicted you're entitled to the dalliance. This resonated with him. He was aware of being more on edge and nitpicky around Julia, reviewing old history in his head of times she had let him down. He vowed to guard against this. As long as he was choosing to live a double life, it made sense to compartmentalize better. To be as kind as possible with Julia, whom he claimed to still love and had every intention of remaining with.

If anything, Peter was emerging out of the delusional haze of the affair, starting to perceive small things about Barbara he found annoying: she left her bedroom cluttered with clothes, watched reality TV shows, listened to music too loud. This clarified for Peter that Barbara was a spectacular person to have an affair with but not someone with whom he wanted to share a life.

As far as Julia went, Peter settled into a "what she doesn't know can't hurt her" approach to managing the affair. He firmly believed she was unsuspecting. Around Julia, he strove to be as engaging as possible, disguising the internal agony he felt managing all his discrepant feelings. His main concern was to be eminently discreet, or as he put it, to create a "firewall" where Julia would not be hurt by the affair by ever knowing about it.

I half joked and labeled this "loving deception." Peter latched onto this phrase, saying it captured the ambiguity of what he was going through. Yes, he was sneaking around, living a double life, withholding the truth about the affair. This caused him considerable distress. It was the psychological price he had to pay for the much-needed affection he received from Barbara. On the other hand, it was anathema to him that Julia find out and be wounded. So, he had to stealthily cover his tracks. He secured a separate cell phone to communicate with Barbara, used only cash when they ate out, and arranged his schedule so planned phone calls and visits with Julia would never be interrupted by time spent with Barbara. He doubled down on his double life.

It all came crashing down about six months into the affair. Julia found condoms in Peter's suitcase and confronted him. Overtly lying was out of the question, at least as far as basic facts about his relationship with Barbara went. He told her Barbara was a work colleague whom he cared about, but mostly got together with for sex. Beyond that, I know few details about how Peter and Julia dealt with the fallout from the affair. She insisted he end it immediately. Which he did. She added that she wanted Peter to discontinue therapy with me because I didn't actively discourage him from pursuing the affair. We had one last visit. Peter used it to process his grief over the loss of Barbara. Sobbing, he mentioned: "I'm having to give up someone I love so much, for someone I love more."

From hurting to healing after affairs

If Peter weren't my client and he and Julia sought me out to deal with the crisis enveloping their life, there's a host of issues I'd be considering to slow down the speeding train and help them assess the salvageability of their marriage. With emotions running high, I'd advise them to defer making any major life decisions around separating, divorcing, or selling property.

Betrayal is a primal emotion and its dark cousin, revenge, can easily get reactively ignited. One way this often transpires after affairs is the aggrieved spouse indiscriminately sharing with family members and friends in ways that can fuel the fire. Infidelity often strikes a moral chord for most people and a background chorus of "once a cheater, always a cheater" frequently muddles reasonable judgment.

I'd encourage Julia to identify a close friend, or cadre of friends—perhaps people who have a neutral attitude toward Peter, or basically believe he's a decent guy—for her to confidently confide in. Until they figure out whether, or what, to jointly tell their daughter, I'd have them be careful about any accidental disclosures.

I'd discourage Peter from oversharing or wanting to process grief from the loss of Barbara, or the affair, in the presence of Julia. Such displays of grief could convey a depth of emotional attachment to Barbara that undercuts the long-term potential for forgiveness by Julia. Research shows that about 76 percent of women would forgive their partner for an affair that was strictly sexual. That number drops to 30 percent for emotional affairs. (Only 35 percent of men tend to forgive their female mate for sexual affairs, compared to 80 percent for emotional ones.)[54]

I'd advise Peter to seek out confidants, or meet separately with me, to deal with residual upset over letting go of Barbara and the affair. During any such meetings, I'd treat Peter's sorrow as a clear indication that he's a sincere, caring person who is capable of close attachments. I would not take a punitive or moral approach to such grief. Reminding him that his affectionate involvement with Barbara restored her hope and credibility in romantic attachments coming out of an abusive relationship might relieve any guilt he feels about abandoning her.

There's a natural tendency to interrogate an unfaithful partner to access all the salacious details pertaining to the affair. Julia may believe she's entitled to this information, wielding an ethic of *full honesty* as a weapon. It's understandable. She's the one who is suffering from broken trust, possibly awash in a maelstrom of grief, rage, and shattered illusions. Possibly feeling like a fool for not knowing she was being fooled. In the face of Julia's anguish, flooded with guilt, Peter becomes ensnared into thinking he owes Julia all the facts as due punishment. However, divulging too many particulars and graphic details can unnecessarily feed unproductive obsessional thinking and needlessly torment a betrayed spouse for years to come.

What gets told in an atmosphere of raw emotion can often be indelibly inscribed in the mind and render it impossible to be untold. Discretion applies. Resisting the guilty urge to vomit up all the facts can be a gesture of love under these conditions—the telling of lies of omission. Holding back from disclosing the lurid or intimate details that have a high probability of undermining hope for marital recovery, when, in actuality, the prospects are good. Does Julia need to know if Barbara wore lingerie, gave Peter better hand jobs, or if sex ever occurred out-doors? Let me reiterate, discretion applies.

There's a *moral sensibility* baked into the true meaning of the word discretion. It involves having the wisdom to dissect information and deliver it in ways that cause needless harm. If there's a context in which the demonstration of discretion is desperately called for, it's around divulging information in couples therapy after an affair. Revealing basic information and global details to reduce confusion and establish a truth-based common ground seems appropriate to me. How did the affair start? How long did it last? How frequent were the encounters? What amounts of money were spent? Who else knows about the affair? Was sex involved? If so, was protection used? Getting bogged down in the details can sidetrack therapy from dealing with the underlying feelings and issues at hand, as well as eclipse a focus on any dormant strengths in the marriage that need shoring up.

I'd take an affirmative approach. I'd remind them that upwards of 60 percent of marriages survive after an affair, and the ones that thrive are able to productively use the crisis as an opportunity to learn how to love each other better.[55]

The onus would be on Peter to provide evidence that the affair is put to rest. The strength of his commitment to the marriage would be reflected in his willingness to agree to an accountability system—established by Julia—to help her regain a sense of trust. This might include: show-ing proof he'd destroyed his clandestine cell phone; allowing Julia free access to phone records, social media usage, and bank account data; having a replacement executive at work deal with Barbara, never him; sharing, unasked, any accidental interactions with Barbara; agreeing to be tested for STDs.

The topic of Peter retiring early, or changing jobs, to ensure he had no ostensible opportunity to interact with Barbara, wouldn't be off the table. I would encourage Julia to perceive Peter's remorseful willing-ness to agree to an accountability system as evidence he felt badly about betraying her and was on course to rebuild marital trust. If Peter were to routinely become indignant and defensively claim: "Why all the expectations? Can't you just trust me? You can be so controlling, just like you sexually cut me off and made me feel I needed to go looking," I'd be less hopeful about the marriage.

The initial phase of therapy would center on turning down the emotional heat. All things considered, I'd lend credence to Julia's raw emotions. Give her ample space to share any rage and sorrow over the betrayal, as well as feelings of hopelessness about the survivability of the marriage. If Peter was largely receptive to this and experienced heartfelt moments of contrition which enabled Julia to dial back her upset, I'd be reassured. Timing when to nudge the deceived partner beyond feelings of betrayal and victimization is one of the most difficult tasks for therapists under these conditions.

What's the statute of limitations for being justifiably offended by a spouse or long-term partner's unfaithful actions? Often it can dredge up examples of abandonment, rejection, and failed trust from old relationships—aware or unaware—that inflame current anger and distress. If this were true in Julia's case, but she was unaware, and persisted indefinitely in punishing Peter, despite his good faith efforts to apologize, show remorse and act lovingly, I'd consider the marriage to be in a red zone.

Assuming therapy was going favorably, and Julia and Peter were able to assume a reflective capacity about their marriage and the affair, to help with forgiveness I might put a soft spotlight on factors that could mitigate Peter's guilt and Julia's feelings of betrayal:

> It's not lost on me that Peter told Barbara that he loved you, Julia, and had no intention of leaving you, instead of lying to her to get her hopes up about any kind of lasting relationship.
>
> It means something to me that when confronted, Peter didn't lie and continue the affair, he mostly came clean. I know he didn't initiate a reckoning, but at least he didn't avoid it when you busted him, Julia.
>
> It may be no consolation at all, but some affair partners can be close friends, or even siblings, and involve husbands, wives, and kids—at least Peter chose someone where the degree of betrayal and the collateral damage were lessened.

The toughest issue might be ascertaining the right moment to prompt Julia to entertain the notion that her unilateral decision to cease being sexually available to Peter was experienced by him as a stark withdrawal of love. That is, without her feeling she was inappropriately to blame for the affair. One small track to forgiveness would be Julia realizing that her pulling back from sex, without mutual negotiation and openness to experimenting with intimate alternatives, was injurious to Peter, leaving him feeling deprived and wanting. This might engender some empathy for him, realizing it put Peter in a state of deprivation, not make her feel unfairly blamed for his unfaithful actions based on that state of deprivation.

If these lines of inquiry were mostly positive, discussions of what led Julia to renounce sex could be had, both the deeper ones—any history of sexual trauma that was resurfacing; her feeling like her sexuality had been hijacked by male objectification; and whether Peter's sexual repertoire or overall inattentiveness in daily life made Julia less sexually receptive—and the practical ones: the pros and cons of Julia locating a responsive physician, or wholistic medicine professional, who could help her experiment with pills and creams to remedy vaginal dryness, as well as the possible need to switch anti-depressants and go off her Lexapro because of its sexual side effects. Restoration of some form of mutually satisfying physical intimacy in their marriage would seem to me to be a prerequisite, based on Peter's acute needs and Julia's possible dormant needs.

Ultimately, the solution to recovering from infidelity is forgiveness, which can be a long, arduous process. It's certainly not a one-shot deal where there's a cathartic display of regret met with an exonerating hug. Traces of the betrayal can persist for years and be re-activated hearing about friends and family members undergoing similar ordeals, relevant movie clips, even the mere mention of the words adultery, infidelity, and cheating. Apologies may need to be expressed and re-expressed.

What I've learned in my decades of work with couples recovering from affairs is that contriteness and forgiveness *is both explicit and implicit*. In the early crisis months, there's much open talk about what occurred, the pain caused, guilt, regret, and tears. With the passage of time, the most fortuitous outcomes are those where the unfaithful partner realizes he or she dodged a bullet—the bullet being the death of an otherwise good marriage due to the affair, especially if there are children involved and a strong preference to preserve an intact family. The guilty relief—fueled by gratitude stemming from the realization that he or she had a moment of revitalizing self-worth from an affair and has a partner who still goes on providing love—energizes the desire to be an as involved, attentive, engaged, and generous partner as possible. This is the *implicit zone of healthy guilt* being put to good use for the betterment of a marriage, or long-term partnership. Over time, receptivity on the part of the aggrieved affair partner to these refreshing loving gestures is experienced as reassuring and engenders similar desires to be involved, attentive, engaged, and generous. That's the *implicit zone of healthy forgiveness*. There's no guarantee, but when there's a restoration of good-enough mutual loving regard, there's a sturdy possibility that whatever feelings of erotic excitement and emotional fulfillment derived from the affair will be relocated in the marriage.

Estimates are that a mere 3 percent of affair partners become marriage partners.[56] That should tell us something. In the grand scheme of things, it's not the affair partner him or herself that's so astonishingly unique and irreplaceable. It's the way that person re-energized the way you feel about yourself. When that feeling of self-enhancement is redis-covered in the marriage, the affair fades into the background.

CHAPTER 7

Getting the right sort of help

Rarely do couples present for therapy with the noble goal of wanting to make a good relationship better. Mostly, therapy is put off until whatever problems exist have reached a boiling point with intimates feeling some combination of embitterment with or estrangement from each other. Studies show that couples deny and avoid their thorny issues for an average duration of over two-and-a-half years before seeking professional help.[1] By the time they enter the therapist's office, the situation has become dire.

The pressure on the therapist to deliver is tremendous: to rapidly instill hope that negative communication patterns which have festered for years can be undone, tired old issues resolved, and parched emotional and sexual connections revitalized; or to simply resist feeling pulled into colluding in desperation with one or both spouses who seem to have shown up for therapy simply to check the box, "done therapy," before barreling toward divorce. As we shall see, if the couples therapist acts too much like many typical individual therapists—being passive and neutral, sitting back and inviting unbridled open communication—the couple and the therapy itself can flame out. Old grudges on full display, back and forth blaming, and defensive interrupting can hijack the therapy, leaving spouses seriously questioning its usefulness. Is it any wonder the veteran psychologist William Doherty once said: "If couples therapy were a sport, it would resemble wrestling, not baseball—because it can be over in a flash if you don't have your wits about you."[2]

All too often, couples therapy *is* over in a flash. Estimates of premature drop-out hover in the 40–60 percent range.[3] Those are dismal numbers. There are others. Only about fifty percent of distressed couples contemplating divorce pursue therapy.[4] This is confusing given the widespread sentiment in Western cultures that calling it quits in a marriage without first pursuing counseling is considered irresponsible. Why are the drop-out and underutilization rates so high? The reasons are myriad. Everything from the stubborn conviction that couples should be able to fix their own problems; the fear that therapy will be nothing more than a forum to be blamed and verbally attacked; the scarce availability of therapists of color or similar religious persuasion; therapists undertrained to provide quality care; the affordability of treatment; and the hold-out opinion that therapy is the place that troubled marriages go to die. Let's deal in greater detail with the last two.

It turns out the available science challenges the myth that couples therapy is where troubled marriages meet their demise. Overall, upwards of 70 percent of distressed couples can count on positive, significant change by undergoing therapy.[5] Yet the myth persists. I suspect, in part, this stems from the standard couples therapy approach practitioners are trained in as regards dealing with clients' decisions to separate, divorce, or stay together. Therapists are trained to be "neutral," which means their sole responsibility is to help couples communicate more openly, clarify what their issues are, and support independent decision making. Yet, for distressed couples seriously contemplating the dissolution of their marriage—about one in three of all couples entering therapy— divorce may be a forgone conclusion unless the therapist is prepared to take an affirmative stance surrounding putting off any decision about divorcing until therapy is given a solid chance.[6]

I'm not suggesting that a slow-things-down and don't-give-up-too-soon therapy stance be prioritized in cases where relational abuse or extreme deception, betrayal, or exploitation exist. Nor am I suggesting therapists overwork to preserve a marriage where one or both parties manifest no ambivalence and have firmly decided to part ways.

What I am suggesting is that in the 30 percent of cases[7] where one spouse remains committed to the marriage and the other tilts in the direction of ending it, or both go back and forth chewing on staying together or ending their relationship, the therapist does well to propose that any decision to separate or divorce be taken off the table for a set period of time as a prelude to serious therapeutic examination of the viability of the marriage.

Therapists often feel they have an ethical duty to be *autonomy affirming*. To help couples make informed choices around maximizing each partner's personal happiness. Frequently, this plays out with the therapist taking clients' decision to separate or divorce at face value, respecting and working with presumed rational choices by independently minded adults. But therapists may have a competing ethical duty to be *marriage affirming*—to advise beleaguered couples to postpone any decision around separating and divorcing until therapy is tried. The rationale here is that an avoidable separation or divorce safeguards a couple against some of the worst life stressors known to humans. The Holmes and Rahe Stress Scale, used by doctors for over half a century to rank stressful life events that predict illnesses in adults, places the death of a spouse, or child, at the top of the list. Number two and three happen to be divorce and marital separation. These are ranked more stressful and illness-producing than going to prison, sustaining a major physical injury, or having a close friend die.[8]

Some surprising statistics might also nudge therapists to selectively adopt a marriage-affirming stance, potentially enabling legions of couples to circumvent one of life's top stressors. Anywhere between 26 and 40 percent of divorced people regret having dissolved their marriage, subsequently believing that either or both could have worked harder to preserve their union.[9]

Under duress, many married people, understandably, presuppose they will be happier divorced than partnered to their for-the-present unlovable spouse. Zooming out, some research counters this assumption. A nationally representative survey tracking over 5,000 married adults over a five-year period found that, on average, unhappily married people who separated or divorced were no happier than unhappily married people who remained married. Remarkably, two-thirds of unhappily married adults who refrained from separating or divorcing rated themselves as happily married five years out.[10]

When the prospect of separation or divorce looms, there's an ethical justification for therapists to stall and buy time with many beleaguered couples, to test whether they're going through a temporary rough patch, experienced for the time being as a hopeless predicament, or are neck-deep in irreversible estrangement or bitterness. For more couples than we want to believe, separation and divorce are later regretted and end up failing to provide the much-needed personal happiness imagined. This says nothing of the stress children encounter undergoing the break-up of their parents' struggling but otherwise bearable marriage.

The best of what couples therapy has to offer holds space for non-destructive partners to slow the break-up train down and take stock of their union. Expanding outwards from there, it helps unsettled couples regain hope by accentuating dormant strengths in their relationship, as well as acquiring kind and respectful patterns of communication, not just refraining from hurtful and fruitless ones. It views an appetite for fairness, as well as one's potential to be the most loving person possible, as engines of positive relationship change. It fosters the use of apology rendering, forgiveness, and humor to lessen ill-will and energize good-will. And, as we shall see, if couples therapy is to get off the ground and have a shot at success, male partners have to be actively engaged. In heterosexual relationships, an affable bond with the therapist is not only key to overcoming male partners' resistance to participating in therapy but can also heighten female partners' hope that their seem-ingly irresolvable differences might not be so irresolvable.

The model therapist

If distressed marriages or partnerships are to survive and thrive—or end, with optimal damage control—they are best treated by a *skilled* therapist, not just a *competent* one. Finding a skilled couples therapist can be more of an ordeal than it should be. In general, psychotherapists are an overconfident bunch, believing they are highly skilled, not merely competent. A study spearheaded by Atlanta psychologist Steven Walfish discovered that 25 percent of mental health therapists view themselves in the top 10 percent and none considered themselves as below average.[11]

Psychotherapists are mere mortals when it comes to love and mar-riage. Studies show their marriage adjustment is no better than that of non-psychotherapists.[12] The same is true of their capacity to be securely attached—to be comfortable enough in their own skin so they're neither overly needy nor detached in relationships.[13] There's even evidence that the separation/divorce rates of social workers, counselors, and psychologists are higher than the US national average.[14] This may explain why a Minnesota poll tapping divorced people's experiences with marriage counseling discovered that only 35 percent believed their therapist seemed invested in salvaging their marriage.[15]

I don't subscribe to the extreme position taken by the intimacy expert Laura Doyle: "Some marriage counselors aren't married. Others are divorced twice or unhappily married. Is this who you want to pay for advice? Would you take fitness tips from a 350-pound personal trainer who just had bypass surgery?"[16] She adds: "If your marriage counselor doesn't have the kind of relationship you want, she simply can't tell you how to get it." That said, I do subscribe to the reasonable position that therapists be forthcoming with clients about their biases around marriage and divorce so clients can make an informed choice whether or not any particular therapist is a good fit.

When asked, or when relevant, I usually disclose to clients some version of the following:

> I've been married for nearly thirty years to a woman whom I adore and is also my best friend. That said, we have been to hell and heaven together, so I know first-hand the trials and tribulations associated with a long-term marriage, raising children and building a life together, what can go right and what can go wrong. Since I am in a very good place in my marriage, having gone through some rough patches where we almost didn't make it, I'm quite hopeful about married life.

If pushed, I don't overshare about specifics, but add that my personal and clinical knowledge biases me in the direction of inviting clients to exhaust all options before separating or divorcing, especially if children are involved—unless there are personal endangerment issues, or the presence of considerable deceit, betrayal, or exploitation.

Other counselors with a pro-marriage approach have gone on record with comments they reveal to clients about their slant:

> The issue right now isn't whether you're committed for life, but whether you can commit to working hard to salvage your marriage in therapy, with divorce off the table for the time being.

> I can see that your hope for the marriage is very low. I see my job as holding that hope for you for a while, until you see whether it's possible to rebuild your relationship.

> I'll be working for your marriage until one of you looks me in the eye and calls me off.[17]

The consensus in the field is that therapists need to be more active and participatory during couples treatment than is typically the case when performing individual therapy. Many inexperienced practitioners assume that what's effective with individuals—tracking and clarifying underlying feelings and needs—can be mapped onto couples treatment. In high-conflict relationships, this can spur rapid escalation of blaming and shaming during sessions that leave clients painfully demoralized and doubtful about continuing in therapy. From the onset, it's pivotal that clients witness first-hand the therapist's ability to gauge how much animus is productive so that aggrieved partners feel sufficiently heard and affirmed due to legitimate past and present emotional injuries incurred by their mate, without sessions repeatedly devolving into mutually frustrating standoffs.

Actively prompting loud and boisterous clients to "own their tone" sets the groundwork for less inflammatory conversations. An often-overlooked consideration with emotionally reactive spouses is how the *intensity* with which they deliver their grievances compromises the *legitimacy* of such grievances. Any shot at grievances being taken seriously—not just being heard, but acknowledged—necessitates a therapeutic focus on reactive clients dialing it back:

> Camilla, it's understandable you are angry at Hugo because he is slow to show initiative at home, needing multiple reminders to help out with the children and do his share of housework. We do need to take a serious look at these issues in therapy. But I think your legitimate concerns get compromised by how loud your tone becomes. Is there a way to dial back the intensity of your frustration and say in a calmer way what you just said?

Periodically, a heavy-handed approach is required to cement the realization that somehow, in some way, on some issues, a couple must find a way to *agree to disagree*. Just this week, I boldly butted in with a couple who for the umpteenth time had become ensnared in disagreement over whether the husband was being insensitive in continuing a friendship with someone who had been repeatedly rude to the wife, or the wife was being too sensitive in perceiving the friend as rude: "I'm not sure hammering away on this issue is getting us anywhere. Can we start from the premise that you both experience this friend very differently and accepting this is, in and of itself, a sign of respect?" A comfort level with assertively disallowing blatant disrespect needs to be part of a marriage counselor's toolkit; even if accomplished softly: "I realize you're furious Billy forgot to pick up milk from the store on the way home—after you had called and texted to remind him. But I'm not sure calling him a self-absorbed idiot will make him remember next time!"

Underscoring with clients how "acknowledging is not the same as agreeing" can lay the groundwork for more active listening and less acrimony:

> Jared: You came home late, greeted the kids and completely ignored me. Of course I was pissed! Who wouldn't be!
>
> Hannah: That's not what happened! You were squirreled away in your office, like you usually are, keeping your distance from the family!
>
> Dr. Gnaulati: Hannah, I know your version of events is different than Jared's. Clearly, you don't agree with him, but can we start by just acknowledging his point of view and feelings?
>
> Hannah: So you think I greeted the kids and ignored you, and you were mad?
>
> Jared: Yes!

An interventionist stance can be as simple as monitoring "air time" to ensure that both parties feel the expression of their point of view, more or less, is evenly encouraged. It might entail the therapist commandeering a chaotic discourse to render it more productive: "It seems to me we have too many issues on the table right now. Can we pick up on one of them that you both feel is valuable to address?" Or: "That issue is so much of a hot-button one, I think we should set it aside until cooler heads prevail."

On a more sophisticated note, savvy couples therapists are conversant at reframing problems ascribed to any individual partner in terms of relationship dynamics:

> Jamal, I hear what you're saying about Grace being sexually unavailable. From listening to you both, it seems more like a dynamic where you, Grace, need to feel Jamal is interested in you as a person, asks you about your day, helps out around the house, is nice to you, to get your sexual motor running. When he doesn't act that way, it lessens the chances you'll be in the mood. You reject his advances. Jamal, you then feel rebuffed and withdraw, being even less communicative, hurting your chances that anything sexual will occur.

Even more sophistication is involved determining and communicating what aspects of each partner's attachment, personality, or communication style is potentially changeable, or needs to be accepted and accommodated as a hardened trait:

> Sam, I notice it comes easier for you to tune in logically to what Tilly is communicating. Reading between the lines, emotionally speaking, is more of a challenge. Being a logical person is a big part of your identity and probably contributes to your success as a lawyer. Tilly, you wish Sam would get out of his head and feel his way into your experience. That doesn't come anywhere as easily to him as it does to you. We have a dilemma here.

> Cameron, I notice when Mary Anne is around more, you have lots of time to hang out or travel together, and have predictable access to her, you are a much calmer version of yourself. When she is busy working, gone a lot, comes home from the office at random times, you are more on edge and apt to become irritated with her. I think this is something for you both to be aware of and work with.

I can tell, Aliyah, you wish you were not so quick to take things personally, to feel insulted and compelled to strike back. This tendency gets in the way of the type of partner you want to be. The good news is that you are aware of it and are committed to damage control measures like taking a personal time out when you know you are in attack mode.

Otherwise, what distinguishes skilled couples therapists is their know-how when it comes to the core procedures endorsed by most schools of thought in the field: keeping the alliance with both partners balanced; unlocking vulnerable emotions; and accentuating client strengths.

Maintaining a balanced alliance involves being watchful to mete out equal support, not overidentifying and siding too much with one partner. When validating one partner's grievance, there's always the risk the other will feel neglected or misunderstood. To even things out, sometimes this entails inviting a rebuttal immediately after providing one-sided affirmation: "I can tell, Priscilla, it's irritating to feel necessary to remind Manuel to help the kids with their homework, wishing he would show initiative and do it without reminders. Is there anything to this, Manuel, or maybe you see things differently?" Mostly, the therapist keeps a mental balance sheet in his or her head, an intuitive sense of how much one or both partners feel sufficiently or insufficiently supported, prepared to rebalance the situation with a nod here, a smile there, a passing supportive remark, or an emphatic gesture of approval.

Therapists are human. The whole enterprise of keeping things balanced implies they ought to warm to and like both partners equally, presupposing joint culpability for relationship predicaments. That's more of a superhuman than a human task. Scholars at the Family Institute at Northwestern University studying these matters discovered that 40 percent of the time therapists engage in split alliances, getting caught up liking and showing preferential treatment to one spouse over another.[18] Often, this gets acted out covertly more than overtly: a muted smile, a half-hearted gesture of recognition, an overly eager expression of praise, restless leg crossing, more animated listening.

Speaking from experience, when I find myself clicking with one spouse and souring over another, I try to be hyperconscious of the verbal and non-verbal signals I send out to diplomatically disguise this.

I consider this a form of professionalism. I don't hold back from conveying my genuine like for the liked partner. For the less likable one, I work at liking him or her more. I find it helps to search for tidbits of personal history that inspire compassion—overcoming the odds to succeed professionally, dutiful in taking care of an aging grandmother, forced into a parental role as a kid due to paternal abandonment, afflicted with chronic pain after a skiing accident.

Strife in relationships is usually fomented when intimates reactively convert vulnerable emotions into invulnerable ones. It's the therapist's job to help client suss out when this is occurring, cuing and prompting them to stay attuned to the vulnerable ones—when pride masks shame; and anger is a foil for hurt, sadness, jealously, anxiety, guilt, or feelings of loneliness:

> I realize you are mad because Helen accused you of being passive, staying in a job where you are underpaid and under-appreciated. Is any part of you also hurt or embarrassed?

> Being called a control freak can't feel good, but I don't think it's productive to go on the offense and call your wife wasteful and materialistic. Is it possible you're nervous about how the kids' college is going to be paid for and whether you are socking away enough for retirement?

> Leona just said you were an uninvolved dad. You reacted by saying she is more married to the kids than you. I'm wondering if she hit a nerve and part of you feels guilty you're not there for the kids as much as you wish?

> Right when Camila mentioned she's lost weight and is proud of how she looks, you rolled your eyes. Maybe there's some jealousy over other guys potentially giving her attention?

The all-important rationale for cuing and prompting clients to stay attuned to vulnerable emotions is that these tend to elicit empathy and compassion—mitigating conflict. Recently, a husband and wife I was treating were bogged down, slinging accusations at each other over whether the husband was too needy, or the wife too cold-hearted. She traveled a great deal for work. Post-retirement, he was nested at home with few outside obligations or hobbies. I probed a little, wondering if his anger masked loneliness. He denied it at first. Then, in the middle of the argument, he jumped ship and declared with noticeable gravity: "Enrico's right. I'm lonely and I miss you." His wife stopped herself and matched his vulnerability: "I miss you too." The fight came to a grinding halt.

Admissions of guilt and wrongdoing can also bring fights to a griding halt. Inviting and inducing clients' guilt for their guilty actions, at first glance, seems moralistic and counter-therapeutic. However, we need to remind ourselves that guilt is a "social emotion," healthily signaling us it's quite possible we have broken a connection with a significant other through our bad actions. Tuning into genuine guilt feelings becomes the emotional gateway to acknowledge wrongdoing and mend broken connections. Therapeutic guilt inducement, as wonky as it sounds, is an important skill for counselors to hone, since it can aid in clients moving through protracted conflicts and restoring positive bonds faster. An example will help.

Hillary mentioned during a couples session that she had taken great pains to make dinner plans to celebrate her and Gabriel's wedding anniversary. On the night of their anniversary dinner, Gabriel had put in a distress call to Hillary, asking if it would be alright to fill in for a friend, refereeing a youth soccer match in the neighborhood. Hillary was galled that Gabriel had forgotten about the anniversary dinner. While revisiting this chain of events during the session, Gabriel off-handedly uttered: "What's the big deal? I came right home after you reminded me and we went out and had an enjoyable dinner, right?" Hillary was livid because Gabriel seemed to be making excuses for his insensitivity, which compounded the hurt she already felt.

I intervened with some therapeutic guilt inducement: "Gabriel, can you see how Hillary might have felt hurt and rejected, having to remind you of the special evening she planned?" Gabriel softened: "You are right. That was not me at my most sensitive." I persisted: "You have said many times in here that you need Hillary to demonstrate more affection with you. She seems to have listened by planning the anniversary dinner." In an abashed tone, Gabriel continued: "I don't know what I was thinking.

Hillary was trying to plan an intimate evening, and by asking to stay out and referee the soccer game, I was being pretty thoughtless."

Crying, Hillary chimed in: "I ended up sucking it up and going out with you when you came right home but having to remind you took all the sheen out of the evening." Gabriel was apologetic: "I'm so, so sorry." He reached over and hugged Hillary, who collapsed into his arms, relinquishing the anger she felt over the transgression, implicitly forgiving Gabriel.

On the topic of accentuating strengths, I resoundingly concur with findings out of Gottman's Love Lab at the University of Washington: in troubled marriages, spouses are often poorly dialed into loving gestures that occur and overly dialed into the ways they disappoint each other.[19] This may explain the logic behind the amusing Bob Mankoff *New Yorker* cartoon where an emboldened marriage counselor announces to a baffled couple: "It may surprise you to know, contrary to your experience, you're actually very happily married."[20] Effective therapists are privy to how beleaguered couples make the worst of a good situation and are primed to step in when either or both spouses show signs of virtuous action or goodwill, no matter how subtle:

> I'm impressed by how well you held back and just listened while being screamed at.

> It's difficult to acknowledge you are in the wrong when the other person is coming on strong, but you showed courage and did it!

> You have a knack for seeing the humor in situations when you could get annoyed. You guys would be in more arguments if this was not the case.

> I can tell you both don't stay mad at each other for long even after the worst fights. Sometimes that's what really matters, not over-talking the issues, letting bygones be bygones, and moving on.

> You strike me as devoted parents who function amazingly well as co-parents. We just have to find a way to redirect some of that devotion to your relationship with each other.

> Even though you find each other insufferable at times, bickering and overindulging your annoyances, you still find a way to have a mutually satisfying sex life. Kudos to you!

Frequently, the task for dutiful therapists is to reframe the negative impressions of clients into positive ones in ways that accurately call attention to benign rather than malicious intent:

> You seem convinced that Bob is being controlling around finances. I wonder if this is just him doing something he has talent at to preserve the financial well-being of the family?

> Jamal, I know it gets to you when Francisco calls you at work to share the details of his day. You say he's being intrusive. What if it reflects his desire to keep a connection with you alive, because he considers you to be his best friend, as well as his husband?

> I know you wish Peter was more communicative and keyed into what you're going through emotionally. But he seems to show his love through acts of service, like making you breakfast and picking up your dry cleaning. That might not seem like enough, but it's something, not nothing.

> I can tell you think Olivia is being unfair by insisting you consider coaching your daughter's basketball team when you are stretched so thin at work. What if this is just her way of trying to strengthen your relationship with your daughter?

As contained in this final example, optimal handling of fairness and unfairness issues in therapy is often at the heart of the matter if couples are to regain hope in their vital bond being reestablished.

The court of last resort

Within days of being released from a rehab center, sixty-three-year-old Landon called me to set up therapy for him and his wife, sheepishly disclosing that his marriage was in tatters; no less, he was determined to save it. His fifty-five-year-old wife, Jill, would be joining in remotely, since she had relocated miles away to her mother's house for safety reasons due to the events surrounding Landon being placed in rehab. The harrowing details were unpacked for me during the extended Zoom videoconference we arranged.

What was intended to be a night out for cocktails with some work colleagues turned into a nihilistic escapade. Landon binge drank until he had no recollection of how he ended up passed out in his car in front of a "gentleman's club," sans shoes and wallet. He awoke the next morning and made his way home, only to discover an empty house. After her repeated phone calls had gone unanswered, Jill suspected that Landon was on another self-destructive romp and decamped to her mother's house. Landon called and pleaded with Jill to return. She was adamant this wouldn't be in the cards until Landon swore he would enter treatment. Distressed and sounding incoherent, Landon pounced back, saying he had a gun in his hand and would use it on himself if Jill refused to return home. Jill hung up and contacted the police.

The dominoes fell from there. Landon was arrested and placed on an involuntary hold at a local psychiatric facility for a week. Once released, he flew to an out-of-state drug rehabilitation center and checked himself in. In shock, Jill elected not to have contact. Both her therapist and her mother urged her to focus on her own self-care, strongly advocating that Jill hold off contact until Landon completed rehab, sending him the unmistakable message that she would no longer tolerate Landon's calamitous and alcoholic behavior. Humiliated and feeling all alone in the hospital, a sense of self-righteous indignation welled up in Landon. Adding insult to injury, he reached out to his mother and demanded she freeze bank accounts in his name to preempt any chance Jill would access them. He persuaded his mother he was bent on divorcing Jill, maligning her as a "gold digger" who would drain their accounts while he stood by, powerless, hospitalized against his will. His mother not only froze the bank accounts but took it upon herself to call Jill and rail against her for being a neglectful wife during Landon's time of need.

Therapy kicked off with a palpable sense it was the court of last resort. The responsibility to heed the ethical pull emanating from clients like Landon and Jill, mired in mistrust and despair, to help adjudicate accusations of fairness and unfairness, is both awesome and treacherous. It's what seriously tempts therapists to double down on aspects of their training informing them to be neutral: stay out of the fray, don't take sides, track and process feelings, just help the couple see "their dynamic." Landon and Jill wanted more than a therapist who observed and helped them process feelings. They wanted a therapist who witnessed, and enabled them to adjudicate, their fairness and unfairness claims:

> Landon, I know you felt abandoned and neglected when Jill remained at her mother's house and cut off all contact, but can you see how this might be her being fair to herself, desperate to get you to finally address your self-destructive relationship with alcohol? All the scary and gloomy times you have put her through with your self-destructive behavior?
>
> Jill claims her relationship with her mother-in-law is broken because you intervened, Landon, pegging Jill as a "gold digger" and turning your mother against her. You tell me, is the relationship broken, or just damaged? Is there anything to be gained by reaching out to your mother and admitting you were out of line, acted rashly in a rage, redeeming Jill in your mother's eyes? Assuming Jill is ready for this, or even wants this?

The reader probably discerned I was unequal in my initial interventions with Landon and Jill, siding mainly with Jill. I made a value judgment. I had to judiciously pick sides with Jill for the sake of the marriage, while not alienating Landon. This was the second marriage for both. The stakes were higher. At bottom, Landon adored Jill and saw a better relationship with her as crucial not only for his sustained sobriety, but also his hope for true companionship in old age. Jill found Landon hilarious (as I did and told him so during our sessions) and adventuresome, and if the marriage worked out, she would be afforded a level of financial security never experienced before in her life. Yet the egregiousness of Landon's actions the night of his nihilistic escapade, and its aftermath, tilted Jill in the direction of seriously questioning remaining married; especially since her mother and friends were lambasting her as nuts for staying with him.

Clearly, I was not acting equally or even-handedly in the initial phase of therapy with Jill and Landon, though I was attempting to be *equitable*. That is, in my mind, Jill's hope for the marriage working out was contingent upon Landon experiencing a real reckoning of the sort where he truly accepted that his culpability surpassed hers. To restore equity, Landon would somehow have to earnestly grapple with how unfair it was of him to leave Jill in the lurch while he endangered himself on a binge-drinking episode; manipulate her to rush home by threatening suicide; unnerve her by necessitating she call the police to ensure his safety; and malign her in the eyes of his mother.

In a sense, Landon owed Jill this sort of reckoning because, for the time being, she was acting loyal enough by agreeing to therapy and staying in the marriage, against a chorus of disapproving friends and relatives. My holding Landon answerable to all these concerns emboldened Jill's belief in the utility of therapy for the possible preservation of the marriage. She felt she was getting a fair hearing.

So much of therapists' training cautions them against stepping into this tribunal role with couples, yet, in my experience, it's unavoidable. In a therapy context, or non-therapy one, it's simply human nature to automatically contemplate fairness concerns when confronted with life stories like that of Landon and Jill's. As noted by esteemed American biologist, Peter Corning: "fairness has a strong, though imperfect, pull on our perceptions and our conduct."

Whether consciously aware of it or not, therapists who open themselves up emotionally to the real dilemmas couples face can't help but get drawn into their ethical agonies: It sure looks like she's under-giving and over-expecting, that's unfair! She's definitely over-giving and under-expecting, that's not right! He's owed more because of how much he gives, that's unjust! He deserves better, look how much he gives, that's so unbalanced! The trick is using these natural impulses caringly and carefully to help couples address imbalances in what is owed and what is deserved that frequently underly marital problems.

One unique approach that subscribes to this way of working is Contextual Family Therapy, formulated by Ivan Boszormenyi-Nagy, a Hungarian-American psychiatrist. Raised in a household with multiple generations of lawyers and judges, he became intrigued with how fairness and justice issues govern human conduct. I had one of his concepts on retainer in mind—for when the time felt right—to tip the therapy scales in the direction of Jill being more conciliatory toward Landon—"merited trust":[21]

> Jill, I can tell you are, understandably, reticent to consider moving back into the house with Landon. You're not sure it's safe, if he'll relapse, if he's serious about wanting to be a kinder version of himself. Does it help build some trust knowing he completed rehab, attends regular AA meetings, and is transparent in emailing you breathalyzer readouts?
>
> I hear what you are saying, Jill, that even before Landon's rehab stay, he threatened to limit your access to family money when he was upset at you for any reason. I realize how demeaning this was for you. His rebuttal is that he did this when drunk and angry and he's aware how demeaning this was. Does that make a difference?

Those working within the Contextual model label the therapist's tendency to shift alliances based on in-the-moment determinations as to who has been harmed the most and is owed support, or whose conscientious efforts are deserving of recognition, "multi-directed partiality." Nowhere does the therapist need to be more partial to a client than when he or she is generous with goodwill. As we have learned from Gottman's Love Lab, troubled couples often overlook kind actions—bids for connection—which can register as mini-rejections fueling below-the-radar, tit-for-tat withholding of affectionate praise and recognition. Being partial to whichever member of the antagonistic couple thaws, showing overtures of kindness, is an important attitude for therapists to adopt:

> Landon, I just noticed that you, somewhat shyly, mentioned it was nice having Jill home this weekend. What about it made it nice?

> You smiled, Jill, when Landon announced he'd be happy to babysit the dog this weekend. Can you elaborate on how this made you feel?

> I'm impressed, Landon, by how well you took note of what Jill said last session about not pulling your hand away in public when she reaches out for it!

If vicious cycles of withholding praise and recognition are to be supplanted by virtuous cycles of outward manifestation of such gestures of appreciation, the therapist's role in prompting couples to flesh out subtle signs of genuine positivity is instrumental. Couples that habitually neglect each other often think pleases and thankyous are corny; yet ironically, these sort of intentional expressions of appreciation are the very antidote to their alienating neglect. The eminent Roman legal scholar Cicero opined: "There is no duty more indispensable than that of returning a kindness."[22] Sensing this duty to meet kindness with kindness, not as a moral prescription, but out of loving desire for the sustenance of a marital bond, can be a turning point in therapy. That is, when it's mutual.

Another turning point in therapy pertains to both parties not only realizing, but showing an ongoing willingness to explore how the emotional baggage from their past shapes their current relationship expectations. Not uncommonly, at first, clients heartily endorse the reasonableness of this. You must be pretty unworldly to be untutored in Freud's notion (not the arcane term itself) of "repetition compulsion," which has seeped so thoroughly into popular culture. It's the global idea if we ignore our past, we are destined to repeat it, at our own peril. The more nuanced version, utterly demoralizing at times, is that we bank on significant others in the present letting us down in the same way as caregivers did in the past. The even more nuanced version is not so demoralizing: we are split between expecting our current loved ones to disappoint us, similar to how early caregivers did, and holding out hope they won't.

Once clients dig into their distant past, they become embarrassingly aware of the grip old hurts have on them and of how often they contribute to new injuries in their current relationships. They wind up souring on historical discussions.

Take the case of Jackson and Sara, both university professors in their late forties. One of their "trigger issues" was Jackson being over-committed to his work as a chemistry professor, which left Sara feeling neglected. Despite his Herculean efforts to enact his fair share in raising their daughter—drop-offs and pick-ups at school, as well as bedtime stories, multiple days a week, fun outings, frequent "math puzzles" time, which his daughter prized—Sara was routinely displeased when

Jackson was required to travel for work, leaving her to "pick up the load." He was a highly accomplished chemist, a rising international star in the research and development of cancer-busting drugs, who broke into a cold sweat when raising the discussion of travel plans with Sara. Sara was no slouch. She was a well-established graphic artist who counted on time apart from parenting and household tasks to preserve her creative juices. Even though Sara tried in her own way to be affectionate and playful, Jackson often seemed blind to this and defaulted to perceiving her as relentlessly critical. I floated the following perspective to them.

It seems to me, Sara, that part of what's going on here is some of this is due to unresolved issues with your father. He was a very ambitious attorney who was gone a lot when you were a kid. You felt neglected and resentful and carry this into the present. Jackson, your mother was often critical and disapproving, such that when Sara shows her unhappiness over your travel plans, you go into a panic, as if you're a little kid in the presence of your mother, all over again.

Like most couples hearing about an "unconscious dynamic" from me for the first time, Sara and Jackson were receptive. They now had a framework for understanding a recurring source of vexation. They felt helped. Before long, exasperation set in due to the uncanny way in which this unconscious pattern from the past cropped up time and time again to disable their best intentions to do things differently in the present. Hence Freud's unhopeful language, "repetition compulsion."

It's one thing to acquire insight into an unconscious relationship dynamic, or to entertain the sober assessment of philosopher Mari Ruti on how the past can color the present for couples: "when two couples come together in romantic alliance they are more or less guaranteed to arouse each other's deep-seated unconscious patterns."[23] It's something completely different to turn it around. It entails a sound awareness that the festering feeling of being owed you carry into the present sets you up to collect from the wrong person, who is a *somewhat* hapless victim.

Jackson may deserve a portion of Sara's ire for being over-immersed in work too, but her rage over this is archaic in nature; it's reminiscent of a girl furious at her father for not being present enough, aggravated by an overidentification with a mother who feels similarly. It may be annoying that Sara defaults to criticizing and disapproving, but Jackson's deflation and panic is that of a boy overwhelmed by a wrathful mother in a family system where everyone's fear of conflict allows Mom to get away with bad behavior.

To undo the tenacious effects of a neglectful past on the present requires committing to a higher ethical ground. It entails heightened sensibility to the fact that it's unfair to hold current partners responsible for mistakes made by caregivers. It involves—out of love for the person whom you attached to in the present—*intentionally and actively* keeping one eye open for how he or she is actually providing what you need, not simply undermining it. That's where good therapy can make a difference:

> I know Sara can be hard on you, Jackson, and that's hurtful. But, at times, it seems to me you confuse her with your mother and get shut down in the ways you used to in the past. You get so shut down, I think, it blinds you to Sara's affectionate gestures and playful ways of connecting to you.
>
> Sara, I realize that because Jackson is such an accomplished scientist, he's gone a lot, leaving you feeling neglected like you used to as a little girl with your father. However, when he's around, I get the impression he's an involved dad and is genuinely invested in his domestic contribution. So unlike your dad!

Therapists need to be mindful of how clients can weaponize historical understandings to avoid taking responsibility for how they act in the very way that a neglectful, disappointing, or rejecting caregiver did, or to be overripe in their accusations that a partner acts unpleasantly, like an early caregiver:

> Jackson: You need to deal with your "daddy issues." I'm tired of being skewered just for being ambitious and furthering my career, which will always involve travel!
>
> Dr. Gnaulati: Of course, it's incredibly important that you be ambitious and ensure your career is on the right track, Jackson. But can you see how when you are

too animated about this, it takes Sara back to some very painful parts of her childhood, leaving her feeling neglected and alone?

Sara: I can't believe I'm stuck in a relationship with someone who is no different than my father. Who is self-centered and prioritizes his career.

Dr. Gnaulati: I realize Jackson's career is all-consuming, Sara. But is it fair to compare him to your father in this way? From my understanding, he's much more of an involved dad than yours ever was. Maybe your dad is more deserving of your anger?

In the therapy court of last resort, proponents of a Contextual model offer some wise counsel as regards a constructive agenda: "To move clients away from the fantasy of unconditional acceptance to the reality of colliding entitlements."[24] In ordinary language, what this means is that effective couples therapy energizes a focus on clients "giving up the ghost," that unmet childhood needs to feel extra special due to inadequate care by caregivers cannot be met in exquisite ways by current partners—who have their own compelling reasons to unfairly expect their current partner to make them feel extra special for similar reasons. However, as we shall see up ahead, if couples can fully comprehend each other's painful historical legacies, they can lovingly commit to honoring each other's "triggers" or "sore spots," avoiding hurting them in all-too-familiar old ways, or caring for them in all-too-unfamiliar new ways.

Therapeutic use of humor

Transparency with feelings of affinity is crucial for therapists working with couples—showing you like them, as well as the whole undertaking of therapy together. Maintaining an openness to humorously engage clients is one way to cement goodwill and positive affinity with clients. Couples tire of their broken-record complaints with each other. They assume you feel likewise. A surefire way to disabuse them of this assumption is to laugh with them. Witnessing them enjoying you enjoying them is enjoyable. It subtly communicates you're all in, unlikely to tire of them anytime soon.

Something as elemental as greeting a couple in the waiting room with a smile, not gestures of over-professionalized formality, tacitly communicates: "It's a pleasure to see you." In her subversive book, *Why Don't Therapists Laugh*, author Ann Shearer sardonically states: "Of course psychotherapy is a serious business. But do we have to be so *solemn* about it."[25] I think: WE DON'T.

Reciprocal laughter, when it occurs, can dissolve any power imbalance, or expected social hierarchy in the relationship, tacitly displaying that therapist and client share a common humanity. Shared laugher democratizes the therapy. It can also promote feelings of friendliness and trust which positions the therapist as a credible figure whose input is valued.

When they hit the mark, humorous comments and exchanges with clients foster an all-important sense of we-ness, or relational goodness-of-fit, that adds an extra quotient of compatibility. A knowing smile, chuckle of recognition, or wry remark conveying common awareness of human frailty covertly reassures clients that you, as the therapist, embody the sort of familiarity with their angst, and confidence in treating it, that augers well for the therapy.

Amusing comments that hit the mark can also reflect acute empathy or deep listening and recognition. They can embody an easy-going sense of I-know-that-you-know-that-I-know mutual awareness, or affective synchrony, that leaves clients feeling non-threateningly understood and better able to relax into the therapy. Due to the spontaneity involved, an element of surprise infuses the interaction, finding clients caught delightfully off-guard. An emotional channel gets changed and clients are primed to absorb sensitive personal information they otherwise would defend against. The playfulness and positive "in-tuneness" shown by the therapist momentarily inoculates clients against experiencing shame surrounding beliefs and actions that might otherwise be shame-inducing. Here's an example.

Percy and Catherine, a middle-aged couple, sought out therapy to address prolonged estrangement in their marriage, worsened after taking on the primary caregiving role for Catherine's ninety-year-old father. Rather than hire in-home health care workers, they decided to sell their house and move in with him. Percy was especially hard done by this. He was well acquainted with how opinionated and harsh his father-in-law was, but believed he'd soften under Percy's devoted care.

Before long, the father-in-law proved himself to be cranky, demanding, and unappreciative, to the point that the living arrangement had become unlivable. Catherine was fine with moving out and orchestrating her father's placement in a nursing home. Percy remained adamant "a promise was a promise" and felt they had no choice to stay put. Sidenote: Percy's susceptibility to passive resignation was a problem in the marriage.

Sessions often played out with Percy railing against his father-in-law's cruelty, reflecting the kind of impotent rage accompanying a sense of passive resignation. During once such tirade, I couldn't help myself: "Percy, you make it sound like you just got handed a life sentence with no hope for parole! Like your old soulmate [pointing to Catherine] is now your cellmate and you're trapped together with no options! Catherine is telling you the cell door is wide open, and she wants to get back to being your old soulmate, not your current cellmate!" They both cut up laughing. When the cathartic moment waned, Percy admitted his passivity was a problem. He surmised that if he and Catherine were to find their way back to one another, not only would they have to exit his father-in-law's house, but he would need to be more proactive in identifying and pursuing sources of enjoyment in his life, preferably that Catherine also might find appealing.

Good-natured teasing can non-threateningly shine a spotlight on a trait that renders a partner difficult to live with, influencing his or her mate to perceive it with more levity and acceptance. Recently, a self-admitted cantankerous husband I was treating referenced that it was hot where he was. I quipped: "Are we talking about the weather, Lance, or your mood this morning?" His wife, who was listening on, smiled, adding: "Probably both!"

A wife I was treating, who had reached her limit with her husband's incessant demands that she exercise more and lose weight, blasted back: "I'm never going to be an ultramarathoner like you!" I snarkily commented: "Heck, you're an ultramarathoner of a different sort, sticking in through thick and thin with a husband who won't let up on these issues!" Her husband smiled and sheepishly admitted: "Ain't that the truth."

Humorous wordplay can be disruptive, pleasantly jolting a spouse to loosen an attachment to some idealized version of a wished-for mate that's getting in the way of greater intimacy with his or her real flesh-and-blood mate. Sixty-three-year-old Betty often bemoaned in couples therapy that her identically aged husband, Peter, was difficult to connect with because he was a "naïve optimist." She, on the other hand, was palpably aware of the tragic dimensions of life. I reminded Betty that Peter had donated a kidney to her for a transplant operation she had undergone: "What can be darker than the idea of electing to serve up a kidney to keep you from dying, I'm no' kiddin' yae [with a Scottish accent]!" This caused us all to burst out laughing which greased the path for a more penetrating comment: "In all seriousness, Betty, after all these years, I think you still get stuck idealizing the kind of man your father was—a whip-smart conversationalist, high-brow cosmopolitan type of guy, full of personal insight and integrity—and by comparison Peter always falls short!"

No doubt, there are risks being comical with clients because there's a thin line between acting spontaneously and acting impulsively. Risk abounds because the message nested in the witty remark is often taboo and the outcome of how it will land, uncertain. With bad timing, bad word choices, or bad intent, the therapist can misread the interaction, alienating couples. This says nothing of humor that is unquestionably inappropriate. When it is used to belittle or mock clients; divert attention away from a difficult problem faced by couples and onto a lighter subject; and when it's tangential to what couples feel is relevant, instead motivated by the therapist's need for stimulation and amusement. All this said, when humor works, the emotional dividends can be great, both in terms of bonding with couples and spurring them to non-defensively look at and accept limitations in their relationship. When the therapy is too staid, formal, and scripted, ludicrous things can happen! Take the joke: Client: "No one ever understands me." Therapist: "What do you mean by that?"

A male-friendly approach

A little-known scientific finding in the world of heterosexual marriage counseling is that, whether the therapist is male or female, a successful outcome relies heavily on the therapist and husband cementing a connection. I suspect, in part, this is because wives are about twice as likely as husbands to be dissatisfied with the relationship, so when therapist and husband click, hope is revived for the wife that therapy might actually make a positive difference.[26] It may feel like pulling teeth to get male partners to agree to therapy. After all, as noted by one counseling psychologist duo: "the requirements of the male role appear antithetical to the requirements of a 'good client'"[27]—keep your feelings inside; appear invulnerable; fix problems, don't just talk about them; get to the point and stay on point; resist getting too dependent. But, in most cases, if therapy is to get off the ground and stay in the air, engaging men is crucial.

The initial façade of resisting therapy often fades fast for men because they tend to rely more on marriage for companionship and life satisfaction than women, priming them to seize upon therapy to help preserve a marriage they've grown dependent on. Some data show the average husband benefits more from marriage than the average wife because there's a greater likelihood she's his primary confidant, link to outside friendships, source of household help, and health-check badgerer.[28] The task becomes making therapy a male-friendly space.

The couples therapy field is rife with models that emphasize skills many women already possess and many men don't. Accessing vulnerable emotions, or "chasing the pain," and deepening intimate connections—twin home-run goals of most models—are more female-friendly than male-friendly. Leading marriage expert John Gottman goes so far as to say: "News flash: Men, you have the power to make or break a relationship." He sees marital improvement hinging on "the extent to which the male can accept the influence of the woman he loves and become socialized in emotional communication."[29] Which begs the question: Does a traditional male have to morph into a traditional female to make couples therapy work?

First off, diversity scholar William Ming Liu at the University of Maryland would argue that failing to treat a male who is comfortable with many of the social expectations associated with what it means to be traditionally masculine is not practicing with multicultural competence.[30] That entails a gender-sensitive approach where men are *treated from within* their masculine predispositions, guarding against biased attempts to superimpose onto them norms that come more naturally to the average woman. Which doesn't mean having to collude around the uglier forms of manhood, or toxic masculinity—turning a blind eye to forms of male dominance, arrogance, aggressiveness, and sexual excess. It involves meeting men where they're at, not shaming them, for displaying what seems to come most naturally as regards masculine identifications.

Terms used to describe men's emotional know-how in the culture at large are often tinged with shame—stunted, constipated, clueless. Several years back, the freelance journalist Tori DeAngelis wrote an article for *Monitor on Psychology* titled: "Are men emotional mummies?"[31] On average, we know men are less emotionally expressive than women, but browbeating them for it is not particularly therapeutic. Many psychologically healthy men experience what Professor Emeritus in Psychology at the University of Akron, Ronald Levant, labels "normative male alexithymia," which literally means, "no emotions for words." It's estimated that almost 17 percent of men embody this emotional style, approximately twice the rate of women.[32] Typically, alexithymic people come across as aloof, drawing a blank when asked what they're feeling, are non-elaborative in their emotional responses (i.e., "How are you feeling?" "Fine"), somewhat out of touch with what others are feeling, overvalue logic, and appear disconnected from their own needs and desires. These challenges tend to be more emblematic of men than women.

I'm reminded of the Randy Glasberg marriage counseling cartoon, where a well-meaning wife orients the therapists about her husband: "He's pretty good at showing his emotions. A blank stare means he's angry, a vacant stare means he's sad, and a distant stare means he's excited." All joking aside, the issue with alexithymic men often is not that they're incapable of identifying their emotions, it's that they're restricted in outward expression of them. That's according to a 2009 Finnish study looking at alexithymia in over 5,000 adults across gender.[33]

The takeaway for therapists is: when interacting with alexithymic-leaning male partners, patience and perseverance are necessary to draw them out emotionally. More directiveness applies, offering emotion word choices and expanded verbalizations (e.g., "I hear you say you're feeling blank, but I'm wondering if you're frustrated since you told me Clarissa forgot to pay the internet bill and when your service was cut off you had no way of conducting Zoom sessions with work colleagues?").

Over the years, I've learned to settle into ambling disclosures on topics tangential to marital problems—the abundance of cobalt in the Democratic Republic of the Congo for making electric car batteries, how inflation drives up wages for workers, China's maritime justification for building the Spratly Islands—as a prerequisite to gaining trust with many men, allowing them ample space and time to communicatively unfold, to edge their way into their emotions. As a masculine-leaning man myself, I can hang in. I'm even guilty of being seduced into joint intellectual meandering. I sometimes ponder what this must be like for the average female therapist; women now make up over 75 percent of the mental health workforce in the US.[34]

Watchfulness over privileging feminine preferences in couples work is important to keep men engaged. One area where this is pertinent relates to how men and women handle stress differently. When stressed, males are more likely than females to experience a fight-or-flight response. Their sympathetic nervous system and adrenal glands light up. A cascade of catecholamines get released into their bloodstream, preparing then to do battle or run for the hills (ancient ways of staying alive and ensuring a healthy number of the tribe survives).

In therapy, discussions of unequal household chore arrangements, lack of sex, or who hogs the channel changer more can result in men exploding or shrinking into themselves. The latter is more common. Gottman claims a whopping 85 percent of stonewallers in troubled marriages are men.[35] When stressed, men more than women are prone to fold their arms, clam up, avert eye contact, and give one-word answers.

Emerging scholarship shows that when stressed, women are more likely to "tend-and-befriend," call their sister, or hang out with friends to discuss what ails them. The release of the "bonding hormone" oxytocin plays a role in their stress response (an ancient bio-social mechanism aimed at building social connections and trust so others will have your back in times of danger).[36]

In couples therapy, heated issues tend to elicit a need in most women to exhaust every discursive avenue to resolve issues. They are more inclined to "talk then walk." When stressed, men are more inclined to "walk then talk." Insofar as a female therapist adopts the naturalness of a "tend-and-befriend" attitude, she may underestimate a male client's need to emotionally withdraw to get his bearings. To temporarily have some immediate silence, change the topic, have it be okay for the therapist and the wife to dialogue alone for a while, hit the bathroom for a toilet break to calm his nerves, or any other number of steps that allow for temporary face-saving, respectful withdrawal.

Another area where privileging of the feminine might inadvertently shut men down involves their inordinate emphasis on physical attractiveness in romantic relationships. A large body of research buttresses the notion that physical attractiveness matters more in predicting husbands' marital satisfaction than wives' in the long arc of a relationship, not just during a courting phase.[37] Most straight men visually zero in on female bodily characteristics, like smooth skin, large eyes, soft hair, full lips, and low waist-to-hip ratio as signs of physical attractiveness. They fret over wives keeping up their appearance as they age in ways that seem superficial.

From an evolutionary perspective, these habits are far from superficial. They're responsible for the perpetuation of the human species. Female bodily characteristics like soft skin and hair texture, and full lips, are considered "fitness factors," signs of youthfulness and health that over the millennia eventuate in greater mating reproductive success. Superficial or not, natural selection designed the male brain to fixate on these "fitness factors." Expecting men to willfully rid themselves of them is akin to asking men to override deep evolutionary brain programming. Which isn't to say men can't curtail, suppress, struggle with, disguise, or guiltily self-sacrificingly renounce their preoccupations over what feels natural to them regarding what they find attractive in females—for the betterment of their relationship with their abiding significant other.

Several years ago, a couple in my office got into a spat over the wife's inclination to cut her long curly hair. She found it oppressive dabbling with hair products and scheduling routine appointments with her stylist, mainly to accommodate her husband's personal taste for long hair. Entering midlife, she felt it was long overdue for her to assert personal choice over how she styled her hair. He thought her long curly hair was sexy and suited her.

I know more than the CliffsNotes version of feminist theory, patriarchy, and male hegemonic sexualization of women. I sat there, stymied. I eventually offered a comment to the husband informed by my feminist-informed intellect, partial to the oppressiveness of the sexual objectification being asked of his wife to leave her long curly hair as is: "It seems important to your wife as an empowered woman to make whatever choice she sees fit in styling her hair and not to be at the mercy of sexist notions of women being valued solely for their looks." Then I coughed up another response directed at the wife: "That said, your husband finds your long hair sexy and I suppose him finding you attractive in this way has some contribution to sexual intimacy between the two of you?" The fact that the second comment followed the first, and I added, "that said," revealed my male limbic brain was over-resonating with the husband's limbic brain.

Following much emotional processing of these concerns, the wife elected to leave her hair as is because it seemed awfully important to him and his sexuality. My male bias infiltrated. The verdict is still out on whether this was a check mark for perpetuating patriarchy and sexism, or one for bolstering the sex life of a couple heading into midlife, where any reasonable measures taken to stoke the fires of love were worthy of consideration. It's tempting to speculate how this exchange would have transpired with a woman therapist and the infiltration of female bias.

Thankfully, the present cultural zeitgeist leans toward dismantling toxic masculinity, holding men to account for entitled expressions of dominance, aggression, and sexual excess. In the midst of this dismantling, it's extraordinarily difficult to cobble together any map of what a non-toxic way of expressing male sexuality looks like. The thesis floated by neuroscientists, Ogi Ogas and Sai Gaddam, in their book *A Billion Wicked Thoughts: What the World's Largest Experiment Reveals About Human Desire*, is disconcerting. They argue the male brain is designed to gaze in sexually objectifying ways, whether it's trained on women in an opposite-sex context, or men in a same-sex context. Men's sensitivity to visual cues—sexually checking out body parts—is rooted to a look-and-lust subcortical brain reward system. They wrap up their findings as follows: "men's brains scrutinize the details of arousing visuals with the kind of concentration jewelers apply to the cut of a diamond."[38]

Just the other day, palpitating with a mixture of panic and disgust, a young adult male client confided in me that during a college counseling visit with a staff person who was his mother's age, he became transfixed on stealing a glance at her breasts and fantasizing about sex with her. As a liberally minded, progressively educated young man he was revolted by this, believing it was deeply disrespectful to his college counselor. I invited him to share more about his fears and desires around this; what it revealed about his emerging sexuality; his relationship with pornography: when it satiates his arousal or turns the corner into galvanizing it; and the key difference between indulging fantasies and acting on them. Telling him it might even be a form of respect that he *stole* glances when the counselor was not looking—rather than *lewdly stared*—and labored to disguise outward evidence of the erotic drama staged in his head seemed to disabuse him of the conviction that he was a vile human being, a would-be rapist.

These are conversations that men, especially in our bring-down-toxic-masculinity era, need to have. Since they are likely to be awkwardly had between male clients and female therapists, I suppose the onus is on female therapists to lean into such topics for multicultural competence reasons, inviting men to share their inner thoughts about what sexually turns them on and off, with due consideration, in couples therapy, to their female mate listening on. It can be shaming to female mates to hear their man prefers they be slimmer, keep their hair dyed and long, or wear clothing that accentuates their physical attractiveness. It's also potentially shaming to men who might secretly need these steps to maximize their sexual attraction to a mate they love, only to be denied airtime in therapy to discuss it. What a Gordian knot! This is the stuff of meaty couples therapy that differentiates the mere competent therapist from the skilled one, male or female.

Loving well as an existential imperative

An encouraging phenomenon occurred during the Covid-19 pandemic. Marriages got better. A large-scale survey out of Brigham Young University discovered that the share of spouses reporting their marriage to be in trouble dropped from 40 percent in 2019 to 29 percent in 2020. Among spouses age eighteen to fifty-five, 58 percent indicated that the pandemic made them appreciate their spouse more, and 51 percent reported their commitment to marriage had deepened.[39] I have a theory about this. It pertains to death anxiety. Confronted with the prospect of losing a spouse, legions of people reached inwards and accessed their most loving self. Instead of bickering over trying to find toilet paper, making and wearing masks, and getting vaccinated, they cooperated. Keen awareness that your beloved can be stolen away due to an illness or accident lends urgency and immediacy to the desire to be a more attentive, decent partner. So too is the nagging realization that death comes to us all and we only have a finite amount of time to get it right. These aren't morbid thoughts. They're existential epiphanies that lessen the chance we will have chilling deathbed regrets.

It's ironic that a recent Merrill Lynch Wealth Management/Age Wave study revealed that it's not the accumulation of wealth and career success that adults fifty-five and older want to be remembered for the most (5 percent and 11 percent, respectively), but "the memories I've shared with loved ones" (70 percent) and "the quality of my marriage/ partnership" (41 percent).[40] Australian motivational speaker Matthew Kelly interviewed a group of hospice workers to document people's deathbed regrets and, not surprisingly, among the most common were: "I wished I had loved more," "I wish I had spent more time with the people I love," and "I wish I hadn't spent so much time working."[41]

Conveying this existential well-spring of motivation to do love better during couples therapy periodically requires stepping into the role of wise counselor. Not in an off-putting, self-important, preachy way. At times, in a breezy, droll, fellow-life-sojourner manner:

> Fast forward to your deathbed. Are you really going to be wishing you had taken fewer vacations, stacked up more billable hours, or pushed more product? That you won more arguments with your wife? Or die happier glad you listened more attentively across the breakfast table, humbled yourself and took more ownership of your part in arguments, did your fair share to help out at home and with the kids, strove to not sweat the small stuff, with your wife?

At other times, with more heartfelt self-disclosure and gravitas:

> At the end of the day, what really matters the most? I don't know about you, but I don't want my wife to die with me left feeling I could have been kinder, more appreciative, more affectionate,

less grumpy, traveled more and created joyful memories. I want to take solace from the fact that I strove to make her life a happier one.

On a different topic, spouses who are parents can draw motivation to work on their marriage from the realization that they have an opportunity to break intergeneration patterns of dysfunctional relationships and set their kids up for a brighter future in the world of romance and love. Paul Amato at Pennsylvania State University conducted a novel study looking at intergenerational legacies and found that when parents get mired in the following, down the road their offspring follow suit: jealousy, being domineering, becoming angry and critical too easily, being moody, and giving a spouse "the silent treatment."[42] A common shibboleth used by struggling spouses to goad recommitment to their marriage is "staying together for the kids." The problem is this often functions as a moral prescription, valorizing self-denial.

A flourishing, self-respecting legacy to hand down is one where spouses fully commit to keeping excessive anger in check, communicating more respectfully, conveying mutual appreciation, and seeing the humor in things. These more virtuous ways of relating can be motivated out of a sense of owing it, not just to yourself and each other, but to your offspring to be more adept at love. Therapists can raise spouses' consciousness of this:

> You know you have an opportunity to gift your children better conflict resolution skills for use with their partners down the road if you can commit to modeling for them more respectful ways of handling conflict.

Finally, in my experience, couples warm quickly to the idea that they have it within their power to avoid reinjuring each other similar to childhood injuries at the hands of caregivers. Desiring to gift each other in this way acts as a motivator to be mutually mindful of and avoid replicating old familiar hurts. Therapy becomes a forum for uncovering and identifying each other's "triggers" or sore spots: broken promises; financial irresponsibility; dismissiveness of personal achievements; empty praise; overprotectiveness; being ignored; being criticized; being raged at; being talked at; being talked over. Spouses then commit as best they can to steering clear of repeating these behaviors.

This is a labor of love. Attempting, where possible, to intentionally correct for childhood injuries is also a labor of love: keeping promises; being financially responsible; celebrating personal achievements; offering genuine, targeted praise; being attentive; talking *with*, not at or over; using respectful, measured language when angry. Of course, this is predicated on the idea that the solution to *getting* the love you've always wanted is to *give* the love your partner's always wanted—to strive for flourishing love.

Notes

Introduction

1. See Gregory A. Smith, "About three-in-ten U.S. adults are now religiously unaffiliated," *Pew Research Center*, December 14, 2021, www.pewresearch.org/religion/2021/12/14/about-three-in-ten-u-s-adults-are-now-religiously-unaffiliated; see Harriet Sherwood, "UK secularism is on the rise as more than half say they have no religion," *The Guardian*, July 10, 2019, www.theguardian.com/world/2019/jul/11/uk-secularism-on-rise-as-more-than-half-say-they-have-no-religion

2. See Damamja Cikaric, "33 LGBTQ statistics for the community and its allies in 2022," *MedAlertHelp.com*, July 4, 2021, https://medalerthelp.org/blog/lgbt-statistics

3. Breanne Fahs and Eric Swank, "Pray the gay will stay? Church shopping and religious gatekeeping around homosexuality in an audit study of Christian church officials," *Psychology of Sexual Orientation and Gender Diversity*, 8(1) (2021): 106–118.

4. Scott Hahn, *The First Society* (Steubenville, Ohio: Emmaus Road Publishing, 2018), 124.

5. Madeleine Carlisle and Julia Zorthian, "Clarence Thomas signals same-sex marriage and contraception rights at risk after overturning

Roe vs. Wade," *Time*, June 24, 2022, https://time.com/6191044/clarence-thomas-same-sex-marriage-contraception-abortion

6.   See Daniel A. Cox, "Emerging trends and enduring patterns in American family life," *AmericanSurveyCenter.Org*, February 9, 2022, www.americansurveycenter.org/research/emerging-trends-and-enduring-patterns-in-american-family-life

7.   See Robert H. Shmerling, "The health advantages of marriage," *Harvard Health Publishing*, November 30, 2016, www.health.harvard.edu/blog/the-health-advantages-of-marriage-2016113010667

8.   Elizabeth Lawrence et al., "Marital happiness, marital status, health, and longevity," *Journal of Happiness Studies: An Interdisciplinary Forum on Subjective Well-Being*, *20*(5) (2019): 1539–1561.

9.   Shawn Grover and John F. Helliwell, "How's life at home? New evidence on marriage and the set point for happiness," *Journal of Happiness Studies*, *20* (2019): 373–390.

Chapter 1
Aspiring to flourishing love

1.   Judge Ben B. Lindsey and Wainright Evans, *Companionate Marriage* (New York: Boni & Liveright, 1927).

2.   Mark Twain, *AZQuotes.com*, www.azquotes.com/quote/880035

3.   Robert Solomon, *About Love* (Indianapolis, Indiana: Hackett, 2006), 101.

4.   Alain De Botton, *The Course of Love* (New York: Simon & Schuster, 2016), 7.

5.   Michael P. Johnson, "The tripartite nature of married commitment: Personal, moral, and structural reasons to stay married," *Journal of Marriage and Family*, *61*(1) (1999): 160–177.

6.   Gary Thomas, *Sacred Marriage* (Grand Rapids, Michigan: Zondervan, 2015).

7.   Ibid., 128.

8.   Judge Ben B. Lindsey and Wainright Evans, *Companionate Marriage* (New York: Boni & Liveright, 1927), 346.

9.   Barbara "Cutie" Cooper, Kim Cooper, and Chinta Cooper, *Fall in Love for Life* (San Francisco: Chronicle Books, 2012).

10.   Ibid., 21.

11.   Ivan Boszormenyi-Nagy and Geraldine M. Spark, *Invisible Loyalties* (New York: Brunner/Mazel, 1973).

12. Mike W. Martin, *Happiness and the Good Life* (New York: Oxford University Press, 2012), 120.

13. Greg M. Epstein, *Good Without God: What a Billion Nonreligious People Do Believe* (New York: HarperCollins, 2010), 115.

14. Barbara "Cutie" Cooper, Kim Cooper, and Chinta Cooper, *Fall in Love for Life* (San Francisco: Chronicle Books, 2012), 56.

15. Greg Eisenberg, *Letting Go Is All We Have to Hold Onto* (Louisville, Colorado, Curved-Space Comedy, 2018), 146.

16. "The 12 required attributes of marital love," *BiblicalGenderRoles. com*, June 20, 2014, https://biblicalgenderroles.com/2014/06/20/the-12-required-attributes-of-marital-love

17. Heather Havrilesky, "A spouse is a blessing and a curse," *The New York Times*, December 26, 2021, 4.

18. Christopher Hitchens, *God is Not Great* (New York: Twelve Books, 2009), 6.

19. Martin Hagglund, *This Life: Secular Faith and Spiritual Freedom* (New York: Anchor Books, 2019), 107.

20. Carlo Strenger, "Paring down life to the essentials: An Epicurean psychodynamics of midlife change," *Psychoanalytic Psychology*, *26*(3) (2009): 246–258.

21. Ernest Becker, *The Denial of Death* (New York: Free Press, 1997), 80.

22. William B. Irvine, *A Guide to the Good Life* (New York: Oxford University Press, 2009), 67.

23. See John Gottman and Nan Silver, *What Makes Love Last* (New York: Simon & Schuster, 2012), 116.

24. Greg Eisenberg, *Letting Go Is All We Have to Hold Onto* (Louisville, Colorado, Curved-Space Comedy, 2018), 176.

25. See Elaine Hatfield and Richard L. Rapson, "Equity theory in close relationships," in Paul A. M. Van Lange, Arie W. Kruglanski, and E. Tory Higgins (Eds.), *Handbook of Theories of Social Psychology* (London: Glyph International, 2011), 200–217.

26. Dennis J. Preato, "Egalitarian marriages prove happier than hierarchical marriages," 2004, http://empowerinternational.org/wp-content/uploads/Egalitarian-Marriages-Prove-Happier-than-Hierarchical-Marriages.pdf

27. Nathan D. Leonhardt et al., "Longitudinal influence of shared marital power on marital quality and attachment security," *Journal of Family Psychology*, *34*(1) (2019): 9.

28. Samuel L. Perry and Andrew L. Whitehead, "For better or for worse? Gender ideology, religious commitment, and relationship quality," *Journal for the Scientific Study of Religion*, *55*(4) (2016): 737–755.

29. Robert E. Goodin, *On Settling* (Princeton, NJ, Princeton University Press, 2012), 40.

30. Quoted in Maria Popova, "Simone Weil on attention and grace," *The Marginalian*, www.themarginalian.org/2015/08/19/simone-weil-attention-gravity-and-grace

31. Charles Derber, *The Pursuit of Attention* (New York: Oxford University Press, 2000).

32. R. B. Zajonc et al., "Convergence in the physical appearance of spouses," *Motivation and Emotion*, *11*(4) (1987): 335–346.

33. K. Daniel O' Leary et al., "Is long-term love more than a rare phenomenon? If so, what are its correlates?" *Social Psychological and Personality Science*, *3*(2) (2012): 241–249.

34. Quoted in Esther Perel, *Mating in Captivity* (New York: Harper, 2007), 3.

35. Karen V. Kukil (Ed.), *The Unabridged Journal of Sylvia Plath* (New York: Anchor, 2000).

36. Chrisanna Northrup, Pepper Schwartz, and James Witte, *The Normal Bar* (New York: Harmony Books, 2013), 61.

37. Dean M. Busby, Veronica Hanna-Walker, and Chelmon E. Leavitt, "A kiss is not a kiss: Kissing frequency, sexual quality, attachment, and sexual and relationship satisfaction, sexual and relationship therapy," *Sexual and Relationship Therapy*, published online 2020, 15, www.tandfonline.com/doi/full/10.1080/14681994.2020.1717460

38. Chip Walter, "Affairs of the lips: Why we kiss," *Scientific American*, January 31, 2008, www.scientificamerican.com/article/affairs-of-the-lips-why-we-kiss

39. Stephen B. Levine, *Demystifying Love* (New York: Routledge, 2007), 8.

Chapter 2
Surviving domesticity

1. Quoted in John Kenney, "Time with family," *The New Yorker*, April 4, 2022.

2. Blake Harper, "New survey reveals most dads wish they were spending more time with their kids," *Yahoo!Life*, January 8, 2018, www.yahoo.com/lifestyle/survey-reveals-most-dads-wish-164905644.html.

3. Kenney, ibid., 32.

4. Ray Romano, *Goodreads.com*, www.goodreads.com/quotes/63411

5. Kittie Frantz, *Goodreads.com*, www.goodreads.com/quotes/226587-remember-you- are-not-managing-an-inconvenience-you-are-raising

6. Quoted in "Adding more sunlight to our evenings is way overdue," *Los Angeles Times*, March 17, 2022.

7. Quoted in Eric Boehm, "Kids aren't rushing to get their driver's licenses—and that's OK!" *Reason.com*, June, 2019, https://d2eehagpk5 cl65.cloudfront.net/img/c1200x675-w1200-q80/uploads/2019/06/topicslifestyle.jpg.webp

8. Quoted in "How much do parents spend on their kids' extracurricular activities?" *Fox Business.com*, May 4, 2019, www.foxbusiness.com/how-much-do-parents-spend-on-their-kids-extracurricular-activities

9. Quoted in "Stress in America," *American Psychological Association*, March 11, 2022, www.apa.org/news/press/releases/stress/2022/march-2022-survival-mode

10. Colleen McClain, "How parents' views of their kids' screen time, social media use changed during Covid-19," *Pew Research Center*, April 28, 2022, www.pewresearch.org/fact-tank/2022/04/28/how-parents-views-of-their-kids-screen-time-social-media-use-changed-during-covid-19

11. Quoted in "Children and parents: Media use and attitudes 2022," www.ofcom.org.uk/__data/assets/pdf_file/0024/234609/childrens-media-use-and-attitudes-report-2022.pdf

12. Quoted in Clair Cain Miller, "Nearly half of men say they do most of the home schooling. 3 percent of women agree," *New York Times*, May 6, 2020, www.nytimes.com/2020/05/06/upshot/pandemic-chores-homeschooling-gender.html

13. Michael Youssef, "It does not take a village to raise a child," *The Christian Post*, March 14, 2021, www.christianpost.com/voices/it-does-not-take-a-village-to-raise-a-child.html

14. Ruth Igielnik, "Many working parents with young children say finding backup care would be very difficult," *Pew Research Center*, February 23, 2022, www.pewresearch.org/fact-tank/2022/02/23/many-working-parents-with-young-children-say-finding-backup-care-would-be-very-difficult

15. Quoted in David Brooks, "The nuclear family was a mistake," *The Atlantic*, March 2020.

16. Simon de Beauvoir, *The Second Sex* (New York: Vintage, 2011), 89.

17. Erma Bombeck, *Goodreads.com*, www.goodreads.com/quotes/454262-my-theory-on-housework-is-if-the-item-doesn-t-multiply

18. Orly Bareket et al., "Need some help honey? Dependency-oriented helping relations between women and men in the domestic sphere," *Journal of Personality and Social Psychology*, *120*(5) (2021): 1175–1203.

19. "National parent survey overview and key insights," Zero to Three, June 6, 2016, www.zerotothree.org/resources/1424-national-parent-survey-overview-and-key-insights

20. Kristen K. Sweeny, Abbie E. Goldberg, and Randi L. Garcia, "Not a 'mom thing': Predictors of gatekeeping in same-sex and heterosexual parent families," *Journal of Family Psychology*, *31*(5) (2017): 521–531.

21. Amanda Barroso, "For American couples, gender gaps in sharing household responsibilities persist amid pandemic," *Pew Research Center*, January 25, 2021, www.pewresearch.org/fact-tank/2021/01/25/for-american-couples-gender-gaps-in-sharing-household-responsibilities-persist-amid-pandemic

22. See Joan C. Williams, "Moms are losing to Covid cop-outs," *Los Angeles Times*, February 7, 2021.

23. Matthew D. Johnson, Nancy L. Galambos, and Jared R. Anderson, "Skip the dishes? Not so fast! Sex and housework revisited," *Journal of Family Psychology*, *30*(2) (2016): 203–213.

24. Sayaka Kawamura and Susan L. Brown, "Mattering and wives' perceived fairness of the division of household labor," *Social Science Research*, *39*(6) (2010): 976–986.

25. Quoted in Karl Pillemer, *30 Lessons for Loving* (New York: Avery, 2015), 139–143.

26. Hazel Barnes, *The Story I Tell Myself* (Chicago, IL: University of Chicago Press, 1998), 273.

27. "Ringspo 2021 engagement ring survey," *Ringspo.com*, www.ringspo.com/engagement-ring-survey

28. Carl Smith, "Average cost of a wedding 2022," *Weddingstats.org*, www.weddingstats.org/average-cost-of-a-wedding

29. Kim Forrest, "This was the average cost of a wedding in 2021," *The Knot*, February 15, 2022, www.theknot.com/content/average-wedding-cost

30. Andrew M. Francis and Hugo M. Mialon, "'A diamond is forever' and other fairy tales: The relationship between wedding expenses and marriage duration," *Economic Inquiry*, *53*(4) (2015): 1919–1930.

31.   Jeffrey Dew, "The association between consumer debt and the likelihood of divorce," *Journal of Family and Economic Issues*, *32*(4) (2011): 554–565.

32.   See John McBride, "Materialism in marriage linked to devaluation of marriage: Study," *Physorg*, February 13, 2018, https://phys.org/news/2018-02-materialism-marriage-linked-devaluation.html

33.   Erich Fromm, *To Have, or To Be?* (New York: Harper & Row, 1976), 104.

34.   Paul L. Wachtel, *The Poverty of Affluence* (Santa Cruz, CA: New Society Publishers, 1989), 39.

35.   See Allie Jones, "The first year has a familiar ring to it," *The New York Times*, August 2, 2020.

36.   Joe J. Gladstone, Emily N. Garbinsky, and Cassie Mogilner, "Pooling finances and relationship satisfaction," *Journal of Personality and Social Psychology*, advance online publication, https://doi.org/10.1037/pspi0000388

37.   Fred van Raaij, Gerrit Antonides, and Manon de Groot, "The benefits of joint and separate financial management of couples," *Journal of Economic Psychology*, *80* (2020): 1–11.

38.   Linda Skogrand et al., "Financial management practices of couples with great marriages," *Journal of Family and Economic Issues*, *32*(1) (2011): 27–35.

39.   Quoted in Wendy M. Troxel, "It's more than sex: Exploring the dyadic nature of sleep and implications for health," *Psychosomatic Medicine*, *72*(6) (2010): 578.

40.   "Americans are hungrier for sleep than sex," *Bettersleep.org*, April 9, 2017, https://bettersleep.org/research/survey-americans-crave-sleep-more-than-sex

41.   Henning Johannes Drews and Annika Drews, "Couple relationships are associated with increased REM sleep—a proof-of-concept analysis of a large dataset using ambulatory polysomnography," *Frontiers in Psychiatry*, *12* (2021): 1–9.

42.   See Christopher Bergland, "Rapid eye movement sleep may have life-preserving benefits," *Psychology Today*, July 8, 2020, www.psychologytoday.com/us/blog/the-athletes-way/202007/rapid-eye-movement-sleep-may-have-life-preserving-benefits

43.   Heather E. Gunn et al., "Sleep-wake concordance in couples is inversely associated with cardiovascular disease risk markers," *Sleep*, *40*(1) (2017): 40.

44. See "Couples that spend the night in the same bed show increased REM sleep and synchronization of sleep architecture," *Frontiers*, June 25, 2020, https://medicalxpress.com/news/2020-06-couples-night-bed-rem-synchronization.html

45. Kneginja Richter et al., "Two in a bed: The influence of couple sleeping and chronotypes on relationship and sleep. An overview," *Chronobiology International*, *33*(10) (2016): 1464–1472.

46. Soomi Lee et al., "Covariation in couples' nightly sleep and gender differences," *Sleep Health*, *4*(2) (2018): 201–208.

47. Terry Pratchett, *Quotefancy.com*, https://quotefancy.com

48. See Mirjana Dobric, "48 surprising sleep statistics & facts to know in 2022," *Medalerthelp.com*, April 19, 2021, https://medalerthelp.org/blog/sleep-statistics

49. Wendy Troxel, *Sharing the Covers* (New York: Hachette Books, 2021), 89.

50. Dana Zarhin, "'You have to do something': Snoring, sleep interembodiment and the emergence of agency," *British Journal of Sociology*, *71*(5) (2020): 1000–1015.

51. Rosalind Cartwright, "Sleeping together: A pilot study of the effects of shared sleeping on adherence to CPAP treatment in obstructive sleep apnea," *Journal of Clinical Sleep Medicine*, *4*(2) (2008): 123–127.

52. Heenam Yoon et al., "Human heart rhythms synchronize while co-sleeping," *Frontiers in Physiotherapy*, *10* (2019): 1–16.

53. Martha Cliff, "Three quarters of couples go to bed at different times due to heavy workloads, hectic social lives and surfing the web (and a third admit it causes arguments)," *Daily Mail*, June 2015, www.dailymail.co.uk/femail/article-3105508/Three-quarters-couples-bed-different-times-heavy-workloads-hectic-social-lives-surfing-web.html

54. Elizabeth Bernstein, "Don't let lack of sleep ruin your relationship," *Wall Street Journal*, March 23, 2021.

55. Troxel, ibid., 92.

56. Bonnie Jacob, "Mommy brain and the mommy mathematician," *Journal of Humanistic Mathematics*, *8*(2) (2018): 223–238.

57. "Surprising statistics that'll make you appreciate Mom," *Personal Creations*, April 27, 2017, www.personalcreations.com/blog/new-mother-statistics

58. Quoted in *BarryPopnik.com*, www.barrypopik.com/index.php/new_york_city/entry/a_mother_is_a_person_who_seeing

59. Sandra Steingraber, *Having Faith: An Ecologist's Journey to Motherhood* (Cambridge, MA: Perseus, 2001), 215.

60. Emma Chapman and Peter Gubi, "An exploration of the ways in which feelings of 'maternal ambivalence' affect some women," *Crisis and Loss* (2019), https://journals.sagepub.com/doi/10.1177/1054137319870289

61. Diana Diamond, Sidney J. Blatt, and Joseph Lichtenberg, *Attachment and Sexuality* (New York: The Analytic Press, 2007), 39.

62. Matthew D. Johnson, *Great Myths of Intimate Relationships: Dating, Sex, and Marriage* (New Jersey: Wiley-Blackwell, 2016), 122.

63. Ibid., 123.

64. Matthew D. Johnson, "Have children? Here's how kids ruin your romantic relationship," *The Conversation*, May 5, 2016, https://theconversation.com/have-children-heres-how-kids-ruin-your-romantic-relationship-57944

65. Joe Pinsker, "'Intensive' parenting is now the new norm in America," *The Atlantic*, January 16, 2019, www.theatlantic.com/family/archive/2019/01/intensive-helicopter-parenting-inequality/580528

66. Daniel J. van Ingen et al., "Helicopter parenting: The effect of an overbearing caregiving style on peer attachment and self-self-efficacy," *Journal of College Counseling*, *18* (2015): 7–20.

67. Peter Fraenkel, *Sync Your Relationship: Save Your Marriage* (New York: St. Martin's Press, 2011), 233.

68. Andrea Fowler, "This is how many date nights you need for a successful marriage," *The Knot*, April 12, 2019, www.theknot.com/content/successful-marriage-date-night-study?

69. Roy F. Baumeister, *Meanings of Life* (New York: Guilford Press, 1992).

Chapter 3
Doing conflict well

1. John M. Gottman and Joan DeClaire, *The Relationship Cure* (New York: Harmony, 2001), 207.

2. National Survey of Marital Strengths, www.prepare-enrich.com/pe_main_site_content/pdf/research/national_survey.pdf

3. Orna Cohen, Yael Geron, and Alva Farchi, "A typology of marital quality of enduring marriages in Israel," *Journal of Family Issues*, *31*(6) (2010): 727–747.

4. Quoted in Sara Eckel, "Value," *Psychology Today*, 48–54.

5. Graham D. Bodie et al., "The role of 'active listening' in informal helping conversations: Impact on perceptions of listener helpfulness, sensitivity, and supportiveness and discloser emotional improvement," *Western Journal of Communication*, *79*(2) (2015): 151–173.

6. Ibid.

7. Quoted in "How happy couples argue: Focus on solvable issues first," *Science Daily*, September 16, 2019, 3.

8. Mike M. Martin, *Happiness and the Good Life* (New York: Oxford University Press, 2012), 120.

9. Jon Richardson, *On Talking Over the Television*, Michael McIntyre's Big Show, December 28, 2020.

10. Deborah Tannen, *You Just Don't Understand: Women and Men in Conversation* (New York: Ballantine Books, 1990).

11. Ibid., 215.

12. Val Daigen and John G. Holmes, "Don't interrupt! A good rule for marriage?" *Personal Relationships*, *7*(2) (2000): 185–201.

13. Gary Chapman, *The Five Love Languages* (Chicago, IL: Northfield Press, 1992).

14. Andrew M. Bland and Kand S. McQueen, "The distribution of Chapman's love languages in couples: An exploratory cluster analysis," *Couple and Family Psychology: Research and Practice*, *7*(2) (2018): 103–126.

15. www.merriam-webster.com/words-at-play/mansplaining-definition-history

16. Jamie Lutz, "6 witty comebacks to mansplaining," *Bustle*, November 15, 2015, www.bustle.com/articles/121583-6-witty-comebacks-to-mansplaining-because-you-dont-have-to-take-it

17. John L. Locke, *Duels and Duets: Why Men and Women Talk so Differently* (New York: Cambridge University Press, 2011).

18. Tannen, *You Just Don't Understand: Women and Men in Conversation*, 122.

19. Lisa Leit, "Conversational narcissism in marriage: Effects on partner mental health and marital quality over the transition to parenthood," May 2008, https://repositories.lib.utexas.edu/handle/2152/3915?show=full

20. Charles Derber, *The Pursuit of Attention* (New York: Oxford University Press, 1979).

21. Christopher Lasch, *The Culture of Narcissism* (New York: Norton & Company, 1979).

22. www.art.com/products/p15063209672-sa-i6844118/david-sipress-well-if-it-doesn-t-matter-who-s-right-and-who-s-wrong-why-don-t-i-be-ri-new-yorker-cartoon

23. Helen Lewis, *Shame and Guilt in Neurosis* (New York: International Universities Press, 1971).

24. Neill Korobov, "A discursive psychological approach to deflection in romantic couples' everyday arguments," *Qualitative Psychology*, http://dx.doi.org/10.1037/qup0000161

25. Thomas J. Scheff and Suzanne M. Retzinger, *Emotions and Violence: Shame and Rage in Destructive Conflicts* (Lexington, MA: Lexington Books, 1991).

26. Daniel Shaw, *Traumatic Narcissism* (New York: Routledge, 2014), 6.

27. John M. Gottman and Julie Schwartz Gottman, *The Science of Couples and Family Therapy* (New York: Norton, 2018), 93.

28. Gwendoline Riley, *First Love* (London: Melville House, 2017), 6–7.

29. Harriet Lerner, *Why Won't You Apologize?* (New York: Gallery Books, 2017), 66.

30. Emmy van Deurzen and Martin Adams, *Skills in Existential Counseling and Psychotherapy* (Los Angeles, CA: Sage, 2011), 64.

31. Gary Noesner, *Moving From Conflict to Cooperation*, The Welcome Conference, June 11, 2017, https://youtu.be/S76abMxQWXg

32. Quoted in Jancee Dunn, "Listen to your family members. No, really listen," *New York Times*, October 25, 2020.

33. Ibid., 3.

34. Gary Noesner, "Negotiating with terrorists," *The Negotiator Magazine*, April 2013, 1.

35. Alan E. Fruzzetti, *The High-Conflict Couple* (Oakland, CA: New Harbinger Publications, 2006), 118.

36. Benjamin H. Seider et al., "We can work it out: Age differences in relational pronouns, physiology, and behavior in marital conflict," *Psychology and Aging*, *24*(3) (2009): 604–613.

37. Enrico Gnaulati, "Fostering mirthful acceptance in couples therapy: An existential viewpoint," *Existential Analysis*, *31*(2) (2020): 368–381.

38. Quoted in *New York Times*, September 20, 2020.

39. Quoted in Rachel E. Greenspan, "'The only person I ever loved.' Inside Ruth Bader Ginsburg's history-shaping marriage," *TIME*, September 19, 2020.

40. Ezra Taft Benson, http://ldsminds.com

41. Herant Katchadourian, *Guilt: The Bite of Conscience* (Standford, CA: Stanford University Press, 2010), 72.

42. Lerner, *Why Won't You Apologize*, 29.

43. Frank D. Fincham et al., "Forgiveness in marriage: Current status and future direction," *Family Relations*, *55* (2006): 416.

44. Frank D. Fincham, "The kiss of the porcupines: From attributing responsibility to forgiving," *Personal Relationships*, *7* (2000): 9.

45. Everett L. Worthington, "Marriage counseling: A Christian approach," *Journal of Psychology and Christianity*, *13*(2) (1994): 167.

46. John M. Gottman and Julie Schwartz Gottman, *The Science of Couples and Family Therapy* (New York: Norton, 2018).

47. Martin Buber, *I and Thou* (New York: Charles Scribner's Sons, 1970).

48. Quoted in Kenneth Kramer and Mechthild Gawlick, *Martin Buber's I and Thou: Practicing Living Dialogue* (New Jersey: Paulist Press, 2003), 85.

49. Quoted in Frank D. Fincham et al., "Forgiveness in marriage: Current status and future direction," *Family Relations*, *55* (2006): 415.

Chapter 4
Humor me

1. John Updike, *The Maples Stories* (New York: Alfred A. Knopf, 2009), 11.

2. "True love." YouTube video. Posted by "Google," June 30, 2020, www.youtube.com/watch?v=PJNliH-MknE&t=51s

3. "Every relationship is a dog." YouTube video. Posted by "Google," August 22, 2020, www.youtube.com/watch?v=o74zupDkFtl

4. "Deleting emails." YouTube video. Posted by "Google," August 2, 2020, www.youtube.com/watch?v=iiZtuR9bF_Q

5. "Mom's used to people." YouTube video. Posted by "Google," July 2, 2020, www.youtube.com/watch?v=pD0NYM-Bu-A

6. Vassilis Saroglou, Christelle Lacour, and Marie-Eve Demeure, "Bad humor, bad marriage: Humor styles in divorced and married couples," *Europe's Journal of Psychology*, *6*(3) (2010): 94–121.

7. Quoted in Jaleesa Baulkman, "The little things: The expression of gratitude, laughter help romantic relationships thrive," *Medical Daily*, February 24, 2016.

8. "Poll: 9 out of 10 would remarry spouse," CBS News, February 14, 2010, www.cbsnews.com/news/poll-9-out-of-10-would-remmary-spouse

9. Lorena Antonovici, "Sense of humor in romantic relationships and friendships," *New Approaches in Social and Humanistic Sciences*, *1*(3) (2018): 37–55.

10. Alice Verstaen et al., "Age-related changes in emotional behavior: Evidence from a 13-year longtitudinal study of long-term married couples," *Emotion*, *20*(2) (2018): 149–163.

11. Quoted in "As married couples age, humor replaces bickering," *Science Daily*, December 3, 2018, www.sciencedaily.com/releases/2018/12/181203185353.htm

12. "Sinbad on marriage." YouTube video. Posted by "Google," May 10, 2019, www.youtube.com/watch?v=xZPCDGH70Ls

13. Liana Hone et al., "Sex differences in preference for humor: A replication, modification and extension," *Evolutionary Psychology*, *13* (2015): 167–181.

14. Quoted in Olga Khazan, "Plight of the funny female," *The Atlantic*, November 19, 2015.

15. Gordon G. Gallup et al., "Do orgasms give women feedback about male choice?" *Evolutionary Psychology*, *12*(5) (2014): 958–978.

16. John M. Gottman et al., "Observing gay, lesbian and heterosexual couples' relationships: A mathematical modeling of conflict interaction," *Journal of Homosexuality*, *45*(1) (2003): 65–90.

17. *Uncle Frank*, dir. Alan Ball (2020; North Carolina, USA: Amazon Studios and Miramax Films).

18. Deborah L. Cabaniss, "Good relationships take hard work," *HuffPost*, March 3, 2017, www.huffpost.com/entry/good-relationships-take-hard-work_b_9358456

19. Quoted in David Brooks, "The nuclear family was a mistake," *The Atlantic*, March 2020.

20. Oscar Wilde, *The Nihilists* (South Carolina: CreateSpace Publishing, 2015), 34.

21. Quoted in Bradley Onishi, "What's behind the belief in a soulmate?" *Institute for Family Studies*, May 23, 2019.

22. Samuel Taylor Coleridge, "The Kiss," https://genius.com/Samuel-taylor-coleridge-the-kiss-annotated

23. Pamela Davenport, "Romantic but hardly romantic: Sarah Fricker's life as Coleridge's wife," *Wordsworth Grasmere*, July 29, 2017, https://wordsworth.org.uk/blog/2017/07/29/romantic-but-hardly-romantic-sarah-frickers-life-as-coleridges-wife

24. Ibid.

25. Ibid.

26. Quoted in Rosemary Ashton, *The Life of Samuel Taylor Coleridge* (Oxford, Blackwell, 1997), 203.

27. C. Raymond Knee, "Implicit theories of relationships: Assessment and prediction of romantic relationship initiation, coping, and longevity," *Journal of Personality and Social Psychology, 74*(2) (1998): 360–370.

28. Spike W. S. Lee and Norbert Schwarz, "Framing love: When it hurts to think we were made for each other," *Journal of Experimental Social Psychology, 54* (2014): 61–67.

29. Alain de Botton, "Why you will marry the wrong person," *The New York Times*, May 28, 2016.

30. Cited in "The Science of Soulmates," January 26, 2016, www.scienceof-people.com/soulmate

31. Quoted in Ana Mc Ginley, "Till death do us part," *Huffpost*, May 29, 2015, www.huffpost.com/entry/till-death-do-us-part_b_7466876

32. Quoted in Steven Pinker, *Enlightenment Now* (New York: Viking, 2018), 53.

33. United States Census Bureau, www.census.gov/data/tables/times-series/demo/families/marital.html

34. Wanda Sykes, "If marriage is a contract there should be a better warranty," YouTube video. Posted by "Google," February 15, 2019, www.youtube.com/watch?v=dSJoJcf0alvu

35. Tamar F. C. Fischer et al., "Friendly and antagonistic contact between former spouses after divorce: Patterns and determinants," *Journal of Family Issues, 26* (2005): 1131–1163.

36. Lara Foley and James Fraser, "A research note on post-dating relationships: The social embeddedness of redefining romantic couplings," *Sociological Perspectives, 41* (1998): 209–219.

37. Kimberly Truong, "What people really think about when they masturbate," *Refinery29*, May 9, 2017, www.refinery29.com/en-gb/2017/05/153673/masturbation-fantasies-research-statistics

38. David Buss et al., "The mate switching hypothesis," *Personality and Individual Differences, 104* (2017): 143–149.

39. *John Lyly Quotes*, www.notable-quotes.com/l/lyly-john.html

40. "First look at the thermostat wars suggests women may be losing these battles," *Science Daily*, November 2019, https://sciencedaily.com/releases/2019/11/191113153127.htm

41. Jo Craven McGinty, "Men vs. women: The thermostat battle," *The Wall Street Journal*, July 11, 2020.

42. "25 funny marriage jokes that describe married life perfectly," *Your Tango*, September 2, 2020, www.yourtango.com/2020336663/funny-marriage-jokes-describe-married-life-perfectly

43. John M. Gottman and Julie Schwartz Gottman, *The Science of Couples and Family Therapy* (New York: Norton, 2018).

44. *Night of the Cobra Woman*, dir. Andrew Meyer (1972; USA: New World Pictures).

45. Leslie Baxter, "Symbols of relationship identity in relationship cultures," *Journal of Social and Personal Relationships, 4* (1987): 266.

46. Carol J. S. Bruess and Judy C. Pearson, "Sweet pea and pussy cat: Examination of idiom use and marital satisfaction over the life cycle," *Journal of Social and Personal Relationships, 10* (1993): 609–615.

47. Daniela Puzzo, "Incredible lessons about customer service from movie clips," *Fonolo*, November 26, 2020, https://fonolo.com/blogs/2018/04/incredible-lessons-about-customer-service-from-movie-clips

48. Jennifer Coats, "Talk in play frame: More on laughter and intimacy," *Journal of Pragmatics, 39* (2007): 29–49.

49. Terry Eagleton, *Humour* (London: Yale University Press, 2019), 15.

50. *Goodreads.com*, www.goodreads.com/quotes/306386-jazz-washes-away-the-dust-of-of-everyday-life

51. Steve Allen, *Cosmopolitan*, February 1957.

52. Neal R. Norrick, *Conversational Joking* (Bloomington, Indiana, Indiana University Press, 1993), 6.

53. Tayari Jones, *An American Marriage* (Chapel Hill, NC: Algonquin Books, 2018), 103.

54. Gregg Eisenberg, *Letting Go is All We Have to Hold Onto* (Louisville, CO: Curved Space Comedy, 2018), 142.

55. Martin Hagglund, *This Life* (New York: Anchor Books, 2019), 44.

Chapter 5
Lust is a must

1.   John Armstrong, *Conditions of Love* (London: Norton, 2002), 8.

2.   Paul Taylor et al., "Generation gap in values, behaviours: As marriage and parenthood drift apart, public is concerned about social impact," *Pew Research Center*, www.pewresearch.org/wp-content/uploads/sites/3/2010/10/Marriage.pdf

3.   See David Masci, "Shared religious beliefs in marriage important to some, but not all, married Americans," *Factank*, October 27, 2016, www.pewresearch.org/fact-tank/2016/10/27/shared-religious-beliefs-in-marriage-important-to-some-but-not-all-married-americans

4.   See Ebony Bowden, "Farmers get it on more than any other profession: Study," *New York Post*, October 8, 2019, https://nypost.com/2019/10/08/farmers-get-it-on-more-than-any-other-profession-study

5.   See Christopher Ryan and Cacilda Jetha, *Sex at Dawn* (New York: Harper, 2010).

6.   Chrisanna Northrup, Pepper Schwartz, and James Witte, *The Normal Bar* (New York: Harmony, 2013), 178.

7.   Amy Muise et al., "Sexual frequency predicts greater well-being, but more is not always better," *Social Psychology and Personality Science*, 7 (2016): 295–302.

8.   See https://crucible4points.com

9.   See "The good and bad news about marriage in the time of Covid 19," September 22, 2020 www.aei.org/articles/the-good-and-bad-news-about-marriage-in-the-time-of-covid

10. See Kaye Wellings et al., "Changes in, and factors associated with, frequency of sex in Britain: Evidence from three national surveys of sexual attitudes and lifestyles (NATSAL)," *British Medical Journal*, 365 (2019): 1–9.

11. Pamela Rogers, "The health benefits of sex," *Healthline*, October 18, 2018, www.healthline.com/health/healthy-sex-health-benefits

12. Jerry Kennard, "Frequent ejaculation lowers prostate cancer risk," *VeryWellHealth*, January 29, 2020, www.verywellhealth.com/reduced-risk-prostate-cancer-with-regular-ejaculation-2328515

13. "Having less sex linked to early menopause," *Science Daily*, January 14, 2020.

14. See Joan Price, *Naked at Our Age* (Berkeley, CA: Seal Press, 2011).

15. NHS. NHS Sexual Health, www.nhs.uk/live-well/sexual-health/benefits-of-love-sex-relationships

16. George Davey Smith, Stephen Frankel, and John Yarnell, "Sex and death: Are they related. Findings from the Caerphilly cohor study," *British Medical Journal*, 315 (1997): 1641.

17. Howard S. Friedman, "Orgasms, health and longevity: Does sex promote health?" *Psychology Today*, February 12, 2011, www.psychologytoday.com/us/blog/secrets-longevity/201102/orgasms-health-and-longevity-does-sex-promote-health

18. Northrup et al., *The Normal Bar*, 218.

19. Ibid., 229.

20. Ibid., 28.

21. Ibid., 46.

22. Gajanan S. Bhat and Anuradha Shastry, "Time to orgasm in women in a monogamous stable heterosexual relationship," *The Journal of Sexual Medicine*, 17(4) (2020): 749–760.

23. See Alisa Hrustic, "This is how long sex actually lasts for most couples," *Men's Health*, September 15, 2017, www.menshealth.com/sex-women/a19535002/how-long-sex-actually-lasts-for-most-couples

24. See Sam Benson Smith, "This is exactly how long sex lasts for the average couple," *Yahoo!Life*, May 16, 2019, www.yahoo.com/lifestyle/exactly-long-sex-lasts-average-141434638.html

25. Environmental Protection Agency, "Save water and energy by showering better," www.epa.gov/sites/production/files/2017-02/documents/ws-ourwater-shower-better-learning-resource_0.pdf

26. Anita Smith, "Workers spend 14 minutes going to the toilet each day even if they don't need to," *Initial*, September 3, 2018, www.initial.co.uk/blog/workers-spend-14-minutes-going-to-toilet-each-day-even-if-they-dont-need-to-go

27. Coral Drake, "Walk your dog: How often, how long, how far?" *Devoted to Dog*, March 3, 2020, https://devotedtodog.com/how-often-should-you-walk-your-dog

28. Tim Sackett, "Anatomy of a workplace smoke break or should we call it recess?" March 11, 2013, www.tlnt.com/anatomy-of-a-workplace-smoke-break-or-should-we-call-it-recess

29. "How long does a pedicure take?" November 14, 2019, www.almond-nails.com/how-long-does-a-pedicure-take

30. "How long should my massage be?" https://elementsmassage.com/elm-grove/blog/how-long-should-my-massage-be

31. See www.adameve.com

32. Quoted in Jane M. Ussher, *The Psychology of the Female Body* (London: Routledge, 1989), 76.

33. See www.adameve.com

34. Liana S. E. Hone et al., "The sex premium is religiously motivated moral judgment," *Journal of Personality and Social Psychology*, online first publication May 28, 2020.

35. Wayland Young, *Eros Denied: Sex in Western Society* (New York: Grove Press, 1964), 174.

36. See https://infidelityrecoveryinstitute.com/religion-adultery

37. See www.catechism.cc/articles/QA.htm

38. Quoted in Robert J. Priest, "Missionary positions," *Current Anthropology*, *42*(1) (2001): 35.

39. Laurie Mintz, *Becoming Cliterate* (New York: Harper One, 2017), 203.

40. Ibid., 9.

41. William Volck et al., "Gynecological knowledge is low in college men and women," *Journal of Pediatric Gynecology*, *26*(3) (2013): 161–166.

42. Fr. Hugh Barbour, O. Praem, *Catholic Theology and Oral Pleasure*, www.catholic.com/qa/catholic-theology-and-oral-pleasure

43. See www.goodreads.com/quotes/310726-chastity-is-the-most-unnatural-of-the-sexual-perversions

44. Nathan D. Leonhardt, Dean M. Busby, and Brian J. Willoughby, "Sex guilt or sanctification? The indirect role of religiosity on sexual satisfaction," *Psychology of Religion and Spirituality*, *12*(2) (2019): 213–222.

45. Alanna Vaglanos, "This is how often women masturbate," *HuffPost*, December 6, 2017, www.huffpost.com/entry/women-masturbation-statistics-fivethirtyeight_n_5445530

46. Mintz, *Becoming Cliterate*, 106.

47. Mark Regnerus, Joseph Price, and David Gordon, "Masturbation and partnered sex: Substitutes or compliments?" *Archives of Sexual Behavior*, *46*(7) (2017): 2111–2121.

48. Sam Allberry, *Is God Anti-Gay* (UK: The Good Book Company, 2015), 11.

49.   Quoted in Christopher Ryan, *Civilized to Death* (New York: Avid Reader Press, 2019), 152.

50.   Mary E. Hunt, "Just good sex: Feminist Catholicism and human rights," In Patricia Beattie Jung, Mary E. Hunt, and Radhika Balakrishnan (Eds.), *Good Sex: Feminist Perspectives from the World's Religions* (New Brunswick, NJ: Rutgers University Press, 2005), 160.

51.   Elizabeth Boskey, "Spirituality and sexuality: When religious clients present for sex therapy," *Contemporary Sexuality* (May 2015): 1–6.

52.   Martha Schick, "How to be a sex-positive Christian," *The Salve*, October 7, 2019. https://medium.com/the-salve/how-to-be-a-sex-positive-christian-97c9fa01660b

53.   Christine E. Gudorf, *Body, Sex, and Pleasure* (Cleveland, OH: The Pilgrim Press, 1994), 139.

54.   Christel Manning and Phil Zuckerman, *Sex and Religion* (Belmont, CA: Wadsworth, 2005).

55.   Ali Ghandour, *Lust and Grace: Sex and Eroticism in the Works of Muslim Scholars* (USA: Ingram Spark, 2017), 27.

56.   Ibid., 38.

57.   Quoted in Hannah Sparks, "Pope Francis: Sex and eating are 'divine' pleasures sent by God," *New York Post*, September 10, 2020, https://nypost.com/2020/09/10/pope-francis-sex-and-eating-are-divine-pleasures-from-god

58.   See Debra W. Haffner, "Sexuality and scripture: What else does the Bible have to say?" *Reflections*, https://reflections.yale.edu/article/sex-and-church/sexuality-and-scripture-what-else-does-bible-have-say

59.   www.brainyquote.com/quotes/matt_groening_107792

60.   www.etymonline.com/word/libido

61.   Terri D. Fisher, "Sex on the brain, an examination of frequency of sexual of sexual cognitions as a function of gender, erotophilia, and social desirability," *Journal of Sex Research*, 29 (2012): 69–77.

62.   Rosemary Basson, "The female sexual response: A different model," *Journal of Sex and Marital Therapy*, 26(1) (2000): 51–65.

63.   James K. McNulty et al., "Sex-differentiated changes in sexual desire predict marital dissatisfaction," *Archives of Sexual Behavior*, 48 (2019): 2473–2489.

64. Gurit E. Birnbaum et al., "Intimately connected: The importance of partner responsiveness for experiencing sexual desire," *Journal of Personality and Social Psychology*, *111*(4) (2016): 542.

65. Lori A. Brotto, Julia R. Heiman, and Deborah L. Tolman, "Narratives of desire in mid-age women with and without arousal difficulties," *Journal of Sex Research*, *46*(5) (2009): 391.

66. Belinda Luscombe, *Marriage-ology* (New York: Spiegel & Grau, 2019), 177.

67. Michael Aaron, *Modern Sexuality* (New York: Rowman & Littlefield, 2016), 166.

68. David A. Frederick et al., "What keeps passion alive? Sexual satisfaction is associated with sexual communication, mood setting, sexual variety, oral sex, orgasm, and sex frequency in a national U.S. study," *Journal of Sex Research*, *54*(2) (2017): 186–201.

69. See John M. Grohol, "11 surprising facts about America's sexual behaviors," *Psych Central*, July 8, 2018.

70. Alessandra Graziottin, "Prevalence and evaluation of sexual health problems—HSDD in Europe," *The Journal of Sexual Medicine*, *4* (2007): 211–219.

71. Bob Berkowitz and Susan Yager-Berkowitz, *Why Men Stop Having Sex* (New York: Harper, 2009).

72. Muise et al., "Not in the mood? Men under- (not over-) perceive their partner's sexual desire in established intimate relationships," *Journal of Personality and Social Psychology*, *110*(5) (2016): 739.

73. Chrisanna Northrup et al., *The Normal Bar*, 127.

74. Margaret Wheeler Johnson, "Half of men say they would leave a partner who gained weight: Survey," *HuffPost*, December 6, 2017, www.huffpost.com/entry/men-leave-weight-gain_n_911143

75. "Do men really care about their weight?" *Motley Health*, www.motleyhealth.com/weight-loss/do-men-really-care-about-their-weight

76. WRNB Philly, "Poll: Do men prefer women with long hair over short hair?" https://wrnbhd2.com/121411/poll-do-men-prefer-woman-with-long-hair-over-short-hair

77. Jessica Benjamin, *Bonds of Love* (New York: Pantheon, 1988), 89.

78. Esther Perel, *Mating in Captivity* (New York: Harper, 2006), 43.

79. Amy Muise, "When and for whom is sex most beneficial? Sexual motivation in romantic relationships," *Canadian Psychology*, *58*(1) (2017): 69.

80. Uzma Rehman et al., "Marital satisfaction and communication behaviors during sexual and nonsexual conflict discussions in newlywed couples: A pilot study," *Journal of Sex and Marital Therapy*, 37(2) (2011): 94–103.

81. Rosemary Basson, "The female sexual response: A different model," *Journal of Sex and Marital Therapy*, 26 (2000): 51–65.

82. Michele Weiner-Davis, *The Sex Starved Marriage*, 10.

83. Matthew D. Johnson, Nancy L. Galambos, and Jared R. Anderson, "Skip the dishes? Not so fast! Sex and housework revisited," *Journal of Family Psychology*, 30(2) (2016): 203–213.

84. Chrisanna Northrup et al., *The Normal Bar*, 73.

85. Peggy J. Kleinplatz, "Seeking therapist collaborators: 'Treating' couples with low desire/frequency by creating optimal erotic intimacy," *Society for Humanistic Psychology*, March 7, 2019, www.apadivisions.org/division-32/news-events/therapist-collaborators

86. Sue Johnson, *Hold Me Tight* (New York: Little, Brown Spark, 2008), 193.

87. Esther Perel, *Mating in Captivity*.

88. Pablo Neruda, *Sonnet XI*, www.pablonerudapoems.com/sonnet-xi

89. Michel Faudet, *Dirty Pretty Things* (Kansas City, MI: Andrew McMeel Publishing, 2016).

90. Molly Fisk, *Late Afternoon*, www.beautiful-love-quotes.com/wild-sensual-poems.html

91. Chrisanna Northrup, *The Normal Bar*, 64.

92. Esther Perel, *Mating in Captivity*, 55.

93. Michael Aaron, *Modern Sexuality*, 135.

94. David Schnarch, *Passionate Marriage* (New York: Norton, 2009), 266.

95. Quoted in Sarah Hunter Murray, "Is sexual selfishness the key to erotic passion?" *Psychology Today*, March 2, 2018.

96. Quoted in Leon F. Seltzer, "Dominant or submissive? Paradox of power in sexual relations," *Psychology Today*, June 11, 2012.

97. Bernard Apfelbaum, "On the need for a new direction in sex therapy," In Peggy J. Kleinplatz (Ed.), *New Directions in Sex Therapy* (London: Routledge, 2012), 5.

98. See "The good, the bad, and the dirty: The iVillage 2013 married sex survey," *Today*, July 30, 2014, www.today.com/health/ivillage-2013-married-sex-survey-results-1D80245229

99. Peggy J. Kleinplatz et al., "Beyond sexual stereotypes: Revealing group similarities and differences in optimal sexuality," *Canadian Journal of Behavioral Science*, 45(2) (2013): 250–258.

Chapter 6
Wrangling with roving desires

1. "Survey says one-fifth of UK couples leave their wedding rings at home," *HuffPost*, January 30, 2014, www.huffpost.com/entry/not-wearing-wedding-rings_n_4691388

2. Janet W. Hardy and Dossie Easton, *The Ethical Slut* (Berkeley, CA: Ten Speed Press, 2017), 16.

3. John Armstrong, *Conditions of Love* (New York: Norton, 2002), 138.

4. Margo Mullinax et al., "Women's experience with feelings of attraction for someone outside their primary relationship," *Journal of Sex and Marital Therapy*, 42(5) (2016): 431–447.

5. John A. Banas et al., "Simmering on the back burner or playing with fire? Examining the consequences of back-burner digital communication among ex-Partners," *Cyberpsychology, Behavior, and Social Networking*, 24(7) (2021): 473–479.

6. See Chrisanna Northrup, Pepper Schwartz, and James Witte, *The Normal Bar* (New York: Harmony, 2013), 219.

7. See Ashley Madison, *Wikipedia*, https://en.wikipedia.org/wiki/Ashley_Madison

8. Quoted in Amber Brooks, "Ashley Madison surveys its users and reveals 7 surprising trends in the extramarital dating scene," *Dating-News.Com*, January 7, 2020, www.datingnews.com/apps-and-sites/ashley-madison-reveals-trends-in-extramarital-dating

9. See Victoria Taylor, "Evangelicals are the least faithful when it comes to spouses, survey says," *New York Daily News*, June 3, 2014, www.nydailynews.com/life-style/survey-reveals-faiths-unfaithful-article-1.1815733

10. Ibid.

11. Marie-Michele Boisvert et al., "Couples reports of relationship problems in a naturalistic therapy setting," *The Family Journal: Counseling and Therapy for Couples and Families*, September 28, 2011.

12. Peter Moore, "Young Americans are less wedded to monogamy than their elders," *YouGov.com*, October 3, 2016, https://today.yougov.com/topics/lifestyle/articles-reports/2016/10/03/young-americans-less-wedded-monogamy

13.   See Esther Perel, *The State of Affairs: Rethinking Infidelity* (New York: HarperCollins, 2017), 18.

14.   See Terri D. Conley et al., "A critical examination of popular assumptions about the benefits and outcomes of monogamous relationships," *Personality and Social Psychology Review,* (2012): 1–18.

15.   See Mark Regnerus, *Cheap Sex* (New York: Oxford University Press, 2017), 82.

16.   David M. Buss, *The Evolution of Desire* (New York: Basic Books, 2003), 127.

17.   Ibid.

18.   Jason S. Carroll et al., "The porn gap: Differences in men's and women's pornography patterns in couple relationships," *Journal of Couple and Relationship Therapy,* 16(2) (2017): 146–163.

19.   Amanda DeCadenet, "More women watch (and enjoy) porn than you ever realized: A Marie Claire study," *MarieClaire,* October 19, 2015.

20.   Lea Z. Singh, "Romance porn: More women are addicted than you think," *Crisis Magazine,* July 21, 2016, www.crisismagazine.com/2016/romance-porn-women-addicted-think

21.   See Monisha Rudhran, "10 (actually good) erotic romance books to read in 2021," *Elle Australia,* September 23, 2020, www.elle.com.au/culture/best-erotic-books-23563

22.   Donna Lynn Hope, *Goodreads.com,* www.goodreads.com/quotes/3176354-people-will-sometimes-find-themselves-attracted-to-others-that-s-just

23.   Charlene F. Belu and Lucia F. O'Sullivan, "Roving eyes: Predictors of crushes in ongoing romantic relationships and implications for relationship quality," *Journal of Relationships Research,* published online January 15, 2019.

24.   Quoted in "Ashley Madison's 'married dating' site grew to 70 million users in 2020," *Venturebeat.com,* https://venturebeat.com/2021/02/25/ashley-madison-married-dating-site-grew-to-70-million-users-in-2020

25.   See Eric W. Dolan, "New study indicates the behaviors of Ashley Madison users cluster together in three main categories," *The Daily Advent.com,* August 29, 2021, www.dailyadvent.com/news/d732868b55ba43b38646ec4d23d25441-New-study-indicates-the-behaviors-of-Ashley-Madison-users-cluster-together-into-three-main-categories

26. See Hara Estroff Marano and Shirley Glass, "Shattered vows," *Psychology Today*, July 1, 1998, www.psychologytoday.com/us/articles/199807/shattered-vows

27. "Is it weird that he likes to be bitten/squeeze/scratching during sex and foreplay?" *AskMen Reader*, www.askmen.com/answers/sex/1698010-is-it-weird-that-he-likes-to-be-bitten-squeezes-sc.html

28. Quoted in Orli Dahan, "Submission, pain, and pleasure: Considering an evolutionary hypothesis concerning sexual masochism," *Psychology of Consciousness: Theory, Research, and Practice*, 6(4) (2019): 397.

29. See "I wanna hold your hand," *Psychology Today*, July/August 2021, 6.

30. Menelaos Apostolou and Michalis Khalil, "Aggressive and humiliating sexual play: Occurrence rates and discordance between the sexes," *Archives of Sexual Behavior*, 48(7) (2019): 2187–2200.

31. Joan Rivers, *brainyquotes.com*, www.brainyquote.com/quotes/joan_rivers_383830

32. Leigh Cowart, *Hurts so Good: The Culture and Science of Pain on Purpose* (New York: Public Affairs, 2021), 195.

33. Ibid., 116.

34. See Molly MacGilbert, "TikTok 'vanilla-shaming,' the glorification of sexual violence and what we can do about it," *Bust.com*, https://bust.com/sex/197991-tiktok-vanilla-shaming-bdsm.html

35. Quoted in Anna Lovine, "When it comes to 'vanilla sex' no two people taste the same flavor," *Vice*, February 14, 2019, www.vice.com/en/article/vbw3bj/when-it-comes-to-vanilla-sex-kink-no-two-people-taste-the-same-flavor

36. See William Saletan, "Open-mouthed wonder. Was oral sex always normal?" *Slate.com*, May 30, 2008, https://slate.com/technology/2008/05/was-oral-sex-always-normal.html.

37. Danielle Page, "Men discuss receiving oral sex," *AskMen.com*, https://uk.askmen.com/sex/sex_tips/men-discuss-receiving-oral-sex.html

38. "The Esquire survey of the American woman," *Esquire.com*, April 20, 2020, www.esquire.com/entertainment/a7290/survey-of-american-women-0510

39. David Frederick et al., "Differences in orgasm frequency between gay, lesbian, bisexual, and heterosexual men and women in a U.S. sample," *Archives of Sexual Behavior* (2017). Doi:10.1007/s10508-017-0939-z

40. Quoted in Anna Swartz, "A history of oral sex, from fellatio's ancient roots to the modern blow job," *Yahoo!News*, May 31, 2016, https://news.yahoo.com/history-oral-sex-fellatios-ancient-153200784.html

41. Quoted in "How do you go down on someone with a vulva and a vagina?" *Healthline.com*, www.healthline.com/health/healthy-sex/how-to-perform-cunnilingus

42. See Evan Goldstein, "How often Americans have anal sex," *Future-Method.com*, October 28, 2019, https://futuremethod.com/blogs/the-future-edition/statistics-on-american-anal-sex-habits

43. Debra Herbenick et al., "Women's vibrator use in sexual partnerships: Results from a nationally representative survey in the United States," *Journal of Sex and Marital Therapy*, 36(1) (2010): 49–65.

44. Joan Price, *Naked at Our Age* (Berkeley, CA: Seal Press, 2011), 51.

45. Vanessa Marin, "Are vibrators addictive?" *Bustle.com*, May 12, 2014, www.bustle.com/articles/24049-are-vibrators-addictive-or-numing-our-sex-therapist-has-your-answer

46. Quoted in Kaitlin Clark, "Why is everyone embarrassed to admit they like vanilla sex?" *Instyle.com*, updated November 2, 2021, www.instyle.com/lifestyle/what-is-vanilla-sex

47. Esther Perel, *The State of Affairs: Rethinking Infidelity* (New York: HarperCollins, 2017), 28.

48. Justin J. Lehmiller, "Fantasies about consensual nonmonogamy among persons in monogamous romantic relationships," *Archives of Sexual Behavior*, Advance online publication, https://doi.org/10.1007/s10508-020-01788-7

49. Martha Kauppi, *Polyamory: A Clinical Toolkit for Therapists and Their Clients* (New York: Rowman & Littlefield, 2020), 232–233.

50. See Arthur Zuckerman, "30 open marriage statistics: 2020/2021 demographics, popularity & health risks," *Comparecamp.com*, May 23, 2020, https://comparecamp.com/open-marriage-statistics

51. Ethan Czuy Levine et al., "Open relationships, nonconsensual non-monogamy, and monogamy among U.S. adults: Findings from the 2012 National Survey of Sexual Health and Behavior," *Archives of Sexual Behavior*, 47(5) (2018): 1439–1450.

52. Frank D. Fincham and Ross W. May, "Infidelity in romantic relationships," *Current Opinions in Psychology*, 70 (2017): 70–74.

53. Quoted in Aaron Ben-Zeev, "Darling, should you maintain your privacy?" *Psychology Today*, May 29, 2009, www.psychologytoday.com/intl/blog/in-the-name-love/200905/darling-should-you-maintain-your-privacy

54. Quoted in Sara Cook Ruggera, "Is an emotional affair worse than a sexual affair?" July 17, 2016, https://couplescounselorsandiego.com/emotional-affair-worse-sexual-affair

55. See "What percentage of marriages survive infidelity?" *Couplestherapyinc.com*, www.couplestherapyinc.com/what-percentage-of-marriages-survive-infidelity

56. See Paul Brian, "Infidelity statistics (2022): How much cheating is going on?" *HackSpirit.com*, March 31, 2021, https://hackspirit.com/infidelity-statistics

Chapter 7
Getting the right sort of help

1. William J. Doherty et al., "How long do people wait before seeking couples therapy? A research note," *Journal of Marital Family Therapy*, *47*(4) (2021): 882–890.

2. William J. Doherty, "Bad couples therapy: How to avoid it," *Psychotherapy Networker*, November/December 2002, 28.

3. John S. Ogrodniczuk, Anthony S. Joyce, and William E. Piper, "Strategies for reducing patient-initiated premature termination of psychotherapy," *Harvard Review of Psychiatry*, *13*(2) (2005): 57–70.

4. Melissa Boudin and Naveed Saleh, "General Couples Therapy Stats," *Choosing Therapy*, October 24, 2022.

5. See Dianne Grande, "Couples therapy: Does it really work?" *Psychology Today*, December, 2017, www.psychologytoday.com/us/blog/in-it-together/201712/couples-therapy-does-it-really-work

6. Linda J. Waite et al., "Does divorce make people happy? Findings from a study of unhappy marriages," *Institute for American Values*, 2002.

7. Ibid.

8. See Homes and Rahe Stress Scale, *Wikipedia*, https://en.wikipedia.org/wiki/Holmes_and_Rahe_stress_scale

9. Alan J. Hawkins, "Minnesotans' attitudes about marriage and divorce," *Family Studies Center, Brigham Young University.*

10. Linda J. Waite et al., "Does divorce make people happy? Findings from a study of unhappy marriages," *Institute for American Values*, 2002.

11.   Steven Walfish et al., "An investigation of self-assessment bias in mental health providers," *Psychological Reports, 110* (2012): 33–2941.

12.   William J. Doherty, *The Ethical Lives of Clients* (Washington, DC: American Psychological Association, 2022), 122.

13.   Burkhard Peter and Eva Bobel, "Significant differences in personality styles of securely and insecurely attached psychotherapists: Data, reflections, and implications," *Frontiers in Psychology, 11* (2020): 1–12.

14.   See William J. Doherty, *The Ethical Lives of Clients* (Washington, DC: American Psychological Association, 2022), 122.

15.   See William J. Doherty, *Take Back Your Marriage* (New York: Guilford Press, 2013), 102.

16.   Laura Doyle, "6 reasons marriage counseling is BS," *Love Works Solutions*, December 12, 2012, https://loveworkssolution.com/blog/is-marriage-counseling-bs

17.   William J. Doherty, "Couples on the brink: Stopping the marriage-go-around," *Psychotherapy Networker*, March/April 2006, 30–39.

18.   Bernadetta Janusz, Feliks Matusiak, and Anssi Perakyla, "How couple therapists manage asymmetries of interaction in first consultations," *Psychotherapy, 58*(3) (2021): 379–390.

19.   John M. Gottman and Joan DeClaire, *The Relationship Cure* (New York: Harmony, 2001), 32.

20.   Bob Mankoff, CartoonStock.

21.   Peter Goldenthal, *Doing Contextual Therapy* (New York: Norton, 1996).

22.   Cicero, *De Officiis, Book i*, 15, 47.

23.   Mari Ruti, *The Summons of Love* (New York: Columbia University Press, 2011), 28.

24.   Ivan Boszormenyi-Nagy and Barbara R. Krasner, *Between Give and Take: A Clinical Guide to Contextual Therapy* (New York: Brunner/Mazel, 1986), 173.

25.   Ann Shearer, *Why Don't Psychotherapists Laugh?* (New York: Routledge, 2016), 2.

26.   Dianne Symonds and Adam O. Horvath, "Optimizing the alliance in couple therapy," *Family Process, 43*(4) (2004): 443–455.

27.   Quoted in Matt Englar-Carlson and David S. Shepard, "Engaging men in couples counseling: Strategies for overcoming ambivalence and inexpressiveness," *The Family Journal, 13*(4) (2005): 383–391.

28. Joan K. Monin and Margaret S. Clark, "Why do men benefit more from marriage than do women? Thinking more broadly about interpersonal processes that occur within and outside of marriage," *Sex Roles, 65* (2011): 320–326.

29. Quoted in John Gottman and Julie Schwartz Gottman, *The Man's Guide to Women* (New York: Rodale Books, 2016).

30. William Ming Liu, "The study of men and masculinity as an important multicultural competence consideration," *Journal of Clinical Psychology, 61*(6) (2005): 685–697.

31. Tori DeAngelis, "Are men emotional mummies?" *Monitor*, December 2001, www.apa.org/monitor/dec01/mummies

32. See Abigail Fagan, "Alexithymia: Do you know what you feel?" *Psychology Today*, February 6, 2021, www.psychologytoday.com/us/blog/living-emotional-intensity/202102/alexithymia-do-you-know-what-you-feel

33. Aino Mattila, "Alexithymia in the Finnish general population," www.antoniocasella.eu/archipsy/Mattila_alexithymia_2009.pdf

34. Garth Fowler et al., "Women outnumber men in psychology graduate programs," *Datapoint*, American Psychological Association, December 2018.

35. See "Self-Care: Stonewalling Part II," The Gottman Institute, www.gottman.com/blog/self-care-stonewalling-part-ii-the-research

36. Shelley E. Taylor et al., "Biobehavioral responses to stress in females: Tend-and-befriend, not fight-or-flight," *Psychological Review, 107*(3) (2000): 411–429.

37. Andrea L. Meltzer et al., "Sex differences in the implications of partner physical attractiveness for the trajectory of marital satisfaction," *Journal of Personality and Social Psychology, 106*(3) (2014): 418–428.

38. Ogi Ogas and Sai Gaddam, *A Billion Wicked Thoughts: What the Internet Tells Us About Sexual Relationships* (New York: Dutton, 2012), 47.

39. See Gary Lewandowski, "The pandemic made our relationship stronger," *The Wall Street Journal*, June 26, 2021.

40. See Glenn Ruffenach, "The battles over who gets what when a parent dies," *The Wall Street Journal*, May 5, 2021.

41.   Quoted in Stephen Nguyen, "24 common deathbed regrets by Matthew Kelley," https://stephenartphoto.wixsite.com/mysite/post/deathbed-regrets

42.   Paul R. Amato and Alan Booth, "The legacy of parents' marital discord: Consequences for children's marital quality," *Journal of Personality and Social Psychology*, *81*(4) (2001): 627–638.

Index

Aaron, Michael, 117
abandonment trauma, 12–13
absolutist language, 66
active therapeutic intervention, 156
acts of service, 58–59
acts of sympathy, 58–59
affair in marriage *see* infidelity
affirmation, autonomy, 153
Affirmative Couch, 130
affirmative responses, 18
agape love, 3–4
    and complex ethical implications,
        9–10
alexithymia, 176
Algoe, Sara, 79
Allbery, Sam, 105
anal sex, 133
Apfelbaum, Bernard, 118
apology, 72, 154
    true, 73
appreciation, 70
    virtuous cycles of, 168
Armstrong, John, 98, 123
Aron, Michael, 111

Asbag, 107
Ashley Madison phenomenon, 125, 128
assertive intervention, 157
authoritative parenting, 48
autonomy affirmation, 153

"back burner" love interests, 124
backchannel-responses, 68
back-up mates, 85–86
Banas, John, 124
Baxter, Leslie, 89
BDSM, 130–131
Becker, Ernest, 11
benign sexism, 31
Benjamin, Jessica, 113, 118
Benson, Ezra T., 70
Berkowitz, Bob, 112
betrayal, 145
Billion Wicked Thoughts, A, 179
Bombeck, Erma, 29
bonding hormone, 177
Bonds of Love, 112, 118
Boskey, Elizabeth, 106
Boszormenyi-Nagy, Ivan, 166

Bradley, Thomas, 12
Buber, Martin, 75
Buss, David, 86

Cabaniss, Deborah, 82
Carlson, Margaret, 39
Carroll, Jason, 36
Chapman, Emma, 44
Chapman, Gary, 59
childhood wounds, healing, 168–171
Christian love ethics, 9 *see also*
            Judeo-Christian culture
Coates, Jennifer, 91
coital kinetics, 98
Coleridge, Samuel Taylor, 83
commitment, 123
      Ashley Madison phenomenon, 125
      "back burner," 124
      changing attitudes towards
            nonmonogamy, 125–126
      complexities of infidelity, 128
      crushes and old flames, 124
      emotional fallout of affair in
            marriage, 145–150
      ethical nonmonogamy, 134–145
      "intimacy–eroticism" paradox, 125
      kinky vanilla sex, 129–134
      literary pornography, 127
      rebuilding trust and forgiveness
            after infidelity, 145–150
      romance literature, 127
      sexual desire and evolutionary
            impulses in male, 126–127
      use of pornography, 127
      wedding band, 123
communication *see also* conflicts
      facial, 19–20
      management, 55–56
communication style mismatches, 56
      "acts of service" vs "acts of
            sympathy," 58–59
      different "love languages," 59
      "duelers" and "dueters," 60
      himpathy, 60
      interruption-is-rude model, 58
      interruption-shows-involvement
            model, 58

      jam session, 57
      mansplaining, 59–60
      one-person-at-a-time, 57–58
      "report-talk" and "rapport-talk," 57
      verbal plumage, 60
Companionate Marriage, 1
compersion, 136, 137
complaining together, 46
compromise, 8
conflicts, 53
      challenge of conflict resolution in
            enduring marriages, 54
      communication management,
            55–56
      communication style mismatches,
            56–61
      confrontational conversations, 70
      humble dialogue, 67–76
      less prideful monologue, 61–67
      marital quarrels, 53–54
      misunderstandings and non-verbal
            cues, 55
      non-verbal communication, 55
consensual nonmonogamy, 138
Contextual Family Therapy,
            166–167, 171
continuous positive airway pressure
            (CPAP), 41
contrition, 71–76
conversational ethics, xvii, 18
      affirmative responses, 18
      leaning in, 18, 66
      leaning out, 19
      respect, 19
Conversational Joking, 93
conversational narcissism, 62
conversations, confrontational, 70
coping with stress, 177
Corning, Peter, 166
counter-reactive shaming, 64
couples therapy, xix, 151
      autonomy vs marriage
            affirmation, 153
      bias in, 155
      breaking intergenerational
            patterns, 180–183
      challenges and strategies in, 151

Contextual Family Therapy, 166–167, 171
death anxiety, 180
divorce pursue therapy, 152
drop-out rates and misconceptions, 152
ethical agonies, 166
fairness and unfairness in, 163–166
healing childhood wounds, 168–171
hope and positive change in, 154
labor of love, 182–183
lessons from Covid-19 pandemic, 180–183
loving well as an existential imperative, 180–183
male-friendly approach, 174–180
motivations for flourishing love, 180–183
multi-directed partiality, 167
repetition compulsion, 168–169
therapeutic use of humor, 171–174
therapist, 154–163
virtuous cycles of appreciation, 168
Cowart, Leigh, 130
crushes and old flames, 124
cuddling, 116
Culture of Narcissism, The, 62

Daigen, Val, 58
DeAngelis, Tori, 176
death
anxiety, 180
awareness and deeper love, xx
regrets, 10
de Beauvoir, Simone, 29
de Botton, Alain, 84
de-moralizing sex, 102 *see also* sex
female pleasure, 102
influence of Judeo-Christian values, 103
masturbation guilt, 105
natural and unnatural sex, 103
non-procreative sex, 105–106
oral pleasure, 104
sex-friendly passages in ancient Muslim texts, 107

sex negativity to sex positivity, 106–107
Song of Solomon, 107
Demystifying Love, 21
Denial of Death, The, 11
Derber, Charles, 18, 61
de Stael, Madame, 118
destiny beliefs, 84
division of labor, 27–35
benign sexism, 31
domestic struggles and unspoken expectations, 27–29
emotional support & views on household labor, 33
equitable division of labor, 30
gatekeeping, 31–32
internalized heterosexist discrimination, 32
mental labor, 30, 32
objective allocation of housework duties, 34
same-sex couples, 35
divorce pursue therapy, 152
doggy style, 133
Doherty, William, 152
domesticity, 23
balancing fatherhood and work, 23
challenges of contemporary family life and parenthood, 24
challenges of modern parenting, 25–26
fair division of labor, 27–35
financial strain, 25
forged families, 27
intensive parenting, 24
materialistic values on marriages, 35–39
monitoring screen time and social media, 25
over-parenting/under-partnering trap, 43–52
paternal guilt, 23
sleep syncing, 39–43
stressful roles of current generation parents, 24
domestic struggles, 27–29
Doyle, Laura, 155

duelers, 60
dueling egos, 75
dueters, 60
Dunbar, Robin, 55
dynamic inactivity, 68

Eagleton, Terry, 91
Easton, Dossie, 123
egalitarianism in modern relationships,
        xiv–xv
Eisenberg, Gregg, 9, 12, 94
emotional
        affairs, 146
        capital, 74
        merger, 117
        mudslinging, 63–64
        support and views on household
                labor, 33
emotional fallout of affair in marriage,
        145 *see also* commitment
        betrayal, 145
        discretion, 146–147
        emotional affairs, 146
        forgiveness, 149–150
        impact of past traumas, 148
        sexual vs emotional affairs, 146
        sexual withdrawal, 148–149
empathy, 7–8
        human frailty and enhancing, 172
enduring vulnerabilities, 12
equitable division of labor, 30
erotic connections, 120–121
eroticism, frenetic, 134
ethical agonies, 166
ethical nonmonogamy, 134 *see also*
        commitment
        affair, double life, and painful
                fallout, 141–145
        compersion, 136
        complex realities of infidelity, 140
        consensual nonmonogamy, 138
        infidelity and emotional affairs, 139
        loving deception, 141–145
        management of jealous
                feelings, 137
        perils of oversharing, 139–140

polyamorous lifestyle in same-sex
        relationship, 137–138
polyamory culture, 136
polycuriosity, 134–136
existential anxiety and relationship
        dynamics, 69–70

facial communication, 19–20
family *see also* domesticity
        American Family Survey, 99
        Bezos Family Foundation, 31
        Brigham Young University's School
                of Family Life, 36
        Center for Family and
                Demographic Research, 33
        contemporary, 24
        Contextual Family Therapy,
                166–167, 171
        Family Institute at Northwestern
                University, 159
        forged, 27
        nuclear, 26
        of origin, 11–12, 63
        and work, 23
female
        libido, 110
        pleasure, 102
        sexuality, 118
        sexual turn-ons, 118
financial
        strain, 25
        togetherness, 38
Fincham, Frank, 73
"fishbowl" experience, 137
Fisher, Terri, 109
fitness factors, 178
flourishing, 13–14
flourishing relationship, 1
        agape love, 3–4, 9–10
        moral commitment, 2
        moral-religious marital
                commitment, 4
        motivations for, 180–183
        mutual love and respect, 4
        non-negotiables, 15–21
        personal commitment, 2

romantic intensity, 2
secular love ethics, 5–15
trial marriage, 1
forged families, 27
forgiveness, 73–74, 149–150
fostering independence in children, 46
frenetic eroticism, 134
Freud, Sigmund, 109
Fromm, Erich, 37
Fruzetti, Alan, 69

Gaddam, Sai, 179
gatekeeping, 31–32
gender sensitivity, 175–176
Ginsburg, Ruth Bader, 70
Goodin, Robert, 14
Gottman, John, 54, 116, 175
Greengross, Gil, 80
Groening, Matt, 107
growth beliefs, 84
Gubi, Peter Madsen, 44
guilt, 71
    admissions of, 161
    healthy, 70
    and infidelity, 139–140, 149–150
    inner, 76
    neurotic, 71
    paternal, 23
    and sex, 104–105
Guilt: The Bite of Conscience, 71

Hägglund, Martin, 10, 96
Hancock, Justin, 131
Hardy, Janet, 123
Havrilesky, Heather, 10
healing childhood wounds, 168–171
hedgehog's dilemma, 119
helicopter parenting, 49
Herbenick, Debby, 132, 134
heterosexist discrimination,
    internalized, 32
high-conflict relationships, 156
himpathy, 60
Hitchens, Christopher, 10
Holbrook, M. L., 102
Holmes, John, 58

Hone, Liana, 80, 103
Hope, Donna Lynn, 127
humble dialogue, 67 *see also* conflicts
    backchannel-responses, 68
    confrontational conversations, 70
    contrition and apologizing, 71–76
    dueling egos, 75
    dynamic inactivity, 68
    emotional capital, 74
    existential anxiety and relationship
        dynamics, 69–70
    forgiveness, 73–74
    genuine appreciation and
        consideration, 70
    guilt, 71
    I-statements, 69
    manifesting curiosity, 68
    paraphrasing or reiterating, 68–69
    real dialogue, 67
    responsibility to self, 75
    transgressor's guilt, 71
    true apology, 73
    "we-statements," 69
humor, 77
    absurdities and grievances,
        83–89, 95
    affiliative and self-enhancing
        humor, 78
    appreciation, 80
    boundaries, 94
    challenging rhetoric of seriousness
        and hard work, 82
    levity leverage, 89–93
    production, 80
    risk of using, 174
    in same-sex couples, 81–82
    self-deprecating humor, 94
    and sexual arousal, 81
    shared laughter, 79
    wittiness ethics, 94–96
humor, therapeutic use, 171
    estrangement and passive
        resignation, 172–173
    human frailty and enhancing
        empathy, 172
    humorous wordplay, 173–174

power of good-natured teasing, 173
reciprocal laughter, 172
risk of using humor, 174
humorous exchanges, 93
Hunt, Mary, 106
Hurts So Good, 130
hyper-individualism, 62–63

Imam ar-Ragib, 107
immortality projects, 11–12
individualism, hyper, 62–63
infidelity, 100
complexities of, 128
complex realities of, 140
and emotional affairs, 139
rebuilding trust and forgiveness,
145–150
insider jokes, 90–91
intensive parenting, 24, 49
interdependence theory, 38
intergenerational patterns, breaking,
180–183
internalized heterosexist
discrimination, 32
interruption-is-rude model, 58
interruption-shows-involvement
model, 58
intervention, assertive, 157
"intimacy–eroticism" paradox, 125
intimacy, unmet, 100–101
invisible ledger, 6
Irvine, William, 11
I-statements, 69

Jacob, Bonnie, 43
jam session, 57
jocularity, lack of, 95
Johnson, Matthew, 45
Johnson, Michael, 2
Johnson, Susan, 115, 116
joint non-negotiable, 17
Judeo-Christian culture, xv, 43,
102, 103

Kama Sutra, 129
Karney, Benjamin, 12
Katchadourian, Herant, 71
Kauppi, Martha, 137

Kelly, Matthew, 181
Kleinplatz, Peggy, 115
Knee, Raymond, 84
Krafft-Ebing, Richard von, 109

labor of love, 182–183
language, absolutist, 66
Lasch, Christopher, 62
laughter, reciprocal, 1
laughter, shared, 79 *see also* humor
leaning in, 18
leaning out, 19
Leit, Lisa, 61
Lerner, Harriet, 66, 73
Levant, Ronald, 176
Levine, Stephen, 21
levity leverage, 89 *see also* humor
finding humor in mishaps, 92–93
humorous exchanges, 93
insider jokes, 90–91
pet name, 89–90
playful banter and endearing
laughter, 91–92
shared background knowledge,
90–91
terms of endearment, 89–90
Lewis, Helen, 64
libido, 109 *see also* sex
disparities, 115
female libido and intimacy
needs, 110
gender differences in sexual desire,
109–110, 112–113
low sexual desire, 111–112
mismatched, 108–109, 114
sexual spontaneity, 110–111
Lindsey, Ben B., 1
Companionate Marriage, 1
moral-religious code, 5
literary pornography, 127
Locke, John, 60
loss of selfhood, 44
love
ambivalence of, 95
labor of, 182–183
languages, 59
unconditional, 9
love ethics, Christian, 9

love's absurdities, 83 *see also* humor
    back-up mates, 85–86
    balancing expectations and
      realities, 87
    destiny beliefs, 84
    growth beliefs, 84
    humor and compromise, 86
    illusion of soul mate, 83–84
    marriage duration, 85
    relational boredom, 88
Love Worth Making, 117
loving deception, 141–145
loving well as existential imperative,
    180–183
Lutz, Jaime, 60

male-friendly therapy, 174–180
    challenge of communicating with
      men, 177
    gender differences in coping with
      stress, 177
    gender sensitivity and
      multicultural competence,
      175–176
    male sexuality, 179–180
    men's emotional styles, 176
    men's emotional withdrawal,
      177–178
    men's perceptions of physical
      attractiveness, 178–179
    normative male alexithymia, 176
    "tend-and-befriend" response, 177
    traditional masculinity and
      emotional communication, 175
male partners, alexithymic leaning, 176
male sexuality, 179–180
manifesting curiosity, 68
mansplaining, 59–61
Marin, Vanessa, 134
marital quarrels, 53–54
marriage
    affirmation, 153
    compromise, 8
    conventional ideals, xiii–xiv
    couples therapy, xix
    death awareness and deeper love,
      xx, 10
    disputes, xvii

duration, 85
egalitarianism in modern
    relationships, xiv–xv
holiness, 3
materialistic values on, 35–39
monogamous relationships,
    xviii–xix
and motherhood, 43
over-moralizing of sex, xviii
and religion, xiii, xvi, 3
sacrifice, 3
same-sex, xv
secular humanistic values, xv–xvi
traditional, xiv, xv
unequal sharing of power, 13
masculinity, traditional, 175
masturbation guilt, 105
mate(s)
    back-up, 85–86
    soul, 83–84
materialistic values on marriages, 35–39
    clash of values and finances in
      marriage, 36–37
    financial togetherness, 38
    interdependence theory, 38
    mental greed, 37
maternal ambivalence, 44
Mating in Captivity, 115
matrimony, 43
McCabe, Charles, 139
men's emotional
    styles, 176
    withdrawal, 177–178
men's perceptions of physical
    attractiveness, 178–179
mental
    greed, 37
    labor, 30, 32
Ming Liu, William, 175
Mintz, Laurie, 104
mishaps, finding humor in, 92–93
mismatched libidos, 108–109, 114
misunderstandings, 55 *see also*
    conflicts
Modern Marriage, 117
modern parenting, 25–26
mommy brain, 43
monogamous relationships, xviii–xix

monologue, less prideful, 61 *see also*
  conflicts
  absolutist language, 66
  conversational narcissism, 62
  counter-reactive shaming, 64
  emotional mudslinging, 63–64
  hyper-individualism, 62–63
  mutual shaming, 65
  pride and shame dynamics, 64
  summarizing yourself syndrome,
   65–66
  "support" and "shift" responses, 61
  whataboutisms, 64
  you-statements, 67, 69
moral
  commitment, 2
  -religious code, 5
  -religious marital commitment, 4
motherhood
  loss of selfhood, 44
  marriage and, 43
  maternal ambivalence, 44
  mommy brain, 43
  paternal jealousy, 45
Muise, Amy, 99, 112
Mullinax, Margo, 124
multi-directed partiality, 167
mutual
  caring disposition, 7
  love and respect, 4
  respect, 8
  shaming, 65

narcissism
  conversational, 62
  Culture of Narcissism, The, 62
  Traumatic Narcissism, 65
natural sex, 103
neurotic guilt, 71
Nicomachean Ethics, 94
Noesner, Gary, 68
nonmonogamy, 125 *see also* ethical
   nonmonogamy
  attitudes, 125–126
  ethical, 134–145
  consensual, 138

non-negotiables, 15
  conversational ethics, 18
  displays of physical affection,
   20–21
  facial communication, 19–20
  finding connection and true
   conversation, 17–20
  joint non-negotiable, 17
non-procreative sex, 105–106
non-verbal communication, 55 *see also*
   conflicts
non-verbal cues, 55 *see also* conflicts
normative male alexithymia, 176
Norrick, Neal, 93

Ogas, Ogi, 179
one-person-at-a-time speaking
   modality, 57–58
oral sex, 104, 132
over-parenting/under-partnering
   trap, 43
  authoritative parenting, 48
  balancing parental support and
   couple time, 50
  complain together, 46
  fostering independence in
   children, 46
  helicopter parenting, 49
  intensive parenting, 49
  maternal ambivalence, 44
  parenting together, 46–48
  paternal jealousy, 45
  path to meaningful fulfillment and
   lasting bonds, 51
  reverence, 51–52
  sharing proud parenting
   moments, 46

paraphrasing, 68–69
parenting
  authoritative, 48
  challenges of modern, 25–26
  helicopter, 49
  intensive, 24
  over-/under-partnering trap,
   43–52

sharing proud moments, 46
stressful roles of current generation
        parents, 24
together, 46–48
passion, 115 *see also* sex
cuddling, 116
desires for emotional merger, 117
erotic connections, 120–121
feeling desired vs. sexually
        used, 118
female sexuality, 118
female sexual turn-ons, 118
friendship without, 97–98
hedgehog's dilemma, 119
mediocre sex, 118
synchrony sex, 116
paternal
guilt, 23
jealousy, 45
Perel, Esther, 115, 116, 136
personal commitment, 2
pet name, 89–90
physical affection, displays of, 20–21
physical attractiveness, men's
        perceptions of, 178–179
Pillemer, Karl, 39
Pinsker, Joe, 49
Plath, Sylvia, 20
pleasure, female, 102
polyamorous lifestyle, 137–138
polyamory culture, 136
polycuriosity, 134–136
Pope Francis, 107
pornography, 127
Poverty of Affluence, The, 37
Pratchett, Terry, 41
Price, Joan, 134
pride and shame dynamics, 64
pro-marriage books, xxi
Proust, Marcel, 75
Psychopathia Sexualis, 109

Quillen, Robert, 43, 76

rapid-eye movement (REM), 40
rapport-talk, 57

ready-wittedness, 94
reciprocal laughter, 172
reiterating, 68–69
relational boredom, 88
religious marital commitment, 4
REM *see* rapid-eye movement
repetition compulsion, 168–169
report-talk, 57
respect, 19
responses
affirmative, 18
backchannel, 68
responsibility to self, 75
Retzinger, Suzanne, 64
reverence, 51–52
romance
intensity, 2
literature, 127
rough sex, 129, 130
Ruti, Mari, 169

same-sex marriage, xv
domestic life, 35
gatekeeping tendencies in, 32
household responsibilities, 35
polyamorous lifestyle in, 137–138
sense of humor, 81–82
Scheff, Thomas, 64
Schnarch, David, 99
secular love ethics, 5
abandonment trauma, 12–13
agape love, 9–10
balancing selflessness and
        self-respect, 9
Christian love ethics, 9
compromise, 8
death regrets, 10
enduring vulnerabilities, 12
immortality projects, 11–12
insights and wisdom from elderly
        couples, 5–6
invisible ledger, 6
love and commitment in face of
        aging and mortality, 14–15
mutually caring disposition, 7
mutual respect, 8

unconditional love, 9
unequal sharing of power, 13
self-deprecating humor, 94
selfhood, loss of, 44
sex, 97 *see also* de-moralizing sex
    coital kinetics, 98
    decline of erotic bonds in
        committed relationships, 99
    de-moralizing sex, 102–107
    female libido, 110
    female pleasure, 102
    female sexuality, 118
    female sexual turn-ons, 118
    friendship without passion, 97–98
    health benefits of sexual activity,
        99–100
    infidelity, 100
    kinky vanilla, 129–134
    life, xviii
    male sexuality, 179–180
    masturbation guilt, 105
    mediocre, 118
    moralizing of, 102
    natural and unnatural, 103
    negativity to positivity, 106–107
    non-procreative sex, 105–106
    nurturing passion, 115–121
    oral, 104, 132
    and relationship happiness,
        97–98
    role in modern relationships, 101
    rough, 129, 130
    sexual afterglow, 101
    sexual desire and evolutionary
        impulses in male, 126–127
    sexual vs emotional affairs, 146
    sexual withdrawal, 148–149
    synchrony, 116
    toys, 133–134
    unmet intimacy, 100–101
    unsynched libidos, 108–115
sexism, benign, 31
sexual
    afterglow, 101
    arousal and sense of humor, 81
    spontaneity, 110–111
    withdrawal, 148–149

sexual desire, 111–112
    and evolutionary impulses in male,
        126–127
    sexual fantasies and, 109–110
sexuality, female, 118
sexual turn-ons, female, 118
shaming, counter-reactive, 64
shared
    background knowledge, 90–91
    laughter, 79
sharing proud parenting moments, 46
Shearer, Ann, 172
"shift" responses, 61
sleep habits, 39
    blameless accountability, 41
    coordinating, 39–43
    human heart rhythms, 42
    mismatched sleep-wake
        preferences, 42
    snoring, 41
Snyder, Stephen, 117
soul mate, 83–84
Steinberg, Laurel, 134
Steingraber, Sandra, 44
Strenger, Carlo, 11
stress, coping with, 177
stressful roles of current generation
        parents, 24
stress response, 177
Sullivan, Andrew, 106
summarizing yourself syndrome, 65–66
support responses, 61, 74
Sykes, Wanda, 85
synchrony sex, 116

Tannen, Deborah, 57, 61
Taylor, Paul, 98
teasing, power of good-natured, 173
"tend-and-befriend" response, 177
terms of endearment (TOE), 89–90
therapeutic guilt, 161–162
therapist, 154
    acknowledging without agreeing,
        157–158
    assertive intervention, 157
    balancing alliances, 159
    benign intentions, 163

bias in couples therapy, 155
high-conflict relationships, 156
in identifying hidden emotions,
160–161
negative impressions, 163
professionalism, 159–160
promoting effective
communication, 157
reframing and personal growth,
158–159
respectful disagreements and
setting boundaries, 157
role of active therapeutic
intervention, 156
separation/divorce rates of, 155
strengths and virtuous actions,
162–163
therapeutic guilt, 161–162
Thomas, Gary, 3
To Have or To Be, 37
traditional
marriage, xiv, xv
masculinity, 175
transgressor's guilt, 71
trauma, abandonment, 12–13
Traumatic Narcissism, 65
trial marriage, 1
Troxel, Wendy, 41, 42
true apology, 73

unconditional love, 9
unequal sharing of power, 13
unmet intimacy, 100–101
unnatural sex, 103

van Deurzen, Emmy, 67
vanilla sex, 131

vanilla sex, kinky, 129
anal sex, 133
BDSM, 130–131
doggy style, 133
frenetic eroticism, 134
oral sex, 132
rough sex, 129, 130
sex toys, 133–134
verbal plumage, 60
virtuous cycles of appreciation, 168
vulnerabilities, enduring, 12

Wachtel, Paul, 37
Walfish, Steven, 154
Walter, Chip, 21
wedding band, 123
Weiner-Davis, Michelle, 114
we-statements, 69
whataboutisms, 64
When Men Stop Having Sex, 112
Why Don't Therapists Laugh, 172
Why Won't You Apologize?, 73
wittiness ethics, 94 *see also* humor
ability to laugh at oneself, 94
ambivalence of love, 95
boundaries of humor, 94
humor in absurdities, 95
lack of jocularity, 95
mortality, 96
ready-wittedness, 94
Worthington, Everett, 74

Yager-Berkowitz, Susan, 112
you-statements, 67, 69

Zarhin, Dana, 41

PGIL2023USA